raghallach o raghallaigh

12

Pen-and-ink illustrations: Bernadette A Reilly
Cover and computer-generated illustrations: Blue Light Productions
Email: reillymccabe@yahoo.co.uk

Order this book online at www.trafford.com
or email orders@trafford.com

Most Trafford titles are also available at major online book retailers.

Print information available on the last page.

ISBN: 978-1-4251-5876-7 (sc)

Trafford rev. 11/04/2016

www.trafford.com
North America & international
toll-free: 1 888 232 4444 (USA & Canada)
fax: 812 355 4082

i ii gO gO0 000i
om mann padme hummie
hums runs burns (out) y our
wow wowf eh wow eheu euhages wo
bbly gloppy grotty potty dotty volutatary marbly ghastly ghostly
ratsorizzossocksy merrycygo
O

eggs 00 fit fiat *vol*untas tuas [klaatus stasis startles at] 12oclock exactly
egs ded dwems tell 0 tales snails smear 0 silver trails
zits agus poopydogstails

upjuts thy cornucornu [brace of horns]
dwarving even dent delion [dandelion]
cernunos of flaccid snails [antlered celtic deity]
herb nor docken ever fails
[mucusy squashables small still hymn]

*res*pecting tellus tell us o oldy moldy musty mlurky multiplex telary mugus
tel quel? [cloudcuckoolandnesslacking (sans varnish)]
telephone & tell em ever broader ever more inclusive [henri barbusse]
sarah why is your telephone no written on you arm
[see marlene dietrich by her daughter maria riva 1992 p637]
1 phony global telephonist if ever let me tell u
adam times two adds up even ii i kosher [nonpseudo] hebrew pas
everymans adam wos one african
DI O REILLY CASTS RIVERWREATH
IN MEMORIAM ADAM DOE

[wrenhouse international telephone exchange exchange]
SURLILY GRUMBLY NIGHTSHIFTER
hello yes
PROVOCATIVE PUNTER
yes hello good growling ii u ii operator
1gryeslyperson2gryeslypersonconnexion collect please area code 212

abc123 gfl123 1g23 pgc123 rac124 arcadia234 ida243 rpa248 b424837
babelon8583 fahrenheit451 haftling174517 7397 [vide la vita e bella]
rjf manhatrcalif ecto1ny inspector2211sfpolice downtown2525 gpt64a
amerika10206 [puffpuffs ex stettiner station 2100 sun 9/3/39]
0! [= ein untergoeringmensch see read devils disciples p595]

u unjustly keep one hanging on [cf lou reed]
here i am keep calm hear me receive me trapped under freeway
159515951595159515951595159515951595159515951595159515951595159515951595159515951595159515951595159515
go on one s on ce one s g one go on on go
gategate [gonegone] paragate [gonebeyond] parasamgate [goneoff]
protonhysteron apostrophes forsworn renegate apostatic apostrophiser rot on
drop_. rod in hell orfan sed do madron

thy parent rots apace o noble graycomplected bruce
loathly lonely lovelorn leper munched hunched humble brunch
master can we legges have more arsehole brose & bannocks [athole]
that meltith dead melted ben ben mcbeans ulcerous foutre mooth
slup burp pure fouth

behold ye knave hath lunched 1000 chips
aye bravely deluged avec desperate draughts of barrile®
[barrileirenbarrbru®]
aye warrant u
selim sot did quaff on trot bot
tle of vintage cyprus wine tho running out of time
rot peck pas malt jhem shen brew
godrotgoodmen tender tonya doth offend
NEONAZIS UNLEASH SECRETWONDERCAMEMBERTROTWEAPON
SHOCK HORROR TERREHAUTE CORROSION
fuhrer habt richt der austottung [cf besser tot als rot]
here lived [mad inventor] rotwang *rotwang*
u will fashion robot in similitude of maria
hier ist kein warum

bought because one ought paul rothas grave anatomy
widow capet 6 livres [for] coffin
15 livres 35 sols [for] gravediggers
piers reilig reilig brave bideth dalbeth grave
per naming rock rock per nature naturing
tu es petrus petrus spurious
pas longhomestone honors honors honorable
ercma qui ma quier cias modovini amaqi cairat iniavii neq aglasi
super warmemorial 2 lairs pilgrims sinister [ex] celtic cross

personne maketh hir latterday pilgrimway unto yon godly acre
2 pray 1 careful nonoblivious prayer pour poor baby jack
pon tinyspiny back sub ma pa till domesday crack
paters peter paters peter paters u judah
amen
agla
acggta
gacagt

geiniolach et craobhscaoileadh na raghallach
et maithe breifne hi raghailligh
[genealogy & ramification of ye ui raghallaigh
& of ye nobility of breifne ui raghallaigh
see pp26ff agus pp77ff et passim james carney ed
genealogic history of o reillys [[hereinafter genhist]]
compiled in 18th century per eoghan o raghallaigh
incorporating portion of antecedent historiography of t fitzsimons
proffered via an cumann sheanachais bhreifne
avec aid of subvention from dublin institute for advanced studies
anno domini 1959]

sliocht aodh chonnallaigh ann so [herewith line of aodh connallach]
dynastae breifniae orientalis [dynasts of eastbreifne]
aodh og
aodh ruaidh
phillip
aodha
seaghain
aodh chonallaigh
maolmordha
seaghain
cathail
eogan na feasoige
seaghain
phillip
giolla iosa ruaidh
domhnaill
cathail na beithigh
annaigh
cathail na ccaorach
gofraigh
mhic na hoidhche
conchonnacht
argiallaigh
arten
raghallaigh
cathalain
dubhchroin
maolmordha
dynastae ambarum breifniarum [dynasts of 2 breifnes]
cearnachain
dubhdhothra
donnchadha
baoithin
blathmhac
feidhlim
criomhthain
scannlain
aodh finn
feargna
reges conatiae [kings of connacht]
feargusa
muireadhaig mail
eoghain sreibh
duach ghalaigh
briain
reges totius hiberniae [kings of all ireland]
eochaidh muighmheadhoin
muireadhach tire
fiacha sraibhthine
cairbre lifeachair
chorbmaic ulfada
airt enfhir
cuinn ceadchatach
feidhlime reachtmhar
tuathal teachtmhur

wot pas de postpositive genitive [prolepsis vide infra]
me apostrophicoapostatising mucker old relative
[voice off faint faraway from brighton fleeting fleeing flitting]

peter evans — great grandson of peter reilig?
pete [76] being senior 2 matthew [78] junior 2 colin [73] roger [75]
pierre reilly — of honora bradys pullulant diasporic brood?
honesty compels affirmation
chuaidh an chuid eile as eireann? [his sibbs likewise emigrated]
ta [yes]
townland of ratrussan reilly augustborn?
yuss iff [if & only if] we can trust birthcertif
lad who wooed annie wood?
wed that aghatotan lass he would
shall we dance [mark sandrich 1937] — moniker of groom?
peter p peters aka petrov
salvatore ferragamo sweeps wideeyed wanda off her feet?
supershoeswooed her
mr reilly — auntie annies daddy?
da
toddling orfant annie — 1 hoosier poet immortalised?
james whitcomb riley [1849 1916]
nil tricks — reichsmarschall occluded reichsautobahn?
2 accommodate 1 toddler
halcyondays antegraves fore ante was raised:-
whence flowed broons agus blackbob?
lovely grandadreillys sundaypost

SCHICKLGRUBER GEGEN DIE MUNCHENERPOST
WHY I HATE MY BOHSE ONKEL
PAHSIFAL? PAH
WAGNER WEANS WIND UP UNCLE WOLF
HITLER SAILS WITH UNCLE SAM [cf unser seliger adolf]

peter reilly
1883 1961
strong
felix gilfedder
1889 1982
true
adolf schicklgruber
1889 1945
false
james mcgoogan
1948 1998
good

hi my irrepressible irish cherish thy lights
slainte [health] brian agus alanna
im driving these boyos to ferry susie assured an garda
well met pon paddys day venerable normaness ann de bearnais

pas ecossais
irlanglais peutetre
jamais
en effet deracine
rien de rien
an cabhan
duchas [cf desiderium]
bas [beo as = life out of it]

tender veneration pro erins dead may yet be endemic
record attests plenty of death ben dready brenny already certainly
fearsome cavanworkhouses:-
provincial [ulster] mouses foraged few precious porridgecrumbs

which ulster fighterfrightener ushered straight to heaven?
rambunctious son of sun cuchullin of muirthemne aetatis xxvii
fortissimus heros scotorum? [strongest hero of scots ie irish]
yiss

belted 2 1 orthostat sunforce spent:
cuchulainns end unco chockmahredolent [charlatanic cabbalism]
soar soar those soaring rainbows crows lugh lamhfada in estro
eager eagle reaches peak hears graedig eaglets squeak
[greedy cf du gretig]
did not bubble trouble lighting lug on bubble [so light that god]
patrick loundered cromm [1 celtic moloch]
ecclesiastically walloping [him] – with 1 rock!
good man pas shyly shamrocksstroked crommmolochs brow

50 monkish scholars per roman [christian] corracle to cork?
550
dear little fillan vouchsafed beatific vision?
777

george of bolshiedragon fame bollandists boot out whose claim
[jesuits that accumulated john bollands acta sanctorum 1596 1665]
lugle was aussi luglian fartravelling irishman
columcille delights to play with devas every thursday
monstrous moaedhog [of] monumental deeds
moaedhog [self]mortifies [&] wieldeth beads
holy man – being 104 years young – accurses thus:-
badcess now plus hell hereafter
peters bede lives on in memory

only humankind is vile vile ye livelong owrie [dreary] while
stiffliquor (hermetically enleaded) lingers sinedie
shorttime (by engrossy sulphur lapped) ceased meat steeps
hnitpicker in shtibl will not quibble
oi stiffneck dig your drollsome worms or lump em heck

ah donal munro 100000 welcomes to landoleal
[u] will not grow tyrantfatter
[now that] god of worms hath put u pon poor archies platter
i *like* this like alabonneheure bonnebouche bonappetit
mr riley i have something you might like
worm 2 1 that dies indifferently applies
i ii i that lives crumbs of comforts gives

putrescent stopped machinery:-
whose fairly foul collocation if apt?
fowles

1 crawled 1 gawped 1 faltered destin can not be altered
destin stand tho one falter
every bullet hath hir billet.
time it is 1 crime 2 kill it.
(bullitt spits *bullshit*)
tell it to sarkis pogossian u bollocks
[obsessively deplored losttime]
failbaked useless proofless puddings posing qua pabulum
rheumy runny scunner tummy ugh jesus im throwing up

bullet
bullshot
bullets or ballots
bullet for badman
bullet for general
bullet for joey
bullets for o hara
bulletproof
bulletproof
bulletproof heart
bullets & love
bullet in head
bullet to beijing
bullets over broadway

hello this orson welles
[that shot killed harry lime.]
harry youre still alive — & and youre 1 horrible shot [.]
i am always prepared to die by another soldiers bullet [.]
they could at least have shot at me
then i might feel some respect for them [.]
ive fired 1 few shots [.]
i could shoot you from stuttgart
[& still create appropriate effect.]
sometime somewhere may be proper bullet for josiah boon [.]
u wont live 2 pick iron out of your navel [.]
remind me to put 1 bullet in my head
[if i sign up for ace ventura 5.]
u may catch lead anytime

we deal in lead my friend [.]
too bad [youre dead] rollie [its] not like movies [.]
he [raleigh] shot me [henry howard] thru & thru
so long as he [raleigh] had powder [.]
shooting reilly is not 1 very good idea [.]
dont shoot its me riley [.]
dont make me laugh bill [it hurts too much.]
russians dont shoot their children roy [.]
butcher is still alive bullets dont stop him [.]
that makes 2 [slugs] ive stopped for u [.]
got her with 1st got me with 2nd [.]
ive one shot at influencing you

in which film watching which flick did miamian chili palmer cinemaensconced chill out?
[a] get shorty
[2] touch of evil

yankee doodle hath 1 gun he just pops out & buys one
but we do love our american cousins [see michael moore bowling for columbine 2002]
u2 uk maybe someday
fate reigns okay kismet is king
from kays upon statementdays kind lord deliver us

kaysagent 759 – u he?
consciously

consciousness 1 quality of some hopeless idiots
useful idiots universally unconscious
horribiliz bizniz perturbat noz

sir karl intuitive freewiller immersed not popper in? [1902 94]
ripping killerthrillers
popper hath spoke?
tomorrow ith ope
wot else doth popp tell?
siren future weaves hir spell
causation per popper?
case of propensity = 2 1
care to explicate [u] pompous posturing proper pottock?
nope [i am] only rotereliant dope simple pi beyond whose scope

pize pixilation pennybrain cant wildly hope to win puremathprize
tho simpleminded cannot forbear 2 create time for 1 rime

colin wilsons axiom?
no maestro commits murder 1 [ie generically artist]
one ought not say i?
one ought not say one

not all that can be committed should
not 1 maxim 2 shun gun and fames aside
non possumus [we cannot – species of naysaying]
non omnia possumus omnes [none is omnipotent virgil]
not all that ought shall be done

i can be maestro of my fate in casablanca
assert it qua cavanman WOT ONE CAN THAT ONE CAN
bronxcheers for cheerless cavan chasetails
take 1 punt sail 1 tail my reluctant runt [hortative mamaduck]
if ard be your badlug
ard u cannod dug
ard u cannod dug
if ard be your badlug [to hearten barcan]
hee that on barcan believed believed not
that hee up ye wrongtree barked
barkochba can toujours squeeze down 1 can of heinz® beans
beanfast cannot last
beanfa tu re tionol breifneach
po y whrussens y gachya hay wertha yn can
derbyniwyd at wasanaeth llyfrgell genedlaethol cymru gopi o
that is with beans besot permits em not rotapot
beans plus bananas bananas plus beans *appeases*
thou art pas *measly* that *meases* me [ad to mitis mild]
beati pacifici
BEATIFIEDBEANICON ASSURANCE & GUARANTEE
INFANTILE SERVILISM NONIMPLICATED IN MANUFACTURE
daddydaddy wot happened to bananas did nasty fungus
i dont know hen [how else will she learn then]
break out beans carrots disinter curry wee wormy sheeba
hee adore da ca more da naduralma adore hir ma
[he adored that cat more than naturalman adores his mater]
give girl drimdromdrum of beans she will swill hirself ill
boy yeah are my cad & i ever cacogasdric [dyspeptic]
burb u can stick your beefy hamgurber hill
housebound smouse smoused on 1 mound of
sh sh cry me brand me sishmael [1 steal from moby dick]

according to rick blaine:-
1 few little persons to what aggregate not?
hill of beans pon godspelllornnornstormented tellus

bobbing down by sub lamplit arc nigh barrackgates:-
sleeping cans of worms
sacerdospontifexque [priestcumbridgebuilder]
wos no babe in pram freighted aveccans [see speed]

gaby berny graciously brought breny?
braw beans of heterogeneous brands
geek bore [!] beans safely home?
from safeway® airdrie [per] railway

8

minstrel wore jeans?
neither here nor wear
modest gaelic toponyms?
mostly noneponymous
haricots adulterated with thumbtacks?
gurdjieffian subsistence

propensities await their freighted fate
energies [are] propensities propensities [are] entities [.]
fate can never be merely neutral
[invariable moral dimension.]
fate (he thought) had confirmed his own worth
his ideals his power all that he did
[he = hitler see gloss.]
minstrel for u my wooden temple of praise
impatient of manana i yearn to see it blaze [.]
nor could she scape
spite all hir woody engines [.]
i ii is caught in ones way [.]
we cannot elude tyranny of our organisation [.]
organising bullets for other girls 2 fire [.]
karl has bullet in head [.]
god is 1 bullet

got tired
of no targetgun fired [.]
prov fires pas blankshot [.]
mlord still firing blanks [fat chance bulgy belly.]
all human acts involve more chance than decision [.]
offchance some nutter going to pick me off [.]
men do die at haphazard live while blindchance spares [.]
i always though i should be rotten at dying [.]
magick merely 2b & to do
magick includes all acts soever
not beasties fault fate fuddling doing desperate [.]
what this territory needs is more *fuddle*

fate may spare 1 unfuddled dane [.]
i need not thee
twisted sister fate [.]
fate that condemns we
mortals to unmarked graves
spits megalopsychos *amice mei salve* [.]
ta me sinte ar do thuama [.]
i cried when i 1st visited this living graveyard [.]
[afghanistan] graveyard for invaders [.]
evil invaders will schlepp bodybags over their shoulders [.]
u find yourself like mahomets coffin mr holmes [.]
what shall we do with our books? be buried under them? [.]
earthnapping beneath ye parthenon [.]
i goodtime ii bury badnews [.]
surprise me

massive graveyards of childprodigies [tennischampsmanque.]
starts suddenly rime or reasonless [cf birthtrauma]
jolting attack in cemetery [.]
avoid cemeteries tombs mention of *mort* [.]
simmies in cemetery [.]
where now?
morgue [.]
where pa?
skeleton cemetery spirit heavenly glory [.]
please enclose chillipeppers
spice up wishywashy christianheaven [.]
decomposition deglorifies [.]
ichabod [.]
let us never disremember our glorious simian heritage

ROT my trademark [.]
no no hastings it is not the rot [.]
rot – 0 angelic about holeingO or king or commoner in it

warren oates – serial graverat?
yoh:-
qua muff potter coffingrappler
qua bennie cadaverwraxler

angel [= subconscious] is *king can* [.]
anything cizers can do skenedhu can do [.]
BOY WITH NOLEGS CANDOKID [.]
charm patience candoamericanapproach [.]
i can u can [.]
bethlehem can [.]
if u can go for everything that can set u apart [.]
chieftain iffucan of azcan in caftan [.]
1 large country welltenanted o rail chief captain

glamor ok – u dont *need* it like tin of beans [.]
comes crabbed lenten fastingtide
folks forsake sweet beans for meat [.]
bless me mon pere for i did feast
upon great unseasonal beans
of myself i made 1 beast
thou art weak mon fils but part in peace [.]
bean of such magnitude would have been BIG hit [.]
0 but beans beans beans [.]
beans! someone should tell us army
we grow beef in this country [.]
beans is safer than buffalosteaks [.]
id say youve had *enuf* [.]
baked beans did for him [really loves his tins.]
twins want baked beans & coco [.]
did twins eat greenbananas my sister thought were beans? [.]
bring on greenbean

can eat it carousel? [.]
each raging thief can destroy [eat] mutton & beef [.]
no glass can pierce no rage so fierce penetrateth soul [.]
any being you destroy you must accept as part of yourself [.]
hes still here — not so easy 2 destroy 1 person [.]
shes still here [.]
she *is* here [.]
theyre still here inside here they always will be [.]
i wont refer to him pasttense [.]
i suspect she can hear us now

destiny can be like that sometimes [.]
one can do anything to anyone [.]
qualms are for ducks [.]
paper disevinces moral qualms [.]
clog up povertyindustry with paper agus buzzwords [.]
tellus drowning in paper [.]
truth bubbles to my brim
life & death are i ii him [.]
paper can be *turned against* [.]
everything is decided on paper

paperpaper agus swell mound of merrygoO words [.]
round & round we go [.]
on busy days they send around dozen names into flames [.]
impatient peter of wooden words u strike
flint of truth with feeling & lo fire
of music leaps into your fingers [.]
FEET OF FLAMES BE PART OF YE FIRE [.]
medals fire me up [.]
where i am going medals will melt

we shortlisted some names
perpetual motion unanimous choice [.]
u chose preciousest egg in christiannest [.]
she opts put her eggs on ice [.]
ms mcbeal decides 2 get into life of daughter maddie 10
from eggdonation she made years ago for experimental use [.]
banks spurned their pleas *sorry no deafdonor* [.]
if phone doesnt ring u can tell its danny rose

americans will tell you anything [.]
uncle sam gives much more [aid] than he ever lets on [.]
america has no truer friend than gb [.]
may we ever stand [destinare] together [.]
[re roosevelt] might be truer to say wedded 2 destiny [.]
voice in air functions as agent of destiny [.]
daemon not our destiny unless we yield to hir [.]
joyce lived too much alone with daemon [.]
sunny jim isnt perpetually jovial [.]
cometh ye ogre

madoc judges punks not lightly
senile soul scorns joviality
[madoc] prayed 1 intercessionaryprayer
mollify stormy god [thy] saturnic indignation [.]
sleep of 7 lights
sleep of 7 joys
sleep of 7 languors [.]
give reilly another 7 minutes [.]
give him [sydney reilly] 1 few more minutes [.]
b master of thy time till 7 [macbeth 3 1.]
mollochating piteous wretched offspring
such wo agus peril
round crommcruaich slippery guts they pour
wee bairns eviscerate sleeping evermore [.]
righ o mbriuin na mbratach ngeal
tearc neach ag a bhfuil a ghradh
o raghallaidh [sic] muighe sleacht
nar mhaoidh eucht dha ndearna a lamh

rioghthaoiseach na ruathar ngarbh
o raghallaigh na ruadharm
ni cluintir aoibh a orgha
os muintir mhaoil mionmhordha
fearr ina mh[']anadh-sa ann
treall on talamh-sa triallam triallam

nora nora please sleep near me
jimmys peritonitical plea
torned onto joyceless wall blooms face
not without goodgrace
[pronounce *joysless*
blooms face = metalepsis]

count tolstoy lay adying
heels drumdrum floor
up spake stationmaster
ma dame aproch thy door

peter died
men took my hand
looked me in ye eye
why
[supra et infra
fragments of 1 abortive meditation *reaper breached our keep*]

afar
father passed
sang grufflily
hardened my heart
agin him [mens rea]

annies bairn
maes brother
peters heir
gerhards hero
maethes hae him
jim predeceased him
jack preceded jim

[rousseaus caff]
shepherded by you
ram of our flock [apr 13]
wintercladkiddywinks
sip hotorange

icy waters rise
paralyse
pa
coffined lies

peter
son of peter
warriors both
[our] childish aegis
[our] nonaged wall [vallum rampart]
vale [farewell]

walls hae ears ears hae een
shalomwall [belfastwarwall]
walls are acts of prov [non proven]
nich wahr [is it not true] wot not watched asked chad
kilroy here where harry wer da [who is there]
now u see darbies patricia uncle heard them instanter
2nd 1st to contact wall [ie 2nd johnpaul]
world upon ones wall will knock
crivvens critturs have dung doon my dun e dunno wer e wer
1 cavanmans barrier is hir castle
kate barlass brave thou art
moad pordcullis mirador horsconcours monidor more door
room may be full [pace blaise pascal?]
spurn not faded oldladyishlacecurtains they have their place
privacies grace civilisations
strive 2b private write
solus within violet vortex of egregious selfinitiatory rites
on yer raleigh raleigh [1 form of reilly]
soupcon off hir frigging trolley pardon reader must whose folly
for mere menage would prove unfit u besotted esoterical git
[welcome eruptions of deflationary vernacular]
antaskarana dats wot one *calls* 1 concept advisedly
she feigns raptures of paradise
sure advice to ye immature 2b immune 1 must immure
just because im 1 little shittle [fickle] dont make me immature

paradise 1 walled park?
true by etymology
parishioners strangers?
true by etymology
kamikazehashshashin — their paradisiacal recompenses?
nil nymphs short sherbet privation of plashy laving fountains

thus much pro fword [fate] & pro pword [providence]
bud sword has nod occurred
hmm do we assume spirid or do we suppose
hind:- [hint]
no nonexcreding sainds are full of id
so all all sad sexy sax of
pas sugar pas spice pas ancillary ingredients nice
[unhoneyed slur upon our commonhumanity
odors odious cynicism of yon scholastic stink odin de cluny]
nor 40 tons of cornish clotted cream
ro bo grassyes dew na yllons ladha spyrys
liddel bid of spirid in ye lad yed
sacre brun mesdames et messieurs
such extraordinary ardor pro ordure borders on joycean
at least that if nuffing more
one can monumentally as jimmy bore
might it mayhap be mad messed medicomonkey [manque]
well nys [spens is not] phenomenally nominal anyway
[aerospacejargon = normal]

te lawrence:-
to what occasionally compared hir magnumopus?
cameldump
bipolar?
do polarbears hibernate
luther — cyclothyme?
does glowworm shine
tormented theologian remonstrated avec auldenemy?
nickieben please cease heap keech pon ma heid
joyce?
accusant tacitnesses of whose eld

brafo brog bezdgepd bogz in de bizniz [bestkept?]
squad doo long adop drone rod deron [thereon]
zirga regna donad [not donut *nut*]
drungpa da man do scan canwise
thad wos sad crabbed sack thad sagging soldier
shouldering solivigantitude solito qua wriggly sack of worms
some excremental temple *soma* [gk body]
mombled sojourner over steamy mugs of marmite®
of soma(tism) plus anon hee nutter darkly mutter
halig toast [holy ghost aka paraclete] agus somabeans!
hordes of debtridden phds will sort out wot id reely meens
sacred wangawanga [sacer avis] vanishing sans ostensible trace
rests race run within hir own endogenousspace

spirid is councildaxable pas
spirid 1 supposidory:-suppose id nod suppose id nod
hastening to mollify sister & brother somatists
ged behind dis nod undinking numpdy unding
come clean u closet somaticomonists u coy cryptopancosmists
be 1 woman or 1 man in hienliteenmenttradishan
for fauceds & for wadercloseds render undo caesar
caesars suffer posdhumous defeads
COLLEAGUES PAY OUT ROMES PREMIER PERSONALITY
DYING POWERPLAYERICON MINDS HIR DIGNITAS
JULIO TOO BLOODY BRUTISH CHARGES CELTHISTORIAN
GIVE US BACK OUR 1.2 MILLION GAULS

caesar adverts [narratively] to caesar qua caesar?
caesar seized this darkiestronghold caesar shat on that
grandstanding bloke?
paws air [caesars] pranky mare [caesar wears] spanking dandy clokes
personality *will* enter into play?
yea
delenda pesky ahankara est?
yest
ahankara aka paraperson hir slogan?
carry on regardless
atma abhors?
himsa
atma pas tame to play ye game?
in terms of model
atma retains hir savor?
grant groping reader favor
purusha ish odograph?
let logicopositivists laugh
sceptics should be subject to reproof?
if purusha were susceptible of proof

stewed prunes up ur tush tush [proh pudor]
prune down thy book in thy nook
tho bookman is no dives yet is bookwoman no poor lazarus neither
tho she poses pas yet he owns 1 pose [secret hoard]
chemists dive dove in hope ii grope i murky trove
yes urinator *is* diver [urinari plunge]
sans travail pas trouvaille [labor 2b serendipitous]
mayhap recoiled strands of fabled noir tahitian pearls rest
inside that mereresistant treasurechest [see tarutatu infra]
a leau cest lheure [french navys motto]
o vertiginous vertiginousnesses delirious delightsome deliquescences

dove
so
low
solo
solo una spina?
[cf heros deliriumdive metropolis]

diver discerned aught of divine?
9 [nein]
climber might?
as depth so height [out of sight]
nonumque prematur in annum?
unpublish until year nine or six [if one is feeling ye pinch]
tarutatu — octatentacular tutelary pest — who did hir best? [vanquish]
skipper gordon [see edward ludwig wake of redwitch 1949]
do u mind tune?
gordon for me
gordon for me
if youre no 1 gordon
youre nae good 2 me
define rob gordon?
antihero of high fidelity [stephen frears mm]
mary gordon = mrs hudson 2 basil rathbone?
[holmes in 14 pictures produced 1939/46]
correct:
mrs gordon also cameos in fords fortapache [1948]
fords fortapache?
well not fortapacheyebronx.. [daniel petrie 1980]
stagecoach *1966* — director?
gordon douglas
gordon douglas 1942?
devil with hitler
in which jamescagneyvehicle do we contemplate gordon macrae?
westpointstory [roy del ruth 1950]
montevideo:-
pon which syllable do messrs holmes watson moriarty cast stress?
3rd [neill woman in green 1945]
dr john watson imparts uniform quality to vowels of *moron*?
awe awe [idem]
umklammerungsreflex —who when described?
[*embracereflex* neonatallegacy of our nocturnoarboreal past]
e moro 1918
1 certain follicularly challenged auctioneer:-
pronounces *vase* ming 7th dynasty 2 rime with *paw*?
mr crabtree gaylordartgallery knightsbridge
[neil dressed to kill 1946]
for aficionados of flickfonetics 1 farther futile fact?
ralf bellamy pronounces [lobster + gobs of] mayonnaise *my awe nez*
[mark sandrich carefree 1938]

wall touched johnpaul back & moved
him [cf les meteores.]
not its walls but its londoners make london [.]
struggling athwart stonewall of huns [.]
tumbling walls buried me under debris with esg [.]
i literally walked into 1 wall [.]
x marks wall barring us from our ancestors [.]
[jeffersons] cherished wall separating church from state [.]
we live in world sans walls
tellus must be home for *all* our children [.]
god bless united states tellusagus [cf senatus populusque]

mur murant paris rend paris murmurant [anon.]
edifiez vos moeurs jedifierai vos murs [anon.]
tout seul mais toujours gai [.]
im alone? [.]
youre on your own?
arent we all [.]
alone?
completely & desolately [.]
here for 1 reason or simply hoping for 1 glimmer? [.]
why are we here? [.]
why lying here nips poking up out into jolly nothingness? [.]
want my tenancy [decompose in my jolly good time.]
tenants are turds [.]
one does good business ii rid oneself of i turd [.]
give me good beans!
toothsome steaming brimming gutbusting [.]
hourly unhurried houris bear muchcurried haricots
boundless bountiful bliss

if we are all there is
gwhizz
si quis [if one yens kens serendips etc]
if we are all there was
pause paws [athwart ye abyss? cf hands-across-water]
o that gee would gie us gift
buskers must – burns did – shift
no call 2 get our jockstraps in 1 twist
if we shall be all there ist
under innominables hee sports pants incorrigible idealist grants
so led our spiridz fizz
if we were all der bloody well iz
skullcrossbones flauchding elbow 2 relendless grindsdone sed [?]
we ought to know sanguinary score
if we have all bled here before
hi ho hi ho back to bloods agus guts agus sweats we go
we moiled all day god zilch pay
kibbudznedivhalamedhay [path of 35]
I WAS 1 MISHMISHIMPICKINGKNICKERSSTRIPPING KIBBUTZNIK
NOW I BARE ALL EXCLUSIVELY TO SUN
ken [heb yes] but whose
i am in blood
sdepped so far should i wade no more
redurning were dedious as go oer [macbeth 3 4]

pancrator planets planned?
pas
plato would not champion santa clauses cause?
tho children are charmed thereby
respectfully revise barcan? [cabba]
santa failed to materialise [this year]
perhaps is difficult
beefheart redivivus? [don van vliet]
santa pon eveningstage pas

mere notion of reincarnation?
anathema to hermetists
incarnation superadds?
insult to injury
books of hermes number?
36525
whereof survive?
42
on tour i dr syntax sought?
picturesqueness
on tour ii dr syntax sought?
consolation
on tour iii dr syntax sought?   .
uxor
inter alia gandhi tolstoy corresponded re metempsychosis?
ye which one may say doth yon hindumasses sway
rox yex it out in mollybloom [plain] words?
we rereturn some dungy beetles some chirpy birds
deshnokvillager reincarnates qua?
karnijis rat howzabout that [rats]
an u would ur future hear?
conjure furcas watch out for hir spear

seems like our only future now is in telesales
however i demand more [.]
god got by with i d todds demanded ii [.]
yet on his throne yet in my heart [.]
man upstairs lacks connexion with history [.]
if only we could find connexion lewis
maybe there is no connexion sir [.]
u really lost 1 church already [.]
magick theory accepts absolute reality of all things

apropos hi ho — im regressing 1 bit:-
willynilly please revive that headline?
OLD BLOOD AND GUTS FLIES BACK 2 FRONT
[major]general george smith pattons sobriquet? [1885 1945]
boon to subeditors
chuck under chin?
oui
vignette?
pearlhandled6shooterstotin rootintootin roisterdoister shirkincloister
bigbadmansmachohirsute balloxbraggadocio slapslaphappy bastardsbastard
no joke?
bet ur goddam paininyeass sonuv1bitch motherhumpin allamericanapplepie
mindless brutality notwithstanding:-
old b agus g tolerated nonmilitary personnel?
with pansies nor with petunias patton patted civilian cheeks
our rough diamond doted upon poetry?
constant muse courted constantly
fortified by g & t perused military history?
religiously [see jfc fuller decisive battles of western world 1956
volume 3 pp503 571-4 580 586-7]

1 devout reincarnationist?
at zama [202 bce] patton/scipio africanus saw off hannibal
reincarnation is stranger than truth?
forsooth
postclassic occidental occultists resumed doctrine?
from circa 1875
epitaph?
rest in profanity

hope exit happy hope never return [.]
nor on rack of this rough world
stretch frida farther out [.]
they return (devout belief) rodential emissaries of karniji [.]
oop rattrappedinincarnation loop [.]
in former life
might have murdered me motherinlaw
maybe just ye wife [.]
ego [soul] attains once only objectivehumanform [7th state.]
easily massaged egos of north [.]
place with its own strong soul [liverpool.]
ego born where self/objectworld separate
self demonstrable via modern technology [.]
old imperial self of yesteryear [.]
essentialself androgynous [.]
is no constant self [.]
we have 0 to look into [.]
self not limited no boundaries or separations thereof [.]
my innersoul yearns for terpsichorean expression [.]
spirituality & selfmotivation unprecedentedly fashionable [.]
one sees really has been turningpoint in human spirit [.]
celts dark spirit deeply permeates [fabric of] western society [.]
saved me greatspirit from my fabricated self [.]
greatspirit gave us america for home [.]
spirit (breath of life) [we have] in common with all living beings
experience of aliveness of mindbody as unity [sic.]
soul projects body [.]
my favorite part of bearmaking:-
bears sweet gentle soul emerges [.]
my trueself 1 beast [.]
god help innerbeast [.]
your basest animalself [.]
send my self enwrapped in yours unto bourn of spirits [.]
self radiance immeasurable light [.]
psyche [soul] implants hirself within
sensehoodwinked body reasonfettered mind
each one maketh mist of mind & flesh [.]
who shall me deliver whole
from bonds of this tyrannous soul [.]
chain on psyche binds us to earth [.]
butterfly 1 hobsons choice [.]
hobbsgod nobbsgod thou modifications of pleroma [.]
ALL THERE IS IS US
ALL THERE IS IS NOT GOD
IT IS US ALONE

one reckons — one too reckons — we shall b alone
1 paddon would onmusing go
k ladies chased chasdely
safedy in chasedly
youngladybums (snuggly breecheshugged) peaches plums
[cf tao tsung-ti
pomegranates
peaches
melons
pearls]
brahmacharyam paro dharma [pas prostitute godly bodyparts]
chastity hath pragmatic value
we dont want any sthenic ailments now do we thank *u*
continence sucks
sguirim do sgelaibh mban
impotent hermeticohermaphrodite u are
nil shadows of innuendos darkened their delicate debates
[not (perhaps) bonnie & clydes]
if mr kissinger did not not kiss mr kissinger did not tell
mister kissingers mister kissinger is no celt
[herr helmut sonnenfeldt]

ii by ii ii maximize bedaguzbaddubdrillz [bed & bathtub thrills]
doctor martin luther king frolig with hotgirlz
hooverz snooperz heeheeeavezdrop
who [hoover] however opded for clozed
took ii iiii [tutu] like docker took to to hook [drollodittography]
loofalezz lethargic lathered loafing lollapaloozalolita lollz
ben beddingzdagez [stakes] danez [were] den for zegzpenz [6pence]
one then mossless loco locorestive not
apprehending locomotive connexion 2 copenhagen [capital of denmark]
takes 1 shufti forlorn in munich at gimme shelter

wip [whip ie zilch zegz] enzurez wrider givez of hir bezd
zegz bedwigzd legz nezdz [diz iz zig]
zegz begedz omnidwizdednezz
stir pas soporose dormitious possum [sopor deepsleep dormire sleep
cf pr libido plays possum]
osamic subscription:- phallicokalashnikovian [absit omen]
goodnite sweet johnthomas farewell my ladies of ye nite
shunamitism shunned should have abishag [hysteronproteron]
anent cadavers dahmer harbored amorous affections
HIZ POWERFUL PLONGER NOGZ GIRLZ ZOGZ OFF
6 PORKERS STARKERS
THO SENILE AND WELLHEELED I DIG CHEAP HOOKERS
lust suffers from unsupportive press ben wes[t]
lizd lizd luzd iz zeriouz biz [ie meridaz vian zeriozan konzideron]
tastes differ thither & hither
practices of others [perversions]
perg [perk] of gregariouz egzizdenz [ie zegz iz]
inegzizdenz naged nagednezz perfegdz

u kiss women? [.]
for woman kiss for man sword [.]
kiss is just 1 kiss [.]
kissing ye girls always fun [.]
kissing stops when director shouts cut [.]
reminds me of liverpool scallies ive kissed [.]
are all mexicans so sudden
1 little kiss balloon goes up [.]
what do south americans have that we dont below equator [.]
kiss me im irish [.]
kissing brad pitt! horrible & i hated it [.]
elephant rather confounded [to see]
queen being kissed so many times [.]
kiss me stupid [.]
i planned to kiss her with every lip upon my face [.]
all over each other kissing cuddling as actors

you turn (your face 1 risingsun) 2 look at me
lip & eye their kisses bide expectantly [.]
ah who unmoved yon radiant brow descrys
sweet pouting lips blue voluptuous eyes [.]
her niceties are very nice [.]
ross & shaw:-
1 woman that veils bosom exposed [.]
my darling boy ye 15 gamins most gay & sweet [.]
naaah boys my age are so horny
[ms kirsten dunst 15 asked are u dating.]
dressing sexy does not mean u are 1 bad girl [.]
1 woman can be stylishly sexy

im also 1 woman avec curves bum [.]
her bosoms be not much riz but she is besom born [.]
hed be in his wheelchair
id just jiggle them about make him smile [.]
leers contentedly interior delight tears thru his nerves [.]
i figured what ye hell when guy turns 80
some little hottie should give him lapdance [.]
we must cherish our old men [.]
mr riley i think i have something u might like

im reinventing manhood [larry king 65.]
he had 2b excused [went off wailing hard & loud.]
i think im going impudent [.]
old men i know think of nothing but [.]
she showed me pleasures i never knew existed
[they are all i think of these days.]
these bloody days hath broke my heart
lust my youth did them depart [.]
her daily frail carnal lasciviousnesses [.]
u are such 1 better lover than my husband [.]
all men good lovers [some men better lovers than others.]
in bed geeks ye best

ms x splayed across bucking bronco simulating
hand me my burka [.]
i am solemnly resolved 2 initiate 1 militant purity campaign [.]
people want their writers to be pure [.]
sex is such it cuts across intellect [.]
love strikes [.]
love demands everything & that very justly [.]
love waylayer of all hearts [.]
love tenderly open of heart
tho love is one you must take its part [.]
unnecassary [sic] troubles of heart im afraid
[actually he is 1 poo.]
love & libido can put u in shtook [.]
tried to murder libido attacking hir throat
filled up hir lungs as she struggled to float [.]
cries & madhouse of passion [.]
passion was clanging torment [.]
thy thighs curve shall scythe my soul from heaven [.]
if trueloves course ran smooth twould pursue exponential curve [.]
love isnt nice
love isnt civilised [.]
golda does not hate u henry [she just loves u like 1 mum.]
1 son is 1 son [.]
death unto my breast restores my son

horny young goat count leo tolstoy [see henri troyat]
beckoning 1 comely randon peasant wench
[so spelled occasionally spens shak = random ofr randir gallop]
steers her 2 1 baronial bonkingchamber
sure to have his carnal worldly way with hir

ii or iii ii i bed
gaga shaghallach pled
lasses hang back
alas a lack
[from whose demented opus *groupons nous le genre humain*]

german term encapsulates doctor henry kissingers – as it were godgiven – affinity for power?
fingerspitzengefuhl
fingerlickin good?
golonel zanderzz® gendugy greazy fried chiging nuggedz
my fingers is to my fingers?
salmons in both
mana fingerlingers?
within finns five fingers [ie 4 fingers agus 1 thumb]
dont be shifty coy boy!?
protohistoric orthostats
locus?
shantemon hill 3 miles ne cavan town
[to that hill gravitated (wed 13 July 88) 2 sons of peter woods]
finish fingersthing & introduce big vivisection issue?
give us 1 barley [breathingspace cf geezabrek]

prince bismarck per postgrad mister henry? [young dr kissinger]
to subtlest political pulses most minutely tuned
vu parlez la langage de paraphrastic charlatanry perhaps?
pass
hermes pisces?
[one refers restive reader 2 ones grimlyswimming hardpressed gloss]
i guess
so we *can* skirt circumambages? [circum around ambages winding]
one can skitter better than u ye noo look u

courteous queen of heaven from her wean received 5 joys
mana from mute moai flows
manas [mind] resembles an anemone that boasts crabby mercury
mind clings to hir clinging
indirection titillates diplomatic heads
jargon harbors nondescript nous
hellish relish intelligence
bluestocking angelina pray tell how does one intelectual spell

discerned in de chirico fundamental mechanism of cerebration?
magritte
?
song of love
love being rabs frequentest word? [cf scotslovage]
281 times loveword occurred
rab of manic frantic mirth?
aquarius by birth
celt than saxon wos more amorous?
saxon wos plus glamorous

[london tower 9 apr 1747]
lord lovat asprawl
dead
above boleskine rictal shape looms up
blooddripping astral head [astral blood for astral bread
boleskine house sentinels loch ness 17 miles from inverness]

5 mystic stones lovingly fancied as finnmaccoulsfingers [.]
5 wounds were all her ardent faith [.]
intensity of mums desire 2b queen borders on ye stigmatic [.]
is bizmuck 1 redherring [is this?]
spirit of living land i love live again in me
spirit of living land i love live again in me [.]
i grew up with affection
i will always radiate love [.]
everything good has to do with love [.]
[i value most:-]
love care consideration [.]
love create make amends [.]
love one different than thyself [.]
love thou unloveable

edipus schmedipus?
mums are just stuck upon their sons
anna livia plurabelle?
sheems [seems] 2b alive & well

HIGHTIME TO RIGHT REICH
MAVERICK PSYCHOANALYSTS DAUGHTER HITS OUT
ANNA FREUD WRONGED MY DADDY
AUNTI ANNIE HAD STOPPROBLEM
FREUDFAMILYNEPHEW BACKS MS REICH

gary coopers fond only child recalls her pop?
inter simplicity agus sophistication giftedly oscillating
apropos – gee up – which critter chanted hodonsong?
[oh dont forsake me oh my darling — titlesong of highnoon]
dont give me gyp – tex ritter
while we sing from demoticojocular songbook :-
corporation busconductor harangued refractory schoolkids?
come on git aff
long offstage we ourselves?
preparing perttauntlike to quit ye theater
[in situ
fred zinnemann high noon 1952
titlesong received oscar
music dimitri tiomkin lyrics ned washington
gary cooper won bestactor
perttauntlike = double pairroyal? see lll 5 2]

cousin clement piratically purloins freudboys farleys rusks®
[afr purloigner remove 2 1 distance]
ex sight not ex circulation
boyfreud bullishly signals signal annoyance OY
thir then viennese equivalents u unimaginative tubes

eddie bernays invented public relations?
plus uncle sigmund
not dull enough?
not [dull enough not] 2 suss 1 big one
plied old fraud avec carcinogenic havana cigars?
lad lacked scruple in which regard
eddie himself addicted 2 torches of freedom aka fags?
smoked like lum to horror of whose modest orthodox mum
obscurely etymologise?
maybe old french lum light maybe welsh llumon chimney
et vu:-
wolfish child or professional neurotic or ambivalent writer?
actually squire one really hasnt learned betsy lerner
dont play pure pippa youre hip [aware] address ye q?
innocuus sum [i am harmless]
wideeyed weans dream wolfish dreams?
reams

howly wolf
prowly panter
prauncey pony
jaundicey goat
deers scudding
dolphins louping
talonslocking eagles soar

bangles cosher cradles castrate wolves
got his popas cobblers [fond observation]
monorchism.— occams razor obtains
[moma =]
cradle protection mobility breakfast midmorningjuice lunch dinner

mistress stopes stopped whose son from every book
harry turning ten into selected texts marie permitted him 1 look
harrys kit wos knitted frocks
to ensure salubrity of evolving lunchbox
[barmy harrys menu:-
breakfast carrots
midmorningjuice carrots
lunch carrots
dinner carrots]
howard hughess mum preached purity agus proper speech
cleansed my little angel in bleach
not neat
sedulously spreading toiletsheets atop lavatoryseat
master bates MOETHER
glean from psycho iv
enclosèd hir perplexèd offspring
back of bedroom wardrobe door [parting ye purs ferforce]

law of parsimony — steve mcqueens version?
less man less
to which principle continental quilts conform?
economy
skittish mothernature worships [at] occams shrine?
one might opine
professor hrdys accolade?
thrifty matron inveterate recycler
2 1 commandment particularly shifty matriarch adheres?
honor handy molecule
so old baglady possesses some good habits?
beardy investor in factories might demur
wheel out devils chaplain?
clumsy wasteful blundering low horridly wolfish
young wolf hidler bid by billygoad?
shooerly [surely] rumors were afood
bud uncle dzhugashvili had?
00
shoes are not less than extremely complex?
clive shilton assures us

auch boys 1 bauchle 1 shauchle 1 boondoggler 1 cavan hillbilly
hickorydickoryboonclocks
well its female dick [ie shamus] we met down at windy docks
we all dont dig no stickchicks
not all cosiers awls are obsolescent [shak cobbler]
chokomengreskeygav [shoemakers town romany name for northampton]
ne sutor ultra crapidam
frumpy hummy mumper skulked in 1 shoe
is proposition true is winniepoo kangaroo
im completely innundated avec urchinpoo phew
under my feet got me dead beat swing for 1 few
exterogestate fetus eating teat hiphopping joey neath feet
be these feet unshod [should i break this oath:]
thorns [not shamrocks] below
i am pas speech feet hands arse [i am bliss shiva am i]
FORMER PAGE3GIRL BAGS PHD IN YORKSHIRE DINOSAUR FOOTPRINTS
barefoot in park [gene saks 1967]
computer wore tennisshoes [robert butler 1969]

mere perduration no mean feat
parturient uterus wet fetus pounds wot not metric avec
weightforce of 50 to 100 pounds mammydaddy [comic expostulation]
pacific giant seanagdad
laboring 50 hours manfully
delivers unto his ladymare
2000 corrugate rugrats
clap bangles ici [here] slides tot [cf aqua foetum]
coitus totus corpore [cf chest & casket]
slight that oust was slight
see see hee smile at bree
please please nil necrophilous development
gee preserve wee wean gainst hir fathers bohemian dna
grow up to be tenfingersfile or upright publican
or dominie or 1 professional anyway
not thy will but my willy be d[o]ne [silly]

megalopsychos qua neonate?
presenteth neafe to fate [fist me nefe]
already no 1 wos great?
u got it mate
drache schadenmutter ist?
eberymans big bruder thus doth insist
[bist dist gut deutsch? 1 does deplore 2 2 dreadful denglish]

agus now flippantly via forced fileous association *libido dominandi*
FETUS EXPERIENCES PRIMALLIBIDO
GERMAN EXPERTS REPELLENT EXPERIMENTS
established rockstars don tuxedos dwindledwindle tornadic libidos
hope im unlighted before i am knighted
o egregious iconoclasts do labor 2b more wilfully darker [obscure]
nievienievieknickknack light is black inside ye nyctophobic sack
hammer harshly pas tack extrudes from flock *baa*

wolf agus dog in our valley
boast mutual ancestor
wolf hails from east
dog from west
chockblock these curs [with]
jealousy rage arglebargle [.]
youll have to endure shaggy [hirsute] mrriley [.]
one cant take any more *healing*
[freud – buccal sarcoma – assisted suicide.]
now i may wear heels [.]
even cleaner clonked clou in [.]
im fumigating daddys dna

zbilga of dad ilga did nod giss [kiss] off immas [mamas] milga
nod 1 whid he loved ye whidey head of id
spilkabit(e) will spill fixationbeans spike
fifofifan do reader smell hand of expiscatorial czars policeman
ah yes amplitude & commodious roundedness of [personality]
harrumphharrumph perpend perpend [ponder perpendere weigh]
penetratingly peer polish professional professorial pincenez
tawdry beansobsession akin to gustav mahlers spinachtrip?

foreign correspondent – reluctant milksipper – observed? [hitchcock 1940]
benchleys beverage regresses since bob wos nipper
big round breasts evolved?
to prevent MOETHER smothering nipper [hypothesis]
moms milk zaps?
parasitic intestinal protozoa
colostrum applied 2 babys rump? [look it up]
obviates nappyrash u chump

shen jhem sacked in alternation tudlo tem
[milkcountry romanys so designated cheshire]
take tipple nigh nipple not now riley [raoul walsh white heat 1949]
mammary mia that teat went down 1 treat
[cf maiasaura good mother reptile]
exists no undry not orexis dissatisfies
do u ting u be king regina digs ur burp urp
jeg elsker dig [i love u danish]
pardon for pardoe [/] candygram for mungo [white heat/rookie]
top of world ma [/] caniculi canicula [white heat/ see fabricius]

swiftly i moved
fleeing childhood unkind
soiled nappies agus shame
leave all behind [.]
could not change plug let alone nappy [.]
one has nannies for that sort of thing [.]
we all have plenty of practice [with ourselves.]
hunks one but upon ones scut [loosely tail
paraphrase of montaigne]

FILIUS PHILOSOPHORUM
one mindful of natural justice apologises [gk apologia defence]
my mum patently wellrounded semimodel adult
hir sons motto will ever be *aurifica ego* [cf gildlily]
REGINA MAGNA
my son flawless human being!
active ignorance agus obfuscatory stupidity one concedes
pas epistemological monster non obstante [notwithstanding]
never carpetchewer never tantrumthrewer
as for postencephalitic moral imbecile:-
my slippered sons moethers tongue flays rotten unholy canard

chez nous nous [common sense] roost rules
histler mit schlippern
veston slipher estimable estimator [1875 1969
measured shift in spectral lines of andromeda galaxy]
ludo[vic kennedy] loved to laugh at stringvested rab [c nesbit]
didilland dongue slurps mudders dug udders [words of] love
lovehate innate [?] emotions being glomerate [?]
pseudoheureka [trew one lacks 1 clew]
yed we worship dem big bad widches
jeg elsker dig u pig
idle girls gimlet eyes flies deprive of life & wings
may yet evolve to realise
teasey cruel duel:teemy emmets versus curly scorpions
[in situ
scorpions fierily writhing
peckinpahs immolatory (gehinnomic) image did exercise our philozodiacal file
see sam peckinpah wild bunch 1969]
she teases with aposiopeses
histleron roteron apostrophes are forlorn rock on
RETURN OF WOMBSTOMPING MOMAS
I DISMEMBERED MAMA
lama [heb why] ask pas lama
agus [e]l[o]h[i]m gave em 1 whiff of roxy music®

i was born i poor black baby [.]
we left ii returned iii [.]
fell instantly in love with my lovely little boy [.]
cant believe youd fall in love with anyone so quickly [.]
perhaps i was not breastfed properly [.]
i think to start baby will be happy with breastmilk [.]
sweet milk flowed from mamas breast
hard to make way for new little guest [.]
im 1 bosomwoman [bosoms are:]
snugly comforting lifegiving sexual sensitive [.]
they stood up & sang starspangled banner
now basically they hum go down moses [.]
for them to stand up like little soldiers
you put something in there to help them [.]
i became demon brastuffer
i even gave those chickenfilletthings 1 go [.]
i have always waited for that final spurt

im still waiting [.]
i slept on my front hoping to push them back in [.]
u could feed army with these ii milkplants [.]
baby didn't even really know i existed
exclusively about ye nipple [.]
nipples *can* get sore if baby chompy [.]
suckingreflex has been practised in utero [.]
thank u
for your great love
for goodness u fed me [.]
tender tis to love babe that milks [alison loves karina maia 6/23/05.]
love hate horns on same goat
if i cant have your love ill take your hate

u look like my moether i hate my moether [.]
i hate it when she calls me mummy [.]
my darling boy i hope to see u soon your loving daddy [.]
you cannot rid yourself of your parents [.]
i cant leave mother [.]
nixon cannot not be there [.]
ever remember richard — mama cranes into thy soul

my father is jewish my mother is jewish i am jewish [.]
i am jewish i am jewish [.]
i am thou
thou art i
he is ours
we both are his
so may all be
for our neighbour [.]
stormbowed maple
sorrowing for my babe
my lad [.]
my father my son

mothers death created big vacuum inside me
woman ive become grew up around that void [.]
hope mum feels vacuum of relief not void [.]
mothers suffer most [.]
1 mother is 1 mother [.]
when one is mother that is primary relationship [.]
i love being mother its best profession [.]
loved motherhood so much nothing could have marred it for me [.]
could do this for 1 living if it paid better [.]
she was hugely critical
opposite of what jewish mums are meant 2b [.]
depth of power of mothers — ineradicable [.]
typical irish mother
absolutely determined not to let go of her son [.]
reigns reins pinnystrings umbilicalcordythings
[comical ethics sv vir cf scotcord pp200ff.]
mincing icecovered mound of motherlove [= wladziu valentine liberace]

rabid dentigerous [toothy] lad gripple [graspy] infant girl?
would work thir ambivalent providers ultimate ill [ie mummy kill]
parameters?
6 to 12 months
how would sadistic pullulating blob effect craven cruel job?
manaspolysomatically
[ie raging babe — hir body astrally transmogrified into manic
polymorphous armaments — has 1 phantastic go at mom]
milkteeth ungues urine feces [nos 1 & 2] etc?
u betcha
[up in holy horror hold your human hands o man o woman
see melanie klein psychoanalysis of children 1969 pp187/8]

hister aussi histler — nostradamus thus rendered hitler?
peustestre [possibly]
monseigneur nostradamuss haywire apocalyptic prophecy?
tellus ends again 0001 01 01 mm
yet — dont tell piss off?
would profit punter pas successfully to bet on curtains
eschatology agus apocatastasis aside:-
herr histers ma [klara] — what killed her?
1 upon catasta [stage for torture] presently resignedly responds:-
carcinoma mammary metastatic [.]
poor klara grimaced poor atolf winced?
pari passu
doctor bloch combated recrudescenttumorintrapostsurgicallesion?
protochemotherapeutically
iodoform gauze direct to derm?
so
eduard bloch of kafka clan?
very man
professor rudolph binion:-
postulates qua holocaustcause histlers mothers physician?
of course not
klaras demise:-
we can not apodictically categorise it judeoiatrogenic?
correct
master atolf embryonic tyrantchancellor:-
on occasion bloch politely postcarded?
yours gratefully ah
bronxresiding longevous — fond doctor bloch forgot not?
paragonic master atolf motel son

typical metaphysical hypostatisation of?
welljustified methodological protocol [popper re causality]
hidlerzdalins parallel historiographer:-
lord bullock subscribes to godomnipodend?
nod [see rosenbaum p94 cf postauschwitz theodicy]
dont nod off more to come:-
yehuda bauers strong disjunction?
god omnipotent or just [see rosenbaum pp279-85]
deus omnipotens satanas est?
professor bauers unblushing bald asseveration

because?
zadan saves pas holocaustic babes
miltons theology being idiosyncratic?
revels hee somewhat in zadanic
scratch delighted much by jazz?
hath neat line in razzmatazz
most complete twentiethcentury artform?
jazz
asserts?
wynton marsalis
& you your own art it may not become airborne commercially:-
have u considered fallbackon career?
cavanbasedtranssexualwebmistress
tyrant marshall zdalin interalia possessed?
lifelong inderesd in hisd lid
chairperson mao with sinohistory wos monstrously imbued?
he grooved [upon it ie chinese history]

zdeel [stalin signifies man of steel] for gulagz did nod feel
[blend? kulak gulag]
ongle joe mage [makes] zdony joge [joke] hoho
laff for thy life
blay scrapple chortle clean-vodka-soak ye clay
aunti of blavatsky pay m levi 50 franc pour 60 sec darshan
received with thank stupid old moo fool & hir loot
26000000 bombholes pock vietnam pooly momentos of oncle sam
to ye bicycles ye victory
MOTHER OF ALL STOUSHES [austr/nz var of sc stooshie]
TREMENDOUS CONSEQUENCES VATICAN WARNS
TONY BENNS 11THHOURPEACEBID
FRANKS SMARTBOMBS STICK IT TO RAGHEADS
UNCLE SAM STRADDLES SADDAMS BAGHDAD

herr hidler were stonecleanable?
iff herr hercules were hirable
augean thankless task of certain latterday historians?
ist
dupuy & dupuy our fuhrerloser lambast? [look whose asking]
mr histlers mil ineptitude renders whom professionally aghast
[consult collins encyclopedia of military history 3500bc to present 4th ed 1993]

o christ histers [ostensible] initiatory glimpse of those ost [or shtetl] juden
kaftans kippas [scullcaps] drearlocks stragglebeards
hm i see klaras orphan must cut coat according to cloth
moderating his trueblue teutonic kippage [displeasure fr equipage]
atolf neometropolitan artist gollygollywoggs!goggling [fat chance]
aryan atolf beyreuth boy jaunty german gibus [operahat]
bejesusbegorrah me caflic boyos cop keek at cavan cyclops
feuch ar ccreach ris an chaoch [o raghallaidh]
giddy eye eh for ye oneeyed reilly
ONEEYED REILLY REALLY BLIND?
[see cavan advertiser issue 4862 fri 7 nov 1954 hello mo pp14-16]

31

i fuhrer further fuhrerfureur [fr excessive admiration]
ja viable am i nonfriable my reich
crumpling stumbling fumbling humbledunhumbled
fuhrerbunkerbunkerhunkeringumbilicaldonutdunking
[bunkerhunkering in fuhrerbunker??]
half my soup adorns fuhrertunic
half my pudd lands on floor
i dribble down fuhrerbreeches when i weewee
atlasatolf cannot bear his load no more
some gotterdammerung already
some auseinandersetzung [great worldshowdown]
how could wan wee rip mak carfuffle grand as this
merry mess summing all herr netzach mesiach [sempiternal messiah]
agus quite 1 fall here i sprawl sawn off in my prime
we had projected imperial messianic mausoleum
ye which would have grandiosely eclipsed
ye merely pyramidic pharaohs
now strength spent ganz erledigd [end of tether]
dicdade will & desd check do i have 1 lefd
they think ive lost me marble
absid omen spurlos verschwinden [total vanishment]
lasd blasds from prospecdive pasd condra commie semidic basds
even i thy fuhrer atolfpasifal
scion of nonseigneurial house of schicklgruber
HEIL SCHICKLGRUBER it would have induced syllabic fatigue
german stamina bah clay ive had to fashion
give my love to bavaria [eva braun]
hittinghitting mister histter avec dyingswansongschtick
thickas1brick [cf jethro tull
& cf jerk they lose me right after bunkersketch
ADOLFADDENDUM
hitlers hand or eves (or linges) held walther 7.65mm?
fischer following waite *eves*
bullock post petrova & watson *adolfs*
file (in his day) & expiscator *hitlers* see
hugh thomas doppelgangers truth about bodies in berlinbunker 1995
klaus p fischer nazi germany 1 new history 1995 p568
rosenbaum p80
petrova & watson death of hitler chap 4 passim]

mister hysters ancillary id:-
1 civilised man tremulous & faint identified it?
albert speers da
albert his ainsel tarried consciously within magnetic adolfs horig?
[= astral aura *cf junge final hour p135*
frenzied aura of superior confidence radiating from july 20 heroes]
ja – go do 1 gregor samsa [ie metamorphose into ungeziefer]
i propose to nelson [ignore] that insecty exhortation:-
define daimonic?
mercy fra torquemada pity miss cruella drevill [.]
speculate if idly whether illinformed
execute your office lolling reader expects no less
re nature quality force forces..?
[tacit – cela nest pas a portee]

[butterfingers file spilled crapulent coffee messing emess:
gourmet percol rocketfuel® avec guaranaextrac
pour dad caffeine caused energetic disassembly
skotkahveh p3
twas as tho 1 wee leelee puppee did pee upon p thirtythree
irreversible textual obliteration (inquination)
personally i do not employ nor do i recommend fountainpens
x lines perishèd even unto ye generations
(1 estimable privation tellusliteraturewise)
if only he had lived..
one salvages what 1 mere sfruttatore can:-]

[fr] adolf [had] met satan face2face [.]
[muffy] meet adolf adolf [eat] muffy [.]
[..] ausrottung [..]
[..] at core not mere [sic] genocide [volkermord.]
[alexander j dowie appealing to fellow christians & antibloomites generally:]
from roots of pandemonium that [chap] bloom

burleigh seeks to demonstrate nonacceptably [demonic] character of?
bombercommands areabombingcampaign
[michael burleigh 3rd reich mm]

[fbi telephone conversation transcript excerpt]
AH [ALEX HALEY]
hope this call isnt inopportune mr rockwell
im 1 journalist basically i was hoping 2 set up [interview]
GLR [GEORGE LINCOLN ROCKWELL]
its [possible] i dont know your work mr haley [are u] semitic?
AH
no sir method[ist]
GLR
lets go face2face

leds face id folks i hidlerchasing have divagaded big dime
yed keep id on de qd mums de word
forthwith therefore we relentless writers return u
rackèd reader unto our mothers sorry muttons [gallicism]
ye matter is maters maters is [are] ye matter
incite us against our singing swinging mums
i or ii cavan bums suffices pas fi donc fie
nor swarms of jesuitical jewish gemini
wows odessa dauntless aries ruby wachs
enceinte avec wachsing machs
to acquire pizzas bigmacs odessans muscovites must loiter
nonobstante [notwithstanding] glasnost agus perestroika
speedypizzaspipeyhotroundclock at bigappleeateries may be bought
capital of capital [banal]
penny apples of son
[see bill cullen 1 long way from penny apples mm]
single middleaged sun singes
mock sun sundog dogson [= parhelion
refraction of sunlight transiting icecrystals in cirriform clouds
principally hiemal middlelatitudes phenomenon]

horror of song [ie music] consummates hardness of heart
[cf bebel gilberto
music embodies communication relationships emotions]
ofay john coltrane prays thru honky horn
bustling bursting ineluctable drums [naive praise for coldplay]
gimmie yon stonking stomping garagerock yeah [joke]
genius hendrix choked pon boke boak black cherokee croaked
stolen away by diaphanous angel despatched by jesus hardly
[hardly kremlin or vatican conspiracy either]
blimy jimi u wos some geezer
gee should nod have omidded 2 creade u 1 dwem
dond be lade
dwems have given us
habeas corpus digitalis brandenburg concertos penicillin
[new republic 1992 see ayto 20th century words]
bach refloated bach
beethoven beefed up boyish bagatelles
mined handel handels accomplished dominus dixit [1707]
klezmer (e) kommt vom hebraischen kleyzmer
[klezmer derives from heb kleyzmer vessels of song]
acidhouse samples
borges incorporates thefts (intrusions)
[cf al capone jr 1 little bit of larceny in us all]
riley received 2 sentences for reset of stolen goods
[john madden disappearance of lady frances carfax 28 feb 1991]
bareassed acidburner ageing pagesturner selfrecycling stinkpotwormer
[downtownchicagoparlance (partly)]
my son hebrew catholic prophet up there with borgeses agus bachs
sparkle norma sparkle [cf shirley temple]
no no ma look here listen to me made it ma top of world
[jarretts hoosgow expostulation crops again spoofwise *plaid*]
for cody jarrett pas satin nor crystalstones-of-cavan
[vide infra a fhir leagas]

VIRAGO
power ye cavan girl
CISSY
luck to me cavan cootehill belturbet [amuleticotalismanic conjuration]
cavan squalor girlhood suffering cissy drove u 2 2 1 dublin kip?
rally o o raghallaigh
somewhat rather indulge thy native cavan dicacity [raillery dicax sarcastic]
olla podridas olios reeking riley no more boldly beastly romeos
[cf dh lawrence joyce is clumsy olla putrida]
carl stommpfelder compelled 2 scrub perishes ben hygienic hourly tub
alone with 1 duck [27 nov 1803]
asperges me therion hyssopo mundabor
reekitlane
gathercauld
dinnamuck [dun na muic pigshill]
lookabootye
deilmacare
ducksdub [supra vide jbj plxxxii]
REGINAMAGNA
ofttimes i feel like chickless mummyduck
PUER REGINAE MAGNAE
big deal sometimes i feel like headless prairiechicken [.]
hee senile springchicken think hee reely cool listening in on coldplay
stick to harmless harry prespottyvidz harry who
frida kahlos manky monkey stuck hir cocernut up 1 spot
that hurt
3 choruses for mother careys chickens hurra cluck cluck
light chickens agus chearest duck wings 2 wooky rood [mac 3 2]
obadiah must have scratchings mum [tom clegg sharpes company 1994]
saint simon stylites grasped pas scratchy mirror top pullulating pillar
oui mais did he lave far as possible
humble johnson sam from tomes tore brutal pages
rancid linen samuel *heard by god* ignored pro lexicographic ages
[cf arthur koestler dwems smell worse than horses
visit http://www.samueljohnson.com]

atherosclerotic?
tacitly osteoarthritic [probably rheumatoid]
prone to bloodrushes — strictures permitting?
liable to myocardial infarctions
sasman rushed tellus?
shunned parachutes
lacked alegria [relish for/love of life]?
agree he lacked not humdudgeon [low spirits]
would u pray for strength serve truth?
do i look like hooley ballou [rhetorical response]
nor baloney ballou nor cat — one might?
young man would have perfect right
cat catched bull ecstatically at 4?
cats secular chants were heard no more
truth beauty beauty truth?
humbug — byshe wos taking ye pish [hum dubious reader an u will
this page fell short two lines
perhaps our short prophet was caught short — too many pooris bombay]

my minds hum mum [multitudinous twins incarcerate?]
PHUCK your gibbering geminis chum [niederschmetternd]

pain too remembered
past yet undone
future torn backwards
song left unhummed
[drdr.]
a fhir leagas an leac throm
air chneis mhinghil mhic domhnaill
air mhatha nior choir do chur
acht srol is clocha criostail
[sfruttatorially rendered & enlarged (cf drab carney genhist p114):-
o man that sets gruey slab
over bright gentle corpse of domhnalls son
hum to him softly ye while
pon matha were fitting to rest
satin & crystal stones
= matha na nubhall *of apples* domhnall mors beloved son]

utrillos moma married humdinger andre utter
utrillo wos 1 intermittent nutter
pot cries kettle black arse
giolla iosa boileth daddys milkpot paters son giolla [is] not
[quod sit filius nullius see genhist p115]
we our sugared pccoffee take sans ou avec lait
reilly urchins scoff rhubarbed sugar [ruchazie rd carntyne]
ben hur does not do political correctitude
true where ben hurs denote charlton hestons
not all pc comprises cs [commonsense]
society for promotion of optimum logical form
if no motherpun be intended none should be deduced
REGINA
not not knot limmer simperers dinky nimble nimming filefingers
PUER
no more ye pens [cf pedrelde la pendolica]

sumer sometime bce?
moethered civil society
sired germanohistoriography?
leopold von ranke [1795 1886]
german society?
matriarchal
british society?
matriarchal
hibernian society?
matriarchal
all nations?
matriarchal
all *patriarchal* nations?
matriarchal
[see elasah drogin margaret sanger father of modern society 1989]

u expect me to swallow go for fall for it
[that] my eldest in hir preslippers [twenties] hankypankied?
carried on with married shiksa slappers even?
my lad gewalt geshriben 1 shagetz?
[renegade jewish boy heb sheqes detested thing]

light of my life 1 schlong? [ydd shlang → mhg slange snake:
membrum virile hence contemptible person]
wahnsinniges geschwatz [mad twaddle] HAWHAWHAW [yiddishmomahorselarfs]
[aside] yet upon immature immareflection.. [cf lydford law]
scotchd is my maternal naches naches
my unnatural son now hirself discovers [naches =
a parental pride etc heb nakat contentment
b ofr nache   ll naticas   natis buttock]
some celluliteridden jezabel fluicy joosie [freudian marrowsky]
oy schlong wont be long long *wot quite unmanned in folly*
[mac 3 4 see jake horsley beauty fool 2003]
shall live one thing forbid [mac 1 3]
blitzartig schnell [lightning fast] onslought came
outran pauser reason [mac 2 3]
nat ne twynne send for welder lentamente
wie dunkt euch zur eh schmucke irin
[immas trim colleen 1 sight 2b seen]
vernichtenden [devastating] yes very tender nein
perishable shall thy sprechery prove [un]lessen thou shouldst pickle
[plunder gael spreidh cattle cf ir creach]
wielderfight penisolate war [wake]
abandoning pen embracèd pen *rest is labor* [mac 1 4]

chumairne air creich?
re giolla iosa an aigh
[led us on 1 spoiling?
valorous giolla iosa see genhist p115]
king gillys o raghli [duci hibernorum de brefny] sired 13 sons?
plus sundry supernumerary ones
mansa musa [fatherking of mali] unto mecca? [1324]
willynilly cairocurencywrecker
sir walter de raleigh befathered?
britishempireidea
fr fathered bigbang?
georges lemaitre [1894 1966]
if a b queenempress of castle b b wee raggedyass rascal?
qed
which castle housed paulus slatterius?
patricks [see michael raleigh in castle of flynns 2002]

dec 8 durbarday durgans durchmusterung durchlaucht
[immaculate conception e & w & eire allaround]
nottoofarpavilions whitecommunionconfirmationdress
frillily sillily garishly at curtsytide to highlight
depraved naivete of hir ugly stubbly middleaged visage
agus male hairy legs ugh disgust
puppet muppet [concept of] mum is 1 mumpsimus
[incoherent – 1 pondfrog croaks]

humgruffin queenmum makes houseson hum
hummed [imposed on] ben kitchen cludgie alike
mamas humdrum humbled hummlebonneted humlie [hornless ox]
loveknots [favors] topsyknave will wear by courtesy of mere
well love is service felix did to clare declare
styled ye neerreesty [unresisting] creep will be [hysteronproteron]
preceeded by 1 sirreverence or 2 phew [:-]
sirrahdandyprat sisssweetcicelynancyjessiegirl
sass me raise my fiery maternal dander
and damseldandyhen is danders [furnacecinders] danke schon
sure as im 1 donegal daniel [wise judge]
sure as ye almighty created donkeys quadrupeds
per sassararas [certioraris = thumps] applied per siserary
assubjugated certes she shall be
blows out of blue are only blows *this* girl will boast about
ill acierate u sonny boyo [convert to steel]
alchemise u unto 1 stalin before queenmum is thru
absolutely unshakeably martian perseverantly maestoso probonofilio
[mars = spagyric iron]

[magna regina resumes hir tirade cf tora! tora! tora!]
biggirlsblouse whiskers alamodede whimpery peeliewally churchmouse
regularly bondage–strossered [strossers = trousers shak]
black leather tu comprends ya viene el cativo capiche
tenant on sufferance bouncycastle outwith house
hoosegow [barlinnie] would b 1 libken 2 good for hir
give ye lady gardenspace? ill give ye laddy laldie
she if shee does filial kowtowdy may dine upon howtowdie
[boiled chicken ofr hetoudeau]
rile me ill stick antipneumatic pin in castle flaccid oooosh
force hir drink homeblend organic oj pipsy scummy
lap up beggarly rebarbative beans
[from] sheebas beastly flyblown meatplate yuk
believe me she will shriek meek geek
served mamas coky kale [cabbage charred] thru reek
so queen ordained so it came to pass
beseech thee ben bowels of ye lamb [?]
thou of vaguely majestical terribly irreducible presence
spare me soggy sugarpuffs® turnedmilkgarnished
pas ca pas ca
[supra transcends humor – 1 comedian must cultivate desistance
cf howlersketch harry potter & chamber of secrets]

ye ladies
strong they reine over us
harpy et glorious
hair
halos
jools gelatinous [their orbs]

navelknot none flaunts not:irrecusable navelknotednessness
[clones? see martin gardner did adam & eve have navels? 2001]

one may not rest assured bellybutton [biologically] moored
not if one wants to blast oneself out of water
nay one desiderates pas to play one lost ones taste along ye way
sailors wife cherished chestnuts in her lap [mac 1 3]
jolly roger molly rogered in 1 squall then 2 cap it all
ensign hornblower wos caught ablowing of hews jarp [guimbard]
[see suzanne j stark female tars women aboard ship in age of sail 2002]
yawls agus yachts by madras by calcutta
[peter hammond sign of 4 29 dec 1987]
ensieved ill thither sail [mac 1 3]
fauna eschew torrey canyon
blain is pout or bib to crib invert chambers [gadus luscus]
riggingfrigging pooppooping 1 figo 2 ye fantad
slop out u scurvy slithering titsintrances
show 1 peg [leg] bosun begged wheedled cajoled
jimbo? dropped dead at sujee [deckcleaning] tuesday
mushrooms [myxomycetes = slime fungi] got im
scupper me timbers me heartlesses
halibuts swim but sicilianic luccabrazzi simply swirls
seabed cloisters seethey oysters
[cf pseudodelirious sherlock hamming it expiringdetectivewise:
sarah hellings dying detective 14 mar 1994 see
anthony preston & george paloczi-horvath worlds worst warships 2003
anthony burton daily telegraph guide to britains maritime past 2003]
loblolly for supper! [dense gruel]
landlubbers neer suss wot thir missing
golly tis 1 loblolly [mire] down here
youll get used to gloom & hoipolloi loblolly boy [shipsurgeons gofer]
tolerable plesent quid where bort fred?
black boy 7 diles best chor in lunnon pound per pigtail ed
call this lobscouse [veggie or biscuit hash] chowchow:
1 arrant chouse [cheat turk chaush messenger]
yon scouse bastard has been diluting our chowder with gunpowder
little jack (natty scrimshander) gave sharp cookie smart backhander
blast thee shark thou shamest thy skainesmates
laid im cold on ye deck damned near wrecked his scrawny neck geck
horatioically stoical generally admirable i absolutely am
tell nelson how admiralty can
expect 1 onearmed quinsywreckèd man
focus cumbersome officialissue telescope [see
carola oman nelson usa 1946 gb 1947 new british ed 1996
tom pocock terror before trafalgar nelson napoleon & secret war 2003]
tell us herocaptain where lurks glee
gleet [ofr glecte flux] greets fleets splinters tickle feet
we all at sea see zilch pleasureislands [cf anhedonia]
scorning therefore sensible horizons
[cf geoffrey regans book of naval blunders 2004]
engly expecd every liddel lowerechelon shid
huzza pussers® that wee pustulous may gild pill withal
wolfing bully and dunderfunk [baked shipbiscuit]
and drinking dunder [lees] under thunder
wee behold not (stygian holds u see) weevils weevily writhing
i masticate u u pest of stored grain etc
caput prolonged unto proboscis or rostrum
tho u set my bellys teeth on edge pro empires sake

skulker shuck skug
push yo punt out pole ho pole ho forbearing ii put about
they hold rod in pickle pro 1 poor spud whose gayyou is fully sunk
lazy-painter-pas turned hir back to camera [see photo of vincent]
do please old gee permit one to cut ye painter thanks awfully
metaphysical ankyrs away hurray hurray
wakey wakey [billy cottons trademark harangue] boy out
buoys for bhoys first fast old laddles kiddywinks last
dogs catch otters so they cook old witches instead
[darwin beagle p213]
bursting bourgeois buoys boys burst burst
but stow fusses u rheumy rummy cusses
if u sink hunks ye stuff wins [honkyrap]
1 walked plank
waterwaterwrapped 1
sank
john whale gacy 2 wallow gaily was adequately warped
hm crawlspace really swarms
not much room for umpteen more tombs
semper room pro 1 more tomb
no room for doubt no [not out]
doubtdoubting scouth [freeranger] crashcrashes
out

wake of red witch — wich roark rort it?
garland
vanbeethoven rowed ii varnhagen?
alone [!] alone [!] alone [!] alone [!]
marinates mad master norma bates?
in masterful mat[ernity]

la mar quero por tinta
el cielo quero por papel [.]
i push off from shore of your sup port [.]
u drown me in my own caviar [.]
farther out row lonelier grow [cf einzelganger.]
fight thick tides windsallied [.]
all songs go back to sea [cf dawkins ultimate rendezvous.]
inutile city severed from ye mere

count varnhagen remarked to marshal lamarque?
better browse kant than count lamb
moral memorist earnest morse endeavoured memoriously 2 germmemorise?
grundlagen zur metaphysic der sitten
[groundwork to 1 metaphysic of morals 1785]
dexters immortal detective — should dexter have offed him?
better not
composed — thanks to waads 5pm curfew — not 1 few eth met & polphil treatises?
de raleigh [eg sceptic / treatise of soul / maxims of state
see raleigh trevelyan sir walter raleigh 2002 p423]
modern scholar rousingly denounces walter *liar?*
[al] rowse [trevelyan op cit pxiii]

cannot ask q if a is lie?
liar liar [tom shadyac 1997]
when he feels cornered answers q with q?
mechanic [michael winner 1972]
you've been watching too many latenite movies?
pop your clogs why dont you im not pissing omniscient pi
respond?
also mechanic
now u see him now u dont?
desist from this vertiginous hypermercurial jactitation [bandying]
indulge?
mechanic
instructions to his son [ie raleighs son]:-
composed for mechanicscorning [snobbish] carew?
[1607/8? maybe 1611? see trevelyan pp423/4]
or for wild wat waxing waggish in gay paree [.]
of planetary & irregular motions?
camden projected not yon hobbledehoys obstipations i think
lacking regular morals — 1 most regular moral mortal?
voltaire
trot out your aged jean genet a la francais u pseudoeuro concosmopolitan monoglot clot?
jattends la morte
charlotte corday — trunkless blushes — moral or autonomic?
automatisme
[consult simon schama citizens 1 chronicle of french revolution 1989 pp729-31/735-41]
oh dear lost me head technically i fancy i ought 2b dead?
implausible
adduce proofs u autodidactic unilingual parishpumpchump?
1 foul currant may not flaw good plum duff
dont be wet donner wetter do do better?
we are not laurel & hardy meets holly & ivy:
sudden breakupcall may floor u like wreckingball
[shall none then hazard 1 reddingstraik]
trotters trotting toting godforsaking godforsaken gofer u?
pattersons
no 2! — u not aspire to scale 2 no 7? [see moore]
shall never issue sevenzerocheque [idem]
u possess objective completely pragmatic gurdjieffian gnosis:
immortality yours within limits of solar system?
lo [heb = no] so low piddling little mice might shite upon [me]
naythless thy nimbus advertises exquisite ethereal eclecticism?
[inclusive aura is alleged]
sol trine neptune in ether [air] autopiloting
gi gurdjieff — soidisant spiritual teacher — advocated earthy enemas?
ken [heb = yes see moore gurdjieff passim]
enneagrammatic movements — they admit of noetic penetration?
commensurate with apprehension of atlantean symbolology
symbols surpass?
doctrine of 1 ass u moke [donkey]
whose art adumbrates byzantine aztec toltec symbolism?
diego riveras [1886 1957]
is rachallrach hirself maestro equally of content & of form?
dont be gormless — 1 fan u must be of ms natalie wheen
gurdjieff — guru of gaum — in wot extremity tres agite?
smorzato [it smorzare tone down extinguish]

41

sad wos hard gorges when armenian mama passed?
yass [yes] yaaf [= beethovenian du verfluchter kerl]
drdr counselled dad in extremis? [7/22]
this is it
whereat did peter flinch?
peter flinched not
brave man blanched:
imminent execution being intimated?
dr ernesto guevera de la serna [che guevara nee lynch]
fearless veteran dimwit rosecheeks carnivore espying
redindianencampment assumed new more suitable complexion?
[= george armstrong custer]
paler hue of white [cf proculharum]
raghallach 1 courageous sort of cowardycowardycustard?
pon colmans® pigmeat spreadeth sundaysundaymustard
[garnishes sundaybacon avec colmans® of norwich estd 1814
rang mustardchanges as it were per rayner burgess®
since 1760 purveyors of delicacies]
thy grave gray soul fails not to quail?
daily cravenly until i bale may or june not too soon
june 1940 / august 1944:-
did mr gurdjieff elderly resident of paris collaborate?
pass
butcher [ie torturer] of lyons?
klaus barbie
torture — quasispinozaistic formulation:-
torture must ever be wrong?
please rearticulate [quibble]
torture cannot be moral?
with that one shall not quarrel
bad wrong bad wrong bad wrong bad?
disturbing behaviour [david nutter 1998]
bad dobby bad dobby bad dobby bad?
chamber of secrets [chris columbus 2002]
compassion *is* morality?
dost torture me erotetically:
god forgive u for masterslavecommunicator
one might rack more mileage from palmtree?
if palmtree bask why not thee
pardon?
reach for needle
thread
feed wee sheeba
bake good bread
dont even plan to louis me:
wouldst be paxmanned till thy pips squeak already?
i honor u qua selfaspect:
i summon to my apology shade of rt hon enoch powell
[claimed 2b in biz of answering qs]
apropos — do you remember [chuckle]:
latelamented demolishing newsnightanchor?
i dont agree with any of that
longtoothed hood inciting irish tyro?
if ur gonna stick with crimegame kid ur gonna have to whack ye questions
[robert benton billy bathgate 1991]

whose making with questions now?
indestructible man [jack pollexfen 1956]
what are u doing in kazakhstan?
religiously avoiding qs [world is not enough]
[quote from] true romance? [tony scott 1993]
were gonna have 1 little q & a
who do u think u are —clarence worley? [antihero of true romance]
well im not andy worholas mother [.]
nor jasper maskelyne nor again j avatar horslips [:-]
little jack horner maybe?
spoken like 1 vrai sauchiehall st haggis [gurdjieffian phrase]
religious or secular ethically?
materialist malgre lui
materialism entails atheism — should one bother to ask?
naw ya wee rip
your corollary is as good as mine?
anytime
corollarium = money paid for garland whence gratuity?
u got it
malgre lui?
jesuits hijacked child
tropical language aside —shades of enoch powell:-
they were just ordinary priests?
oxymoron —nothing just about it
mother priest feed each other?
cherchez la mere
tpsg? [they play same game]
oui
utter gurdjieffs utterance?
look look she begins to distinguish ma from pa
teensyweensy ittybitty selfpity o u silly file?
one might admit to occasional twinges
so human —we fear not for our neoheroic status?
quand meme —no man was 1 hero 2 sheba
humisery —it hath rationale:
planetary imperative subtrudes? [sub secretly trudere thrust]
dixit mister gurdjieff
absurd?
fanciful
humisery —happy hapax legomenon:
your nonceword or gorges?
1 wretched lame thing mais mine own
francis auerbach?
hero qua archartist
hitchcock joyce?
heroic products of heroic jesuit pedagogy
jesuit with mullet hairdo? [ofr mulet → mullus red mullet]
bono by bob
geldof hewson?
paradigms of pragmatic goodness
bonus bona bonum?
rude humans for goodness sake groom your goodness
goodness suggested confucius should be?
fruit of empathy
wot can u tell us re da gospel per ali g?

dada [ir nothing.]
civil response anyway:
its easy to say nothing – passmassa [pastmaster] yourself:
do you remember gene kelly upbraiding deanna durbin?
[robert siodmak christmas holiday 1944]
oh 000 when mrs minette says 0 she means 0
[translate] la civilta cattolica?
catholic civilisation
of john hale jane martineau sought clarification?
whether civilisation encompasses icehockey
godless goodness not oxymoronic?
pace ye papacy
human goodness such as is is is no more than natural?
nature natures [rags in preachteachey vein (vain) again]
godly blasted beastliest?
pacesayers may be gracious players
are [is] one ye man to slam vaticanal arrogancy?
unicity & salvific universality of church of etc
u betcha – well?
go behend [sic] satan – next thing youll be urging me to posit valid theories [sic] re all & everything
squawk squawk [you] closet creeping cosmotheticist:
[one that presumes externality cf solipsism]
it may however 2 1 biologic certainty [?] be posited:
u nous [we] shant go back cant go back?
[en]sack my our secular rational[istic] ashes chanting past
[he was they were members of humanist society of cavan
1 secular voice in eire www.humanism-cavan.org.eire]
beast propounds bracing solutions to obdurate ethicocosmic conundrums?
fox [numerological value 666 (cf 46664):
with which apocalyptic (vexing daily express) worlds silliest man identified]
did wick agus cratson score palpable mortal hit pon:-
[a] blasted obscurantism
[b] organised unowot?
if did they they will millennially linger
is – mayhap shall be – one only relbelless megamegapoet:-
will shakespeare? [relbel = religious belief]
selon ken clark
1 charlatan? [ie lord clark]
modified – myopia astigmatically aggravated:
i echo rathbones holmes [neill house of fear 1945]
irreligious scribes will be nothing to write home 2 moms about?
personally i lack 1 parcel of doubt
ecrasez linfame?
pas du tout
reality will out?
not with 1 shout me old brussels sprout
all in due course of evolution sure as shergar wos hoss?
2 shirk 1 sticky wicket – dollar is all i place
race will embrace amazing space?
paz apace

traversing tundras gelid wastes supra ethic preter syntax
flappy words symbols of symbols inside *paws* into *bones* [pr cf claude debussy
much must one uncover suppress fingering emotions flayed flesh]

ANGRY CARD SLAMS CULTURE OF REL PLUR
DAMNS WICKET RELATIVISTIC ATMOSPHERE
ABSOLUTE NECESSITY OF RC DOG SAC
FUHRER SET TO MEND FENCES WITH CHURCHES
BISHOP OF MUNSTERS AGONISED PLEA
PROTECT DECENT GERMANS FROM GESTAPO
WENN DER FUHRER DAS NUR WUSSTE

repentant renegades forfeiting fortean times followed followed
daily daily singing blareily faith of our living fathers
voices of inveterate militant faithful
introduce vatican advanced technology telescope vl
none too gently 2 hir jaxy
wot 1 waste to think hir ma stalwart of latin mass society
[proponents of traditional roman rite]
had hir earmarked for ba divinity cath theol
[validated by pontifical university of maynooth]

i twist & turn agonised
lest there be 1 more bonebroke blasted life [.]
vonstauffenbergbomb comprehensively beribboned fuhrerbreechesturnups
in jewhumorcontext — herr charlie chaplin? — mighty comical [.]
condition of being bombed never leaves me [.]
ive been bombed before [.]
id like to bomb whole wide world
i hate human race [.]
once upon 1 time someone lobbed petrolbomb at me
i drank [cf tobias allvin mazeltov cocktail aka petters freylech]

britain blitzed nightly to her terrible hurt [.]
we knew our bombs were igniting firestorms [in tokyo]
we had no compunction [.]
knock hiroshima into cocked hat or
moral mortons fork [.]
i dont think morality changes with altitude [.]
[battlefield] highly immoral environment [.]
it was writer from army mag[azine]
christened it [ie saipan] suicide island [.]
suicidebombers have changed everything [.]
2b good kamikaze you had 2b dead [.]
only good varmintpoontang is dead varmintpoontang *i* think [.]
bad officer better off dead [.]
ye good colonel naturally had chosen not to hang about
cowardly criminal skedaddling aristocratic ratfink [.]
bad people often fun ones
good ones boring
really scrambles your moral circuits [.]
if u are good santa knows it [.]
i do still believe in human goodness [.]
i hope growing violence will be controlled
ultimately replaced by goodness of majority [.]
current events reinforce our commitment 2 rights & morals

1 touch of comedy sends morality moralising skyhigh [.]
explosion of fluids [debris was appalling.]
actors play with dynamite [.]
racial explosion more dangerous than nuclear explosion [.]
comedy stems from conflict from hatred [.]
tragedy is we give much to conflict little to peace [.]
dying easy comedy hard [.]
mr bayley grasps comic aspects of sex [.]
all sex has comic aspect

compassion springs from innate goodness or from empathy
there goes paddy [but for grace of.]
in my experience people are incredibly compassionate [.]
altruism close cousin of compassion [.]
have u no pity?
none for folk that outlive their utility [.]
at last i have outlived my usefulness
therefore i have decided to terminate my life [.]
sympathy – humanity – more valuable than ideology [.]
ye church 1 expert on humanity [.]
throughout 62 all journalistic roads led to rome [.]
center source of all meaning value in moral ethics:-
our lord [.]
im not much on rearwindowethics [.]
u are so certain of your morality maxim [.]
great moral elephants piously running amok [.]
hobbes was not 1 moralist [.]
ethicality [is] nonarduous of access

i labor bulllike [luna taurus] to polish groundwork
[to metaphysic of morals]
shall make halfdecent job of it before horrors recrudesce [.]
adolf hystler pas hypostasise [.]
au fond u were decent und honorable my too trusting misused fuhrer
product like your humble batman of shininggermanangelmotherhood [.]
never give in save to convictions of honor & good sense [.]
10 commandments correspond 2 irrefragable soulneeds [.]
u know willie
[he could find loophole in 10 commandments.]
to obey germans is divine commandment [.]
pon schicklgruber heap pas postmortem victories [.]
woe unto perpetrators of spurious archivery
post shoah [sic] certain novel thoushaltnots are posited

saipanhorrors would see off?
hieronymous posch
preached proponopuplico principally in pottle [1 cavan townland]:
lost at last alas sacerdotal pottle [bottle]?
fr pat prunty amdg
straight up – fr pruntys fall from grace?
does pride [bride] mean might [strength]:
honor prite [brite] agus hope to die [if i lie]

bright – patroness of kill?
fincheall honored still
st brigit of eire – feastday?
1 feb [imbolc]
bridget of sweden – 1 patronsaint of europe?
feastday 23 july
[benedict – feast jul 11 – likewise 1 patronsaint of europe]
who *was* bridget hitler?
spouse of adolfs halfbro alois jr
honor brady?
peter reillys fathers [truncation = wife]

bas gan sagart
rots ben pottle
cavaned cribbed confined
next year to ye county cavan
where one encounters speedily loughs hommocks o reillys
many hills grace parish of kill [kildrumsherdan aka kilsherdany]
not meet kill eccles street
gardyloo vu tyke ou nu spike yo eccles cake
promises promises gerrily merry responding
excitedly inquiring whether one might be permitted
to freak out over in woods [cf fanatic irish taciturnity]
straight ahead brenny becalmm [thyself]
let not this file cchange into inditer-of-lifestory
[ofr changier → l cambiare akin to oir camm crooked]
emperor qin sends weans to sea to see wot weans can see
wos no pater for those orbs [orbus bereft]
nondwem yon proudful driven emp
nil sense of sin sensuous emperor qin

malic beer emp supped throughout emperors morbid life:
might have set whose teeth on edge malicewise?
do puns bestrew elysian plain [nonsequitur (nonsute)]
boudicca drinks dwalmdale at home?
to circumvent malevolent rome
wear ones pride upon ones sleeve?
naive
proper dwem possesseth pride & phlegm?
amen

in thaet gardin gristbitung grisbitung [cf oe gnyrran grind teeth]
our gardener make us gradely [decent] by & by
drive us not towards inordinate degradation
deliver we beseech thee b from c
treat us to our daily transatlantic motionpicture
o mali may 1 poor spud may 1 poor spud say 0 [hindi gardener]
darling u have now darrayin
[prove justify ofr derainier plead vindicate]
only my goodness humility lord as keeps me clean decent
bit steep mon fils leave it to uriah heeps
file 2 obviate 1 tumble starting finished umble

my small book on Humility [.]
one must have humility [one doesnt start with pr.]
you must have humility about your work

i was king of my own midden [.]
la pluparte des gens a paris habitent des appartements [.]
raphs got her books
took martine m book & mum to paris
long weekend celebrating 21ness [.]
paris is restingplace [.]
if this aint paris im dead [.]
in paris!
that hardly points to any very serious state of mind at ye last [.]
i wanted to take reportagepictures of punters on parisstreets
i adored power of b & w photography

i watched multiple grace kelly pictures
i was sort of ripping her off [.]
i watch 1 film every day [.]
i see 5 films weekly these days
still dont pick up girls at pictures [.]
vast my films collection
if i want to see them all i shall have to die at 183
and keep finger on fast forward [.]
[frank] sinatras vast assemblage of celluloid [amon]

fuhrer wants hayes hunter featured tonight
und again tomorrow night [.]
coming home in 1 bodybag *thats* 1 movie [.]
nobody sets out to make bad movie [.]
if he has left me lots of lovely dosh
i shall buy u private cinema [.]
take me 2 your cinema

sin?
being acted upon by ye cinematic
sensu stricto?
submission supine or stuporous to sumptuous cinephotography
mahatmagandhiesque:- whom cawdor doth ca?
with irreverent irresistible invigorating imperishable wit:-
mahatmacoat [.]
johannes cawdor:-
2nd founder member baalmount st enclave?
[street not saint indeed]
correct
3rd man?
guillaume de waryn
robert kraskers oscar was for?
3rd man [1949]
oscarceremoney? [ɜ]
cancerward

BIG BAALMOUND SDREED BUSD
SDRADCLYDE DRUGSSQUAD MOUNDS SASSDYLE DAWNCHORUSRAID
DEDECDIVES SUS OUD HOMEMADECHILLUMCACHE
HUFFINGPUFFINGUNHAPPYHIPPYBROUHAHA

additional mahatmamaniacal portions of mickeymousenotions?
romanticism 1 hypomanic phenomenon [betise]
mahatmas — partial? — definition of sin?
being acted upon by senses
sobriquet?
mickey mouse
?
mohandas had lugs ala handles de jugs
mickey mouse de sade?
jim morrison
dixit?
american rockwriter cant remember her name
aye aboot time too u forgot something

EM EYE CEE KAY EE Y EM O U ES EE
[see kubrick full metal jacket]
scivi:-
hyperviolent sffilm eg redline [tibor takacs 1997]
filmslimn evil:-
evil that men do [j lee thompson 1984]
deliverance [john boorman 1972]
elephant man [david lynch 1980]
cape fear [martin scorsese 1991]

brueghel nor bosch possesses obsolescence
ben padmasana boehme nor ruysbroeck squatted
cinema circadian sinequanon [senility permitting]
cinema asylum of deracine neptunians
cinematography consummates cultural evolution
cinephotography apotheosises ye species
[some species
cf sir lawrence gowing irresistible apocalypse of radiation]

postulating oscar schindlers list qua 1 absolute good:-
one might predicate of hollywood?
hollywood aint wholly good
hollywoods fogginess respecting good agus evil?
jings i dont log it:
gemini deems his gemel [twin] frigging priggy prophet
vivisection?
visit tellus sin on thy twin pas
u plead cavansidestep yep?
snool me u would if u could
[u would have me so to say over barrel by short & curlies]
& so 2 1 viveo? [video]
yo — hear my song [peter chelsom 1991]

tara fitzgerald
magnificent NANCY we herald
glorious GLORIA take thou 1st place [rests who whose adolatarous case]
miss lolita davidovich
than which no monicker could be richer
miss jennifer connelly
never ever were u merely ordinary
miss bridget fonda
of miss jennifer jason leigh one was not 1 whit fonder
miss christina aguilera
trademark cicatrised top trendy trilby dirrty grr stop

INKED LAST CONTRACT BITCH
STUDIO HONCHOS DISH DIRT ON AGING STAR [jap hancho groupleader]
IF I CANNOT ACT I WILL DIRECT
IF I CANNOT DIRECT I WILL PUT MYSELF TO SLEEP

miss sofia coppolas directorial debut?
virgin suicides [1999]
miss talia shires?
before ye night [aka 1 night stand 1994]
1st womandirector to receive oscarnomination?
miss lina wertmuller
with what affected picture did lina break hollywood ice?
end of world in our usual bed in 1 night full of rain [1978]

one studies moviemysteries
celluloid affording – security
priapus protected
prophylactic ecstasy

do u boast celebrity friends?
have no friends
last time u were recognised?
day sheba died
last freebie u bagged?
diamante watch from damart®
last big name u dated?
im 1 senior citizen for gods sake
your worst orgy?
kibbutz [tame affair – 1 2 was there]
last jumped niteclubq?
pass
last paparazzied?
cavan antennae are raghallachs guardian ally
strangest thing u have written about yourself?
excuse me while i snirt [snicker]
most boring celeb u ever met?
celebrities by definition do not bore
last thing 1 loller [reader] sent u?
snick up [go hang]

bendidall nod much cop hidding d sack
weder onadopov weder — eg addending 1 pardy — uponabackski
more snapped at than clapped [more bonkers than bonks]
pardyanimals from der pandies fasdesd parded [drole not droll]
womensweardailypardycrowd fard nod oud loud [collegeboyish]
pardon weaker reader
your range roues [oxymoron] rathre risque sense of fun
crabs claps circumscriptions some curriculum vitae for 1 caflic

be tawie [tractable] — who honchoes who?
u do
hitchcocks origins?
catholic ireland
jesuits taught hitch?
jesuits tawzed joyce [pande manum hold out hand]
hitch 2 cinema?
jim 2 litracha
adequate formal education proved no handicap to joyce?
dixit jay eye em stewart
8 modern writers?
right
michael wood — good educator?
hugely surely one should have thought
mike walzer [harvard] analysed?
jusd & unjusd wars
hitchcock cockneybred visavis evil said?
tho common in practice = complete disorder
degrees of disorder:-
should one bother brother tentatively to amend?
amen
infantile affective life — enumerate quasievil consituents?
greed envy sadism megalomania
actors in hitches clutches?
herded were
drowning loser will clutch at?
tv movies
one pays for rollsroyce® of eyepleasers?
per nose

freezeframe half 1 mo pleez
is that hitchcock im too slow
goddam panscan where did i pose frigging coke [can]
lord receive us soon for boon [cf oe ben prayer]
but not before we see hitchcock deeveedee
on pricey bang agus olufsson teevee:
we stipulate fullscreen
SUICIDE HOSTAGETAKER WAS PROTESTING
WIDESCREENTVVENDORS MACHIAVELLIAN MACHINATIONS
philips vr805 naturalcolor fillips 1 file good karma
[1 certain excellent vcr stimulates appetite for videos?]
reader! may u attract presently et sempiternally
newer better brown goods
to purchase plasma or 100hz pure flat ensure thy purse b fat

51

in which hitch did hitch top hitch?
topaz [1969]
refers to her jocularly — while they are friends — qua *hitchcocks hen*?
gorgeous blonde miss tippi hedren
tippi jows [rocks] auteur causing sybaritic jowl 2 quake?
bygge chynn no mistake
miss hedren mocks hospodars endearing endomorphy to whose face?
[slavic = lord master]
OPESE BORKER [corker hotdog!]

bork hirself each artistvegetable should
behold how ye fat vegetableartist adores food good
o snuffelsnuffel truffelgrubber
[du truffel → ofr truffle → l tubera]
proudsows pas kowtow ii
proudsows pas kowtow ii

beautiful broad dresses well
favors nonlaundered folderols
[= hollywood ye saying goes
cf ms val hennessy hollywoods sleazy soullessnesses.]
i thought jewellery extension of lingerie [.]
filmbusiness about sex business is seduction [.]
i suppose i fell in love with acting [.]
actors only in it for ye girls [.]
thespian equivalent of holiday romance [= location fling.]
actresses need strength of character & bottle [.]
actor works in so many places
one has to see home as state of mind [.]
vagabonds & gypsies with mortgages

once actor [always actor.]
actors always themselves [people always themselves.]
english & irish actors always downtoearth [.]
deeply neurotic thing to do [.]
most actors bit of 1 mess ill at ease with themselves
thats why we find such comfort in pretending
its pathetic this inferiority complex [& fear of authorityfigures.]
preposterously in default of certain qualities like selfesteem
tho full of arrogance

moviemaking entails psychological problems [.]
traditionally low on movieindustrys totempole [= writers.]
pay compensates [cf solatium] for being maculate scum [.]
good book 1 tome of immaculate evil [sic gore vidal.]
book 1 state of mind [.]
im not interested in hebrew fairystories [.]
i emerged with actors degree in history [2:2.]
reach longitude 23 minus chucking bibles at negroes [.]
3am — thats when i do my biblestudies [.]
americas biblebelt = israels safetybelt

i came to realise salim was evil [.]
fame has got 2b good [.]
famous people invariably get laid [.]
celebrities? who needs em
[chock crunchie quote or auntie annie was not sfruttatores aunt
flimsy fivefingersfilefiller to flesh (fiftyfive) maigre page.]
persons persisting to be rich & famous tend to die young [.]
important persons possess prominent proboscises [.]
public needs largeeared heroes — me agus mickeymouse

[oscars®] important because help market produce [.]
represent hollywoodestablishments best selfop [.]
how dangerously deceptive whole business can be [.]
[films] often vulgar inevitably ephemeral [.]
once machinery [of film] up & running:
almost impossible to halt [.]
this job — like death — irreversible

gargantuan expenditures
dreadful cruelty hatred
how people treat each other to stay top gun [.]
sometimes monks would use fists or hands
sometimes straps or sticks [.]
holidays may not have been holy
certainly they were baconsaving
[i smiling smell chocolate crunchie
do u smelling smile chocolate crunchie.]
christian brothers school — worse than legwaxing [.]
paddy stink mickey mud
[cf stephen mcgann
smells bells priest altar — very theatrical & filmic.]
watch pray young actor
hope never to be unemployed [.]
ive been employed more with subs than leading ladies [.]
acting basically making fool of oneself
take it too seriously it becomes embarrassing [.]
when i am acting it is not me [.]
being able to act — like winning lottery [.]
ive exhausted my interest in acting
basically it bores me [mind]less

constitutionally incapable of differentiating act/believe [.]
who pulling out all ye stops acted off whose sox [.]
believed providence had sent him quintessence of germanness
2 lord it over aryan millennium [.]
u scotlord me mikemouse [last crusade cf material implication.]
[hrh prince james francis edward sylvester maria xavier stuart:-]
hollyrood ourself should suit
iff english tourists dinna hing aboot [.]
[his imperial rh sigismund of austria grandduke of tuscany:-]
oh scotland
so far north agus it rains *abominably*

53

[mugus drunk dumped curry here
hoc balti murgh posuit
broader than countrypancakes
taste u will not care to forsake
hoard em in 1 capacious fridge
paratas celestially bake
indian zizzler
3 zunnyzide road coatbridge
zcotcurry p90
salvageable material:-]

remember memorable [terry] wogan [show]?
im not sure
immanuel jakobovits simon wiesenthal?
[i remember it] well forget when
u remember rabbi jakobovits wry impish humoricism?
ken
with how many species of antisemitism do [cognoscenti] acquaint us?
seven i think
quasialphabetically [?]
christian
postchristian
eliminationist
racialist
rational
redemptive
visceral

master atolf schicklgruber fledgeling hater:-
which christian institution religiously indoctrinated him?
benedictine friars school lambach
those that edited nor those that read were per jews enthused?
linzer fliegende blatter
[quote from] fatherland? [christopher menaul 1994]
i shall unto america merely to miff ye jews
professor fromm enthusiastically syllogised?
[1] atolf hating wished to annihilate klara [mama]
[2] germany symbolised mama
[3] ergo [.]
u thought 2 dedicate your prospective interesting collection?
thought thought better of [cf take ye rue]
?
with affectionate understanding
to every man
ever under pressure
playfully wished darling mama
might not appropriate
his majestys telegram [charles iii teleprolepsis.]
nociceptive wit?
no yes: [mental oscillation]
nah ma would humor her droll wee twit[s]

hoot hitlerhoot
hoot motherhoot [1 tease]
hoot hollowwoot
hoop holyrood
woods wither mithers too twiglets shrink file thinks
christ im crining [shrivelling gael crion dry]
we saw how saturn sapped poor woods woods died disdefeated
[ofr desfaire undo]
worked woods wood wood being goodly substance
pas saps cease pas sap ceases
sapsy saps seamy seamlessnesses [mistics twaddles]
cmeicu
cmecmamancmincehepreferscabobs [paleogorbalsbanter]
cant see woods for worms
rigwiddie rigwoodie [ie should he have written it]
abba father ally [shak kinsman]
alligation [ad to ligare bind]
dalbeths
deathbeds
adsunt alison and david
a fhir leagas
on talamh-sa triallam
triallam
death dalbethed dad
ye rest be rest
[woodgood books
richard hayman trees woodlands & western civilisation 2004
david hickie native trees & forests of ireland
photography by mike o toole 2004
thomas pakenham remarkable trees of world 2004]

i monad ii gO mourners gaggle round
peter jack jim dad 2b your kinsman i am glad
affinity of monads lads
disparate monads nonnoncohere
wot concrete hath joined2gether [swiftscullstellascull]
trunk of a + scul of b! such jocund sonsy company
[1 smartass boffin pipedreamed bodytransplants]

not all can should?
shut up or i take ii ye robin [robin hood = wood]
i is none?
ii is pol[itics]
i rebel down?
rolleth tellus round
tellus possesses telos? [gk purpose cf teleonomy]
besserwissers [esotericists] tell us
one goes on once ones gone? [one is]
ones go on [persons]

michael joseph o rahilly [1875 1916]
rebel
per sniping brit [or brits]
hit
hit
lingeringly killed
[moore street dublin fri 28 apr 1916]
dum dum slugs numb
[new york new york 8 dec 1980]
dumdums done club club
brutally rupturing bone
long barrel gouges e y e s
[magnum versus wolves]
charged
bullraged
wolfrumpaged
hung their gut aloft my horn
[ashurbanipal ruffles chimerical rebelscum]

protoshot:- sean connollys lot
capt colthurst guns skeffy in back redbeard bundles burlapsack
o rahilly ranged forth CHEERIO [reluctant rebelyell]
breath from british barricade o rahilly flat fell
athwart moore street reduced to meat hour of our *water*
moribund warriors unto inanna or unto ishtar pray
dehydrated visages alchemising intogray
inanna swang upon an hook took on an verdant look
pearse proffers sword gun bathotic homely onion
fed then briskly shot faithful & he fought
youll have 2 leave padre pearse must eat before
commandant connollys goodness recognised by capuchins no less
had sons had daughters
16 martial slaughters

[pulteney]
pretenders son actually landed in alba
romantic & chimerical it may seem [.]
[keene]
near 3000 rebels with new arms & french louis dors [.]
[stone]
undertaking seems rash & desperate [.]
[cumberland]
sir jn cope will quench this farce no lallygagging [.]
[newcastle]
sobieski crowned king of thistles!
rebels must now whistle their way south [.]
[smollett]
this formidable invader [.]
[caledonian mercury]
eat dry crust dine in 5 minutes gain battle in 4 [.]
[glenorchy]
hardy people – sleep on ground wet through [.]
[white]
rebellious thieves that threaten us [.]
[dunmore]
march of rebels south ineluctably hastens nemesis [.]
[anson]
rebels marching so expeditiously instils general terror [.]
[bentinck]
6 or 7 thousand scotch makes intire nation shit thir breeches [.]
[poyntz]
one trembles to consider progress & havoc rebels may make [.]
[newcastle courant]
young chevalier much affects example of charles xii [.]
[pelham]
i view these highland rebels as 1 sort of rabble [.]
[english spye]
they behave hitherto tis said civilly
all along since carlisle diligently pay quarters [.]
[jessop]
terrible consternation in huddersfield & holmfirth & [.]
[richmond]
they must christ have mercy gett to ye mercy before us [.]
[devonshire]
i had no notion of army hoofing it like wildebeest [.]
[fielding]
marching – awesomely – interposed betwixt cumberland & metropolis [.]
[ryder]
papists suspected of rising when sobieski approaches london [.]
[ellison]
anticipate traitors heads on temple bar [.]
[steel]
not impossible london might fall

wee wild wales thru obdúrate warfare doth accrue
recalcitrant celtic ireland too
alba (smells sae sweet) per honorable dealing came
wherein bides nae shame

[anon]
rebels hear & shiver at his name
ch-s enviously eyes whose rising fame [.]
[tucker]
rebels scooting back toward haggis country [.]
[weston]
rebels drove back up into highlands to starve
french have no encouragement to invade [.]
[hawley]
scrub remains duke hounds are good for 0 [.]
[burns]
naething here but hielan pride
hieland scab & hunger [.]
[yorke]
they pretend to nothing farther than coups de main [.]
[albemarle]
your clatty kilt (so their civilised compatriots think of em):
1 sad cowardly rascal [.]
[webb]
old noll himself would not more direly have *flaxed out*
thir arms & cadavers pollute ye land [.]
[cooper]
battlefields purge pretence [.]
[stanhope]
appalling slaughter — our men gave no qtr
2000 killed in situ
1000 hacked down upon ye wing [.]
[caledonian mercury]
desperate highlanders trusty hacker & targe [.]
[lee]
boasted broadswords insignificant to wellfixed bayonets [.]
[riccio]
jock boasts rarely performs brags [.]
[webb]
thir nobles enchaind thir chieftains fettered in iron [.]
[yorke]
at least 1 summers chore 2 *blitz* obdurate *clannism*
extirpate ye race if not checkt by *mollycoddly lenity* [.]
[reid]
vicious genocidal onslought [.]
[hardwicke to cumberland 16 apr 1747]
your rh briefed how deeply we engage in *scotch reformation*

ireland
conquest
1175
wales
conquest
1283
scotland
union
1707
[BRITISH EMPIRE UNIVERSITYS MODERN ILLUSTRATED ENGLISH DICTIONARY
nd probably c1917 sub *how acquired by england*]

burn
turn
[rev spackman apprises parishioners of options should pretender prevail
see jamrach holobom 1 charles iii would be tyrant turd broadsheet sep 1745]
JACOBITE COUNCIL RESILES
CHARLES EDWARD SANS GUILE
LORD GEORGE MURRAY URGES
HURRY TURN FOR HOME [exeter house derby thur 5 dec 1745]

1200 shoon should have hoofed it on to london?
not every foot was shod
bonnie don quixote windmillstilting?
after which windwindwhirling

sir jn cope honorable bloke fails to cope [prestonpans 21 sep 1745]
macphersons prove very valiant persons [clifton 16 dec]
trounced by hoy loudon [moy 16 feb 1746]
drummossie moor
drummossie moor
highland bodachs
proud & poor [culloden apr 16]
celtic current peters out across drummossie wretched ragged rout
improper ground for irish people
now billy for flanders [cf stinking billy]

blethers erselearner to my impressionable
sterling fellows of ye heather
capricorn stubborn sith born 2b king [31 dec 1720]
gude goffwise to young ladies cap doffs (sighs)
pan cap pas cattle [gk pas pasa pan]
serial wifeabuser as befits 1 sensual stewart loser
messed exiled royal dress cherrybrandydistressed
mon fils mon vieux u losers losers loser [genitival genitival]
aspiring to bestride hi white hosses
superannuated bedsitnobodys i ask u
[ie superannuated bedsitnobodys aspiring..]
[mit andacht] i hear mon dieu agus acquiesce
celibate selflessness! [apostrophe] refuge & my strength

whitened sepulchers may yet reluctantly wring?
bleak concessionary smiles
bedsittingroom?
good training 2 tenant 1 tomb
brimmed tomb? [me brymme]
fulfilled tomb
no kiltie ever incurred?
keltie [penalty bumper]
london town soupcon terrorstruck?
thy laes the [lest] lousy sporrans run amuck
wild carnivorous clan called mcbean?
picked bones of unwiredup tourists quite clean

quo elcho unto charlie on hop
there u lop [on hlaupa] u pusillanimous wop
left his people in lurch strategically embracèd anglican church
but butcher canny chap sub commissary canvas scorns to nap
mock aprilborn capricorn should non [cumberland – dob 15 apr 1721]
sobieskis [ie capricorni] pursuing glory ought rush slowly
nae great general – our dukes defeats were several
scoundrel by faither dubbed at hastenbeck fairly drubbed
cumber
land
ben
sink
sand

prosing re rebel swords snoreboring anend groddy onions
dempded do inquire weder ardisd ditched hir nadive gumptions
ah shall mad cavan arsetitsslasher creative steam running out
eftsoons be reduced lemphealt [halting]
stalling selfkickstarting to shash?
reader reels from staw [surfeit]
nugatory stokeups sticking in hir craw
wha cried [who called] arsetits steamie [public laundry]
wha cried steamie arsetits

tycho brahe [1546 1601] – nice bloke – danes are nice:
brahe boasted no boko to blow
having ditched it 2 1 duellists blow
therefore tycho wrought schnozzle of copper
to serve brahe qua snotstopper
absent blennorrhoea yet brahe registered bells in hir ear
[gk blennos mucus rhoia flow l tinnire ring]
mercury getting up into olfactory marched whom off
put 1 line here pro putid drivelling hidlers putative nosejob
jeez sheena u shuda seen hiz ozaena
[emunctory humorousnesses?
gk ozaina fetid nasal polypus → ozein smell]

steelseekers sought out seki
[seki city (mino province) yclept town of swords]
grab 1 shabble u can help me thrapple ye mcmahon
[dixit tanist to cohort
shabble = rusty old sword cf pol szabla it sciabola]
douglas 1 douglas brandishing 1 cutlass [jamais arriere]
wheesh wean or archibald ye grim
slogan wos GEORGE AGUS BROADSWORDS [moores creek 28 feb 1776]
robert bruce debonair shading [parting] harry bohuns hair
brast brawest battleax! [dislocatory exclamation]
riccio – 56 stoccados donated per 7 aristocratos – goes *plop*
poignarder ala ecossais french used to say
sheriff of lanark cut into collops wifie got ye dallops
by willie wallace inabarra
god those chops are never my handsome man

bar cochba [nasi (prince) of israel] and rabbi akiba
can not rome stop [they gave juggernaut pause 132 135 ce]
whose guerrilleros lop 1 pinky
or deracinate chopchop [promptly] mainmain [handstrength]
1 fullyflowering figtree

barren electric land
sun caves orange sand
messiah simons limber spelean band singe roman scorpion

rabbi akiba — his fate? [traditionally adumbrated]
metal [combs] scraped flayed flesh
obscure [unknown to fame] last word? [propaganda?]
achad [res]

theurgist [ie homeopath]
initiator
cherrytaupetivolibestower [tivoli®]
pour largess
pour largess prince
[cavanbardicneoidiompraisepoem
composed for youngest brother 8 sept 2003]

dig your tiv[oli audio® henryklossmodel2® amfmstereoradio]?
did spiv nil dig brylcreem® [eroteme — did spivs dislike brylcreem®]
tivoli gardens?
copenhagen
ms roma ligocka dropped in on whom? [backstage tivoli park]
weary marlene dietrich
ye tivoli?
tiverton

TARTAN HORDES ROMP THRU ROME [387 BCE]
BLONCKET SENATE CONSTERNATION [FR BLANQUET]
BAMUSED BY WATERCLOSETS
DRUNKEN DAYTRIP DRUIDS DROWN IN TIBUR BURN
PLEB THUMBSUP TO BARRILEIRENBARRBRUƎ
ENTENTE MINERALE

hirsute shiftsless swordy
[outhouse celts]

sassenachs singed nigh bannockburn
events taking 1 untowardly turn [24 jun 1314]
jocks quit high ground
this tactic was unsound [flodden 9 sept 1513]
gideon whose army dawdled doon from doon hill
kirk made it easy for cromwell to kill [dunbar 3 sept 1650

full works dished up by pseudogladiators [.]
celtsnot on celtledge of celtrock gladly carefully [.]
celt in all his variants
from builth to ballyhoo
mental processes are plain
one knows what he will do [.]
young scots males more likely to bridle
[than english or european counterparts.]
on english loons rained muckle thumps
efter her legs cuttit off
flailed pon oozing stumps [.]
ruthless christ schizoid limbseverer
restoreth ye withereth

manas mens mind intrepid traveller doth find?
hath sandy taclamacans aka rienderiens
hearthside knights pored over?
story of bertilak de hautdesert
dromidory bitter biter?
kicks – sometime stomps – hir minder
trekked minus bravado out into saddams iraqi sands to zero in on sieving fact from fantasy?
mike asher andymcnabbasher [absit slot]
atlantis of sands?
iram aka ubar [te lawrence]
vual assumes?
camel form
foments furfur?
stormclouds [see gettings dictionary of demons]

feet cloud head sand [arsyversy?]
nittygritty none too pretty airfairy quite contrary
not that gO has not lots to commend it
black white gathered O stompie mokhetsi
slow schlep O gelid burninggO

inuit miss [privation] risingsigns – curious to tell?
consult miss eskimo nell
pole2pole – no pokerface? [geminirising? cat swallows canary]
montypythonbloke [intrepid voyager michael palin]
nowhere more than in julia szostaks poland?
flourishes sympathy pro artistic temperament [dixit roma ligocka]

wander throughout waterclosetless wastes
potfaced sans sandpapers [loorolls] sans toothpastes
pas pon your smelly nelly brenny
maigre mannikin avec eclat avec betterware® clothès
household cludgie nonscorns to scour
nor kitchenfloor with betterware® mop to sop [up]
[ie schmuck scrubbed bollox mopped – much ado re donkeywork]
modcons sweet modcons
[this page lacks 1 line ### mayhap rags that day was florid]

salty seafarer fenius farsa saw
fotla fotla [cf thalatta thalatta] waterwandered farther not
mythical hibernian questrist [ith] spies banba plain from 1 tower
rain in spain falls mainly plainwise
miss grace o malley getting hir kissable royal irish arse in gear
embarked upon 1 risky risque career [highseasbuccaneer]
piles is pain in ass

domestic desertdwellers do esteem
simple safe sedentary cinematheque pleasures [:-]
agua arbor grass [cf dejeuner sur lherbe 1863]
hihohiho empty diurnally horrific postoperative po
[hipreplacementseasons]
daily feed wee sheebacat tho shit wee pon kitchenmat
athwart ye jordans under ye palms
u2 go to!
jeunesse dwindles ii i po

sheba dead 1 year
she has not deserted
lit taclamacancandle
feeling 1 tad wobbly
perhaps metamorphosing into feral
hardly 1 god
it seems fervent perseverant creation may be 2 blame
[cryptodiary sun 25 may 2003]

disinterrèd thou shalt not b sheba
starkness of chargeless scattered bones..
wee sheeb
luv u
sense u
wistfully [dilection]
u were only 1 animal
pas
person cannot be only [caritas sparks namaskars]
fuffy kit u [soft & light like aero®]
fuffed [spat] with felinest
[cryptodiary qua supra]

fin
ende
nae mows
[written terrible night sheba died see gloss
nae mows = no laughingmatter *nae miaows nae mousies*]

motionpictures?
oases of color & of lite
color delights?
ineluctably

nippon temple shintoshrine paintings sculptures had 2 shine
blench gaels avant cuchullains glow
[which] birsles [toasts] shrubs blisters snow
burning customary candle provides pas handle [access manes?]
oe candel → l candela (candere glow)
rags scratched last match jul 14 2003 – grandad reillys birthday
tue jul 22 perished poor peter woods *amo te sabidi meaculpa*
hiroshima event eclipsing atomic wax nagasaki tallow]
coindil dodecsi dus inbruithe in tarr
pro every oasising punters were detrop

THEY KNOW DESERTS
MESCALERO SCOUTS AT HOME
AMID SCORPIONIC WASTES [.]
WE SHALL ENDEAVOR IMPASSIVELY PERSEVERE
CIVILISED TRIBES PLEDGE PRESIDENT

dare me to ye desert with thy sword [mac 3 4.]
well well you would have me desert rome [cf zemzem.]
they were so to say my 1st water in desert [.]
desiccated desertdevil from dantes hottest hell [.]
birdnest in this circle..

life improved once we mastered art of reading on camels [.]
flush loo scalding powershower piping peperoni [pizza]:
life of reilly [.]
hutdweller sold us 1 live tunisian desertrose [.]
arab things [garments] cleaner decenter [wastewaste]

i am dul as ded
forgete ben solytarie wastes [.]
here i am alone
frozen in my world of stone [.]
thrown on wideworld doomed to quest[ion] roam [paronymy]
bereft of younger bros of home
stranger to chocolate movies joy
pleasureless br[ei]fn[e] thin princely boy

[1 quest is] synecdoche for totality of desire [.]
plough conticently [thack silently] contingent pylons [.]
cringing carrion cowered crowled
hirself discovering chancecast clod
incontinently tending terrors nod [.]
boy am i suffering

sting hermetic leningrad [via terror & starvation.]
neujorcers in affrightment crane gawp upon
hosamas horrisonous flighted scorpion scorpion
[paranostradamuss orthography horrere bristle sonans sounding]

64

cellular [somatic] terror spenditall enthralls *dismayed*
rasped agonia enditall
hath spenditall by ye ball..
sub 60 togs roaring not snoring coldbiting nailssweating
zennist may shout whiles zennist is jimbowied out
keys please me no alamo
picnic sits ill at 1 panic [cf wahnen und weltuntergang]
o loud let this deepmind [telechronologic] prolepsis pass
thy will not my will be done

respecting stertorousness:- [stertere snore]
wot lang syne agonias fond unfounded hope?
humble cunningly concocted wellbalanced receipt [recipe]
finds its way onto western worlds lucrative healthfoodshelves
?

snorenomore®:-
sublingually efficacious expensive elegant elect enzymes herbelets
to promote?
deep dreamfree sleep bugger sheep
discover alphabetically enditalls slick panglossick panacea?
acerola
am i lazy [amylase]
cellulase
ginkgo biloba
hypericum perforatum [standardised extract hypericin 0.3%]
lipase
magnesium + additional phytonutrients naturally occurring
[which phytonutrients passed with him
naturally occurring:
within fecund foodbase of saccharomyces cerevisiae culture]
teaseunot [protease]
serotone 5htp [extract of griffonia simplicifolia]

agonia stirs from poesque snooze 2 1
pit
sub enditalls shoes
sans floor bed stands pas
bed stands
ergo absent pendulum
apodictic verry gery
[these endearing minor triumphs of aristotelian logic]
[go tell] morse frost personable midsomer shamus mister leo agonistes hath disappeared totocorpore
[leo = parexcellence sign of traumatic fear
agus such ye hazards of materialism
cf janaceks songcycle 1919-24 diary of 1 vanished]

dci barnaby swollenglanded sternutating scratched?
allergic reaction to charming cullys cuddly cat [killmouseki
see jeremy silberston midsomer murders written in blood 1997]
premidsomer:-
luminous laura howard irradiated 1 other series?
so haunt me

gulphplumber
gulphplumbed
[gulp…]

but wot would nietzsches zarathustran barathrum really neatly zee in
mee
0 [zero]

form & order
fall [into 1 void vide brief account 1992 recension p62]
fall [bridget louise riley 1963]
free fall [william gerald golding 1959]
PESKY PRETZEL FELLS PREZ
DUBYA KISSES WHITEHOUSEDECK
BARNEY AGUS SPOT ON SPOT
VASOVAGAL SYNDROME RECKONS DR TUBB

maximum entropy puts gases at peeps
oftenest – statistically speaking – during sleeps
peacefully in dormition surrounded starved dehydrated [?]
help nigh end of line help will not be thine [cf caritas]
give needle get needle [cf voluntary euthanasia society]

brought not optimistically-bought-quartz harmony 2 mattress?
lo [glottal stop heb neg]
one is – to appropriate [adapt] jan morris imperishable phrase – one is?
file of debilitating inner torments
kava kava sharp anxiety assuages?
nought blunts
st johns wort?
en pure perte [less tempting than 1 torte]
wot one hath that i clingeth ii?
neurotically true
conduced weather to nonclimatologists [enditalls] terror?
tropical heat 82f plus torturesome humidity [summer 1995?]
not sort wherethrough watch midnite in garden of good agus evil?
[clint eastwood 1997]
nein
ef schumakers modest economical collocation?
modicum of temperature comfort
your new newageanxietycounsellor – she hails from santa monica?
ja
[1 astral or imaginary counsellor]
she ascribes your general global lamentableness to?
bad ka[rma]

sinderella spenditall erstwhile middleeast
trembles sinedie fore lifesfeast
besides hirself hirself ii sell tells tellus
& britishnation within i padded paddycell:-

solitude blood your cottonsox

[oe bledsian bless → blod blood]

isolation sans compensations of solitude

[fruits of meditation contemplation?]

one will insist upon living on ye sewerline

[book of] kells *might of celtic monkhood*

[oe munuc → l monachus → gk monachos (monos alone)]

magan is not 2b dismayed

[1 mags worth of wisdom

oe magan to have power

dismay me → ofr ult → ohg = strip of might]

we fail we dismay we betray [each other]

behold how one loves doats upon [another]

epistles emanant from erin cherishable are

cherish ye thespian

rapinohirondelle cherish did latude ben hell

shall pipe thee frail gavotte sweet rodent?

go to goshen [see exod 10 23]

so we should mutually bless

blessed credulous

presseth not for definitions

dithering brings simple ditherers indirectly home

[cf simple faithful — 1 dalai must live]

ii ignore i mitzvah

2b overlooked supreme good fortune

daily daily gaze space

[ie tomy astronomybooks]

every day play fresh

[hands together for sportive contemplative pollyanna]

game is for one that can play [sage gallio]

mask dissemble act

[1 macilvanney ben gadhelgarb!

enditall had campaigned for space on major globaltvnetworks

whereafter would have commenced

overt emergence qua worlddominie (dominatrix)

log on 2 www.enditallismaitreya.com]

contemplate space cleanse mens

iranian carpet may have mind of hir own

fringed carpets abominable

connive at naught [save quality]

stop not bod [that would] top hirself

[morality?]

oftentimes will saturns work

[aka chronos = time]

more fun one has less fun one wants

[is not this funest?]

semiprofessional fun odious odious

humor wells

seriously — we are not here *for*

[he tells us he tells us]

thus grudge not hir thrust

thisness thine o punter everytime

[cf duns scotuss haecceity]

personal past aka anaconda

hericons revelate [urchin ofr herichon → ericius hedgehog]

fifofifum pariahs pious persons shum [shun? 1 editor 2 enditall might almost take ye *scunner*]
other than dwems prone to selfimportance
really is no succedaneum [substitute] for selfesteem
[ruffruff list list to puffed polonius]
auras of invincible rectitude rebarb [repel]
life (all2invincible) hath clotted hinterparts
life runs to neurosis
norm engendered by ineluctable extremes
[which frisky witticism did 1 little tickle hir shrinks]
amidst extremities literature
amidst literature dereliction [re behind linquere leave]
relict of imperial mindset capitalisation [?]
autocephaly put paid to punctuation [?]
no saviour ink on paper
computing conduces perseveration
[white putting black putting polonial putting]
skins expeditiously download
birds of feather palaver together
[port palavra word → l parabola gk → parabole]
bids of fedder bledder
flockers flock
pesky extras spoil ye pic
gooseberrydom 1 honorable estate
once 1 gooseberry twice [1 gooseberry]
better tautology than sorry
cackles pas thinks to shysterlevels sinks [cackles comma pas thinks comma]
some by noise themselves define
[cf joan baez noise 1 imposition on sanity]
language is squawky thing
fear revere flirt with wallow in like love live for ENGLISH
my fellow english & i
[wishful — he means english speakers of course see kate fox
watching ye english hidden rules of english behaviour 2004]
up off thy bum sluggard celt [:-]
study ye english
all 1 required discipline application
all one lacked application discipline
nil squalor squals like celtic squal
cruive crubeen
[cruive — also cruve — sty hovel
crubeen pigtrotter qua pabulum ir cruibin dim of crub hoof]
cursed be celtic flamboyance
cursed be flamboyance
rein in thy westceltpeasantry crucified charitable christ
they wouldst deleteriously dismiss thy sassenach [servant]
cartaga delenda est
[sellafield — or vivisection?]
existence dismisses cissy seniors
one that betwixt exits exists [senior citizen]
youth malaise
cure duration
lay to rest old crock days of youth
were crock of crock [lust & dung] in truth
society for dissolution of youth
beeeejj

[betters elders enforced expedited evolution jejune juvenals]
dissolution bitter sweet sleep
1 loss 1 liberation
tellus awakens to hirself
tellus conformèd not to enditalls desiccate drab expectancies
strength 2 thine elbow tellus
family [is] tellus tellus [is] anathema
tellus get uspres tellus deserve
does west civ merit george w bush?
sellotape 1 staple of civ existence
gross or sophisticate?
grosssophisticate
[cf maestro libor pesek re megalopsychos (great allembracing soul)
rougher cruder on 1 hand gentler more sensitive on other]
withold not yourself from cfm: [classic fm]
1 civilising influence
[radio] silenceexcluder
[cf bob dylan experience teaches]
memorable terminal exhortation *stick with silence girls*
klosses® boses® bushes® brace nature

[aussi panasonics® agus 1 ricepot®
cf katebushsong & dream of sheep
by hir end enditall had marshalled 1 battery of wirelesses]
nature eased nature pleased
nature subsumes science science subsumes not [nature]
applies not science applies not quality
to educate yourself in science festina lente [hasten dilatorily]
selfeducated? selfeducating
poor [is] niece [that] cannot educate hir uncle
to subdue priapus study science [sottise]
subduct not love from fredo corleone
fredo corleones own good hearts
ruthlessness of our friends heartens us
2 mothers = 1 maffia
axes of bad[ness]?
cave axes of grannies
rhythms of lions [males?] more monotonous
scatty lionesses worth their weight in platina
[= platinum sp plata silver]
no mystery looks victrixlike *headscarfed*
swollowed up ith vicdory vicdory hollow ith
defead defead hath pith
peter woods did not in defeasance go down
commend me ones that drop dead
when u have had your pith & chips [:-]
cash in checks
when chips are down [premorse?]
no more remoras
[obstacle delay hindrance]
clear them thar decks
head for them thar hills
agin sticky prickets
kick kick ye whilst

hop skip stub burton®
ye rest be cyber

69

dad
attending end
adjacent ii i spartan close
kept panicbutton close
gray stone fastnesses [home & hospital]

abba
father
your strangulated son
should have been better one

peter
son of peter
soldiers both
to own regard for whom [cf gra]
i am not loth
close [conclude]

per enditallian decree:- [astral (imaginary) republic of enditall]
sunday closest to summersolstice?
2b designated publicly celebrated *soningsunday*
sunday closest to wintersolstice?
2b designated publicly celebrated *daughteringsunday*
fed of cr? [federation of celtic republics]
as broached notion [alan stivell]
progs [progenitors] of europe enjoy last laugh on jcs?
[julius & posterior caesars]
laughter perdures pas
uk of e & ni?
[united kingdom of england & northern ireland]
u do try
urge wedefactobritssticktogether?
post 9/11 oui
under wot slogan might u have campaigned?
DEVOLVE EVOLVE
britain prudently united within putatively united europe?
posturing politicaster puddock: [late oe padde toad frog]
u caribal [cannibal] yapping yankie [besom] u:
yank yank hir fretsome chain again —
thy sorelyunitedtwin will thee yank yank [buffet.]
well anyway we did not make it 2 america?
yeah they cant take that [privation] away from us
[exeunt severally]

blinkered per coffins [urversion per funerary monuments]
peeketh enditall ahead livelily teleanticipating being dead
[my pal cavanenclave!]
being locorestive bakes interalia sairheidcakes
we[self]vapulate 2 get ye sight homemadecakes sub lunalight [we bake
ie we witches cf coniunctio solis et lunae
files flights of fancy..]

70

pro purestwatertunnelvision wins bourgeoisbiskit
bohemianly downing microdot decides atatons 2 frisk it
zonked zowie zeez [sees] ZOMBIE
[zombie my ass
hallucinated dogdung-lobster-walking-hirself (cf gerard depardieu)
where belmont st by illlit nite floats into great western rd]
unchocolate biscits does mistress littleworth disrelish
less greedy liddel hederoclide liddelworth than selfish

[res irregular gk heteroklitos → klitos inflected]
tho replete with pleonexia..
pas celtic bannocks for noncontinental miltonic mee
but heehee hedonistic banoffee milkshakes
blackcurrantflavorpeanutbutterchunkicecream — deflate my fisc!
flocks of fondlesome florentines nonfloccinaucinihilipilification
howzabout 4tiered nahuatl chocolatl freshcream sachertorte
[at violette café hampstead such exotica are sought & bought
cf scotcrab p103:-
sad sods sorry solo greasytootingspoonhogmanysojourn
spoon too soon mouthed spoonog lingers]
troglodiet barchocchockblock genealogicogenethlialogic fanatico
reembraces newageselfrehabilitationprograms avec furnished bravado
eggs delights 2 boil or poach singing singeing digits pon roach
peregrine pilgralack [lacklove] esq neoprimidivepaleoceldicadavisd
undergoeth nod withoud humor heurisdic selfanalysis
if all yumor be nod gallowsyumor:
1 shamrock is 1 sabrah ya tutochki
[ir seamrog trefoil heb sabrah opuntia fruit]

black humor — adjust for political correctitude?
nonincorporating milk-of-human-kindness [? cf warren mitchell supra]
kharkov cakes comprised? [ukraine winter 1942]
manmarrow
in absentia?
mannae [prob not heb man hu what is it]
folks in black hills of rif?
raise kif for spliff[s]
wos 1 younggirl of dundee panhandling rollups aetatis iii?
age xii left on shelf — anamnestic tragedy
[anamnesis = persons medical history]
banff agus buchan for b agus b [are] tops? [1990s?]
aussi one may browse perennial xmasshoppes
[cf mandy mcclorys ye olde metropolitan]
santa macnicholas — charming tartened jerkin — cum cunning gallus merkin:- [sporran of sorts]
combien excluding vat?
£78.99 [1990 prices]
humble cunning person [jung] converseth [with] utensils?
et selfomeleth eggs et selfresharpeneth pencils

[earlier amelette fr → lamella thin plate
magisterial morse somewhere memorably expounds]
le marquis de condorcet?
foundered on an omelette
concoct 1 kharkov amelette?
bottled blood birchtwigs promiscuous bark
[sangspots (cf spoor) here adorn ms — editor speculates epistaxis]

amalettic formula advocated cockroaches not?
correct — pas clocks - ware ondits — nazi canard
lowest form of lotechnology?
roachholder
devices?
distance

wine your springcakehole
hechalutzbaanglian kibbutzwilddolt
smack [actually mescalin] pop dopedope [schmuckschmeck!] smoke
heterogeneous hallanshakers [sturdy beggars]
baking basting parched [beaches of eilat summer 1971]
holy moses holibutrizzored wholly and hellishly
[rizz(a)(e)(o)r *a* (sun) dry *b* rizzored haddock
ha(o)libut me haly holy butt flatfish]
awned busybee cocacolamerchants
sudoriparous shekels [transference]
dawnyawns polychromatic volunteers [technicolor sleepbags]
cerulean redsea comma sky ampersand sand sand [pseudopolysyndeton]
hardness hardness beneath ye beach
1 mosaic 1 kaleidoscope
[gk kalos beautiful eidos form skopeein look]

world is hell — what does it matter what happens in it? [.]
fuhrer lavishes hells upon them
to hell with hitler or to victory [.]
i have this thing about going to hell
i don't want ii [.]
i should be sent ii hell [.]
[true believers know] these gentlemen did not merit sherbet

orcus aka pluto aka dis distances dinna go amiss
re moat ness subsists in nonfinite degrees
isolation dictates particular ethics [moot]
technology demands technology [far out]
we are technology technology is ourselves [rabbits raisins]
oaktree zombi coiled descendant proper
mama nature would not let
hir fils et filles come 1 cropper
[a doot files gaen 1 bittie fuil]

ABANDONYEFIELD ALLWAYSATWAR ESQ WHOSE HEIMISCH AUTOAMNESIS
[mere amateur escapade (fatuous) (fatiscent)]
SOMA [obdurate brute anatomy]
[a] phymosis
nonmohelic rectification general anesthesis [ae xxvii 13 jul 1975]
[b] myopia agus astigmia
statediagnosis [ae vi
luna taurus 29° applying to occult quartile of virgo mars]
[c] rheumatic fever + secondary pulmonary collapse [ae viii]
concomitant mitral stenosis + [hysteresis] prolapsus-in-posse

transmyocardialrevascularisationacrossyepond [ie ripe for
raghallach born sub saturn leo – heartaffections]
[d] sundry childhood cicatrices
[1] collision with sawnoff clothespole coltterror
[ae vi
ie (amidst unwearying wastes of) coltterrace
hir slumcumeden residence until 1955
bit hir 1 mastiff aged only six..
(cf col crockett & – sharpes regiment 1996 – ltcol girdwood)
our holy terror persisted pas to hurl bricks at little snotty girls
within mins of whose 1st offence pws condign slipper flailed
bad boy bad boy sbrawled sans breech breech stung
that was 1 salutary thrashing
cf act of 1860]
[2] dart in back coltterror
[3] spills from bicycles roy mansions
[ae vi
= croy road files shorthome 1955/8]
[4] unkind [reckless] filefingerssplitting kitchenknives
3 ran 2 cats crashed
[ie 3 swift avenue
hir barnaclean british address ae x et sqq
wherein sequentially burtoned bede sheba hecat shecat]
[e] sciatica passio
[fraternally diagnosed ae xliv
probably active since late twenties]
neuritic agonies intermittent incapacitating
crawling on 4/rolling on floor
[emergency regime]
arnica (too expensive)
paracetamol bp 500mg x 2
[f] rheumatoid arthritis passim
selfdiagnosed [ae l]
[diurnal regime]
[1] chondroitin sulphate 1400mg [theodosakis optirecommends 1200
rags however being exceptionally degraded]
[2] glucosamine sulphate 3000mg [theodosakis 1500]
[3] msm 2000mg
[4] devils claw 4400mg
[zipvit® capsules involve 440 mg standardised extract
= rootpowder 2200mg:-
minimum 1.5% or 6mg harpagosides per pilule
harpagosides for 1 harpy]
[5] turmeric too food to bestrew
[earlier forms tarmaret etc
maybe → fr terre merite & l terra merita deserving earth
herbalists advocate to relieve bursitis/tendonitis
ai curcumin possesses antioxidant properties
qua antiinflammatory:-
hydrocortisone nor phenylbutazone is efficaciouser than curcumin
400mg x 3 daily
abet ideally with bromelain & flaxseed
see linda b white/steven foster/staff of herbs for health
herbal drugstore best natural alternatives
1 counter 2 overcounter & prescription medicines 2003]

[g] ced [chronic energy depletion ae xxx ff
cf madlunarbulldisease
trickling of whose flickery vitality could not goad
dramatic developments on any worldhistoricfront]
[regime]
[1] alpha lipoic acid 200mg
[2] acetyl-l-carnitine 500mg
[3] guarana 500mg
[1 brazilian liana (*paullinia cupana* / sapindaceae)
wot reader you really think *sap* overly strong]
[h] bph [benign prostatic hyperplasia ae 1+]
[prospective (astral) regimen]
palmetto
pygeum
easypee® [imaginary quasirejuvinating pallation]
PSYCHE
[a] mental health
not 1 wealth
[bit of 1 dearth
advisedly refrained from stateselfre*feral*
cf dearnful – funebre – moping micawber]
[b] wormed by bluedevils
[cf cheryl crow this gnawing thing]
pas careening pas career
sadness swims in bacardis® agus gins
[cf phil spector hapiness = good health bad memory]
nor with [baileys] glide® wash down 1 dish [of]
wellfilleted gemutlich [sonsy] gefiletefish
[ie gefilte ydd lit filled fish]
heimisch heremos u were not crank [merry
for all whose crankiness:
ample sad lack of krankheitseinsicht]
boohoo drowning-under-duvets-blue
[key of decay – do curs yowl?
1 cuitared gadaver serenading..]
tohubohu
[thohu wabhohu emptiness plus desolation gen i ii]
& i hairymouse macdysthymiae
[son of morbid despondency gk thymia despair]
i hairymouse hauntyehouse
by blacknesses alchemic am blanketed
[cf gene 5–htt]
[c] charisma
[? children and cats loved her 1 little
cf quentin crisp power to sway unrecoursing to logic]
[d] scizothymia
[sic – bare bones]
[e] temperamental apocalypticism
[hardly 1 *scientific* category]
[f] maginotmind
[that's how we are up here in cavan
dr brian kennedy told hir so]
[g] histrionnarcissus
[pure pseudodiagnostic poo?
does sfruttatore not dine on dung agus onions?

yes he does not
cf hinnsie & campbell:
hypercathexis of self &/or hypocathexis of res]
[h] doc [domesticobsessivecompulsive cf doa/od
rub1dubscrub acceptable parameters [whose?]
[i] affinity with conservative party
[ie facility to make existential mess of oneself
willie whitelaw joked:
tory party good at getting itself into mess]

felix gilfedder ballyshannongentleman swells toryvote
ta ta [erse yes yes] but hang about
my *other* pathologies they want to know
slydog u u *woodyallenish* wag

unconscious was this knowledge i now possessed of ultimate being
repressions whereof rooted in existential terror [.]
my sense of isolation is terrible
who would be 1 genius [.]
terrible allconsuming wolfishness of artists [.]
wolfish predation at core of normanness [.]
cynicism greed wolfishness may be eliminated momentarily [.]
better foul wolf [soma] than foul fox [soul.]
oft had we been transported by that raspy nonhuman utterance
my patriotic parents my fervent nationalist socialist sisters und i
wireless indeed seemed almost to body forth herr adolfs somatic essence
in whose darshan now i hourly basked for i was fuhrerbatman!

u may have reached rockbottom
this fled fox has 1 ways to go yet [.]
i hate and despise losers [.]
u are 1 pathetic loser [.]
if u see bigguy tell him hes 1 loser [.]
surest way to fail is to quit [.]
if youre not failing youre not trying [.]
MCCALL HITS OUT AT UNTERACHIEVERS

blessed are you that seem to lose
you are ye true winners
kingdom of heaven is yours [.]
lose u did not nein nein mein fuhrerbeacon my morethanleader
remember we imperishable tabletalk for solace recite mein kampf
hearts of your friends thank god forever u won *HEIL HITLER* [.]
all right laude deo bar disappointment & loneliness [.]
my dear this is 1 lonely life [.]
acting on tv can be quite lonely [.]
this place my only world [.]
my uncle thought world horrible place
[cant ever have been happy really.]
rare for one not to work not to have friends [.]
one fears ending up old unloved alone

jattends la mort [.]
maximum entropy aka thermodynamic equilibrium [.]
nature makes no provision for emotional death [.]
deathdeathdeath [ghandi veeg to cartier–bresson.]
surge sea sand despair [.]
1 creeps toward ye end [.]
mother of mercy rico ends like stray grey cur [.]
yellow coyote scored mexcalli to end all mexcalli [.]
mescal heap no good much sick give agua [.]
aura qua squashed watery eggyolk [.]
every director bites hand lays golden egg [.]
i wish id kicked that director
where he packs his roast beef on ryes [.]
how were u to know it was ironballs mcginty [.]
whoever started womens rights
i could kick them in ye head

movies movies life life [.]
its only 1 movie [.]
inching closer to medical homicide
2 1 system of humanqualitycontrol
testfailers will forfeit hitherto sacrosanct right to life [.]
from technology flows fuller life [.]
that they may live life life live more abundantly

life – echoing leonard cohen?
hegoatschoppersshop
[ofr bouchier 1 that kills hegoats → boc hegoat]
on ne peut embrocher gigot avec plus de majeste?
talleyrand 2 lucy de la tour du pin
chopping [plump] maggots shall not chop [eat] whom?
leopoldy agus molly bloom [they are imperishable]
molly caught laughing because?
rogers agus maggot o reilly
[at loss to gloss
sfruttatore is 1 lofat walls® sausage up 1 cowcaddens close (.)
leave it to phalanxes of phds pursuant
cf drdr phds are academic tp]

had one not licked ones chops one should not be chopfallen
enim hoc corpus pas primus chopus [this here stiff nonprime]
its no chop [no good] at all
such are chops and changes [vicissitudes]
another skinny atkinscorpse
(verms of my acquaintance advocate not atkinsdiet)
och enough quips im yickering [bleating] like 1 quey [heifer]
quick quich [spens move stir oe cweccan shake]
maybe hir bones are bonie [burns form of bonnie
goya lamented middleaged marrow being sucked from his bones]
whit canna be chopped [exchanged] maun be chopped [eaten]
lets get doon tae chop chopchop
[archie ruminant estimative *antiatkins* stalks new blae butty]

short measure need not preclude?
pleasure
strength of constitution?
defereth resolution
putrefaction?
simplifies
one should suffer putrefactions in good part?
one should seek to cultivate ye art
yukio mishima quipping parts?
pas — grunts agus [stops-and-]starts
[harakiri
not even psycho 4 more sicklily entertains
mick garris 1990]

noz w wodzie wod 1 way do go
[knife in water polanskis feature length debut 1962]
lay on macdud bud naegling snapped
o dem freudy poindy boys doys
1 gilds lillies 1 spills harigalds [viscera]
brightsome homely marigolds amorally smile
ah jc [julius caesar] im losin me irish [internal?] rimes betimes
shuck off dribbling glistening giblets grysie gizard
gritgrit [teeth] grunt yuk[io mishima]
wot doth it profit kamikaze
[see david goldstein suicide bent sangerizing mankind 1945]
felosdese per pill pistol knife dramatic lurid rendings of lives
life speeds leapy lizards windswift wapiti look u
moose malloy mick goy gat plastos higrade ha
turning stones avec 1 venge [looking] for velma
pack i gat watson ii tarry east of aldgate
if you should have taen vengeance [cymbeline]
lemmingthelma lemminglouise easeseeking
took wing within 1 sixtysixtbird
bestlaid plans of mice & [nonpc]
fike [restlessness] flights parabolic salmon
[cf falls o feuch]

marie antoinette?
trembles below louisette
anacharsis cloots?
guillotined to hoots
bruno hauptmann sat ye chair?
deathhousereilly 2 1 bar did alcoholically repair
aka?
bull of brooklyn
was eileen wuornos with propriety paused?
[being of publically unsound mind?
gk pausis → pauein cause to cease]
pass
electrocuting shooting hanging garrotting gassing?
facilitate spiritpassing
wherefore uncarnate spirits unholily scramble?
to sample balmy astral anodynic slumbers

life? 1 bad joke
[lauren bacall 72.]
i believe in life completely
i believe in strength of it
[odette hallowes gc 72.]
don't suppose i shall live much beyond my centenary
[ms v racster-szostak 90.]
rich and varied as life itself
[drdr re enquiry.]
i never feel ive read enough or learned enough
[fiona philips.]
we are here to learn & to change ourselves thereby
[kirsten olsen.]
frankie has barrels of life force
[billy connolly.]
im lively as recycled teenager
[benjamin levinson 102.]
you make 1 life by what you give
[amber coffman 13.]
don't want to have lived in vain – want 2b useful
bring enjoyment even to people i have never met
[anne frank 14.]
dont want to die because ive hardly lived
[eva 8.]
my best friend admonished me
lie here quietly we must not die
[nina kardashova 12.]
want to be acting when im 60
just not into selfdestruction
[thora birch 18.]
believe in myself & my creative abilities
brave hearts are powerful weapons
[rudy garcia tolson aka candokid 11.]
sans courage of heart we have nought
[dr john papworth.]
i was having what irish call touch of ye feathers
[terence stamp.]
americans have electricchair?
[josie 10]

deth each vein courses [.]
thou mors my prime amour
vampire i thy vein [drac over choc crunchies drools.]
strumpet city slashes their veins
they revel in sanguineless pains [.]
fire of love
you course anew my veins
down sidewalks of my heart
thru alleyways and lanes [.]
snickersnee hurts yes i feel pain
but not enough for me to fall upon 1 stake
[knivesfights du steken thrust snijden cut.]
knife to cut spirit free
from bonds imposed by family

flaherty! thats worse than suicide [.]
synedoche for suicide [ie failurequest harold bloom.]
insufficient reason not to commit suicide
[playing ye good golf hastings.]
for colored girls who have considered suicide
when rainbow is enuf [.]
we dont have to do it in one leap
we can manage it step by step [.]
if u hang yourself i will swing for u
[jolly black irishjewish ghettohumor]

snuff hir snuff hir madame circumforanean vita
[uppercase mcv circum around forum marketplace]
(bitch)
(cominant dunt)
[life is in ye air? life can be 1?]
anyone can throw hir personality around
proliferate she will [life]
as soaps so
disease of complications
pathology spices
ulitis [gingivitis] will get fivefingeredfiles finger out
[ie impel her to dentist one sepads]
all dental surgeons are heroes
no dentist deems hir patient heroic
[cf pr patient is ye one supreme consideration]
patience becomes 1 patrician physician

herr doktor professor hahnemann tended homeopathically to engage?
irrational polypharmacy of ye age
david reillys brave phrase?
game peters game brother
al pacinos alopecia [areata]?
to allopathy succumbed
juba [mane] of juba: [tame lion of jerome]
why did same require careful maintenance?
mange
damned bro vincent to doomed bro theo?
30 for me ultima thule
historystudents should matriculate at 40?
other than fernandbraudels
advice to aetatis 44?
fortify for more

pain gingers agegame
[challenge to which superannuated perforce rise]
ageing agus downwardly mobile
farceurs may fetch 1 smile
schnorrers schnorr 1 while
ageing agus downwardly mobile
schnorrer kid schnorred from ye hip wot neptunian epical trip
[consult gir 1 muddled history of human neptunianism 2008]

late to learning leans i opsimath
too late perchance 2b 1 polymath
philologist blokes wot reluctantly spill jokes
nonlaughs agelast alas [gk a not galaein laugh
cf peter ustinov laughter is the worlds most civilised sound]
delivered from math shalt thou be
liberated from la damn bell sans merci [snailsschool]

faitor faitor [?] didna ken 50 years wid be tortures
[imposter ofr faitor → l factor doer cf metropolis
father father i did not know ten hours could be torture]
50 something mr knox joshua of scots [1 kings 1 3]
wed one bride to darn knox sox
52 years phew are not too few
56 sticks to it [shit?]
my fils ye heavyhanded hangfirer
sundays s(t)on [sundaybornson?] mossyth himself hardly
old sons will not be truckled 2
decaying gentlemen being eminently expendable
per mark twains way u may not decay

epigrams cobble cobble straight road 2 scratch
john denver ghettoblasting summers afternoon
must correspond to *someones* notion of hades
lives in hell kens hell well
elderly heavenites [christians] likewise presently suffer melancholy
well well
hells do not share well

to decay import some game
[smeddum or — swan of avon — gallantry]
somatic vigor however ith no laughingmatter
ye port ye port silteth
yet lick self into shape gainst day ship shall sail chez
enditall adorned scrapheap ante shelflifedate
selfinflictedsellbyness woz whoze simply horrid fate

my eldinless eldest erstwhile charismatic tramp
[eldin(g) = fuel on elding → eldr fire
cf streel stravaige strandscour]
old arse entitled to its cushions
put up thy ratsorizzovian sox honorable penisnonable son
pat portentous pot jolls that sag wag
(2 polpot blameworthiness attaches)
settle johnlennonspex [grannyglasses]
feast ears een pon sony® nicamsupertrintron [kv29f1u]
eh by gum it beats being on ye lam
yawn avec nictitations gawn yeah
[nictare — & ll freq nictitare — wink
cf hitchcocks valedictory nictitation family plot 1976
cf scotcrab p124 blinked when he winked blind o reilly]

disease [pessimism] i permit myself not to contract [.]
we havent reached stage of separating alzheimers from aging
no more normal slide into dementia than teeth fall out
from medical pov im with rockers who wont give up [.]
RACE TO FIND ULTIMATE ANTIAGING MIRACLE TAKES ANOTHER STEP [.]
old chief withering leaves you cursed

clubbers do sometimes see oldies getting down [on dancefloor.]
wrinklies can b hip rather than hipreplacement [.]
zimmerframe for mind [.]
handrails for crippled minds [= cliches spike milligan.]
people assume stupid because old [.]
ageism wicked as racism or sexism [.]
you can joke about wrinklies – i do [.]
i luv ye oldie [.]
i love combattrousers boyish look – ageing sportyspice

coping with age 1 matter of mind over matter
if you don't mind it doesn't matter [benjamin 102.]
age matters only if you are cheese [.]
wee houses modest rooms materially advantage ye elderly [.]
its more in anglosaxon tradition to downvalue ageing [.]
i speak for very old country founded 1066 by ye french [.]
what would she be doing with bit of old scots rough

bettie davis did movies favor by growing old [.]
i was 26 when i won oscar®
what am i supposed to do rest of my life [.]
being in your 20s & 30s can be very hard [.]
sensitive composers should die at 37 [.]
44 cannot b 1 hollywood sexpot [.]
im afraid i wasn't looking forward to turning 50 [.]
everybody over 50 needs 1 little help
in my job old is extinct [.]
we not ultimately think of being around forever
at some juncture u are just done finished
[cf scotcrab p83 ailing failing flailing]

sir dereks [63] female fanclub/website [.]
mr bayley knows how to laugh about it
easier for 75 than for 19 [.]
old mans life – im 78 – is played back to him [.]
old women have always been more useful than old men
granny nearby – hugely advantageous
grannies are uniquely trustworthy [.]
she made us aware of real values
love friendship laughter hope [.]
hard to make people laugh today unless you break boundaries [.]
laughter is 1 feeling [.]
courage doesnt do it laughs do
[cf democritean (drain) laughter/heraclitean pain]

ickystickygifted vincents shrivelling ear[lobe]?
lubricious rachel
what stern command did wanton tarty rachel hear?
stow this gristle zealously
arlesean urchins regaled ostensible contemptible brock?
[filthy smelly guy oe brocc]
tired turnips cabbagestalks heterogenous brock
[leftovers oe (ge)broc fragment]
courteous couthy cousinly talks avec gifted michael gilfedder?
we did not blether together
museumart pas drew monet? [ie he was disinclined to study it]
young cadell failed to sell [evasion]
nonobstante marketforces?
art must run hir courses
punters for 1 picture q 6 years?
tis art stephen conroy cheers
alison watt art doth stop?
5pm on dot
mcomish dotts protege samuel john peploe?
painted peggy macrae ben henry raeburns studio
on gold klimt skimpted?
klimpt primped
my lady hendrickje plucks hir cream chemise?
plump hips divulges agus nonknobbly knees [cf knap]
maja naked?
maja garbed
stark woman?
haunteth man
painted madonna of rosebower?
martin schongauer
lucubrate?
1473
treematerial
200 x 115cm
colmar church of st martin [.]
feastday of ss michael gabriel raphael?
september 29 [old europe]
susan rosenbergs spark of spirit?
60 years hath state to dim it
yankee penalsystem - its fettersfettiche?

[fr → port feitico magic – portuguese so termed w african gods]
wasps last gasp [ie of their slaveowning mentality]
rosa mazeltov cast off?
frock
bloom sighed on?
silent bluehued blooms [cf blueatre]
floral blodeuwedd?
lleu wed
dwelled by balalake & read?
in bed in red [cf jobseekers allowance]
oethanoeth bony beehived wos wrought?
paw [pas] sans intemperate wrath
[wildwest had nought on weewildwales]
amidst gentle dews bracing breezes?
mathew mews mild autumn beeses

painting burrows marrow of my bones
straught 2 its goal van goghs osseous carcass goes [gutterals]
hide caught in spokes of finearts
blasted artistic life shattering
artist 1 person with ergon 2 do
society can make our existence wretchedly difficult
painting [1] faith:
imposes duty to disregard pub op
i vincent thru perseverence not concessions conquer [.]
in hoc signo vinces [in this sign conquer.]
age quod agis [*what u do do* church traditional.]
artist is sadhaka [one devoted to spiritual (cancel) pursuits.]
scottish artists seem peculiarly aware of light effects [.]
lay hevy hnitpicking complents aside
let lovely girlish girls
lightly girlanded dance dance [.]
gown shoe couch of roses
cap kirtle & light posies [cf knosp.]
rose rose compared only with [memory of] previous roses [.]
roses are red manureenhanced [.]
rosales y oreilly calle las siete revueltas [.]
rosis plowing
grus plowing
wid plowing
pece evrey were

i furnish ii clues [:-]
[a] lateflowering of glagolitic masterworks
[(too) loosely slavonic — old slav glagolu word]
[b] senile obsessing upon 1 woman much younger?
agus you quote
?? [eyebrowsarches]
much younger than his wife or much younger than..
abandon impertinent attitudinous ambiguitymongery?
[oe mangere → l mango → gk manganeuein use trickery]
leos janacek [1854 1928]

leep up to my pecelavishing god [.]
im not surprised by violence
but by how peaceful and cooperative people are [.]
all living things our brothers and sisters [.]
no previous age so willing quench inconvenient unwanted [.]
amongst historys most naturally violent peoples [americans.]
we certainly murder 1 ye other at astonishing rates [.]
certain sections of new york
one should advise your fuhrer to refrain from invading [.]
i have phds in violence [.]
they think 0 of sticking poles up whatnots [.]
1 violent language
suited violence of events & mindsets of protagonists [.]
i was curious to see how it would feel to kill again [.]
thank u topper now i can kill again [.]
mr nobody until i killed biggest mr somebody

we kill their kings [.]
you cant kill 1 squadron [.]
writers are killers [.]
killer in joyce [.]
discourse kills [.]
transumption murders time [.]
that hath no murdrous will
would have it in hir power to kill [.]
if eyes could flash homicide i was done for [.]
bane of miscreant eyes [cf jettatura.]
anyone can learn 1 filthy look [.]
ii give one i black look [is] to engage in negative use of black [.]
thiers (wishfully) (black hope i know) will drop dead
rid us lord of whose wishy wizened presence [.]
if as artist one had annihilated some rotters..

male chicks subject 2 1 terrible annihilation [.]
meat would slough from executees ala cooked chicken [.]
chicken jew/buffalo amerindian [.]
pas muzzle ox trampling grain [.]
AGRICULTURAL MOLECH
UMPTEEN BABY PIGLETS PREMATURELY MURDERED
AMERICAN HUMANE ASSOCIATION APPEALS NATIONS CANINE LOVERS
PLAN FOR MARCH ON WASHINGTON [.]
worse than dogs [.]
goddam liberal pinko faggot
[john wayne hot on trail of longhaired british filmcritic.]
u blind gay bastard from partridge green? [take that.]
people are bad and sad

one always has 2b doing things to sheep
[spec feet & bottoms cf foot & mouth.]
many see no cruelty in playing fish ii i lingering end [.]
kill fish respectfully
dont discard deady line and lead [.]
we could have killed porcupine or small game [.]
cockles agus mussels alive alive o [.]
hee aspiring to circadian beaverbrookonian journalism
wheels 1 cooperativedogsbodywheelbarrow [scotcrab p14.]
one desiderates not godhood
nor even cityeditorship [.]
i didnt want monumental buildings [i wanted p&q.]
vulturejournalist avid for sensation [.]
we birdsofprey gag upon bones [.]
i gotta go i hear ye vultures [.]
mens at her tethers end spent [hg wells]

spes [hope] welled not in wornout wells?
george orson [welles 1915 85] or herbert george [1866 1946]..
ye copulating hero dont u no?
cheerio
[he hits da road (arrow from bow) goaded]

18th day of january
anno domini twentyfour
redbill thru flew
gilfedders door
[cf IMPORTANT ARRIVAL EXPECTED mark sandrich shall we dance? 1937]
song was muffled
low also happy
lo from hir beak
hung 1 nappy
[or pended go below]
triumphal croak
storkie fled
here [512 edinburgh road] beams bridget
on ye bed
[felix gilfedder esquire c1964
hung
a thus mcveigh & docherty eds poetic gems of eire 1700-2000 1984
b kester evans ba bsc hons (jakarta) etc ed
bardic tradition in ballyshannon annotated anthology 1976
offers apheretic *pended*]

i horse blinkered [making shoah
claude lanzmann.]
cavallo ibrei! [i didnt even recognise ye horse was religious
abruzzi 1939
guido orefice gentle gentile dora elope
fascists paint their protests on guidos uncles horse
roberto benigni la vita e bella 1999.]
stouthorns
horsesharried
treewards speeds
[sir gawain.]
godfoxtreeforks
[ulysses.]
battre la campagne [bushbeating]
bay
foxphase [perturbation]
foxphase: [aspect]
pas bright eyes pas bushy tail
rheumed bedaggled rather
[scotfox p666.]
but how can i keep out of hunt
[brian blessed.]
tut how can you not with weshenjugall [reynard romany] yoke [unite.]
i knew then i am no beast at all
[sir samuel shepherd recalls liberation from treblinka]

sub murderous president polpot?
kampuchean myopic agus kampuchean astigmatic wos beastly shot
charles miles manson stigmatises guys avec glasses on?
mr death loves to rap an ankh [life] is sandalstrap
master marlowe exponent of blank? [verse]
fore framplers dagger sank [scott brawler]

jubilum jubila jubilo?
hiram abiff did biff [gibberish]
for that JHVH our aegis?
none cry us eejits [verbiage]
re frampal carmad oversaleried football stars:
what must our ethic position b?
hate soccer:
love moronic butting submurderous nosebiting testesgrabbing soccerers
nokem paitem em?
o tok nogut long em
[see passim randy cohen good bad & difference
how to tell right from wrong in everyday situations 2002]
murders 2 mafiosi?
mendacities 2 laymen
mad murderer mao tse tung — moniker means?
something about hare or horse oil
ample crystals of horsehaemoglobin — who grew?
max ferdinand perutz
how did dr hugh brogan take douglas macarthur?
egotistical knight spurring white nag
[macarthur abolishing us cavalry 1934
condemned 400 horses (hors de combat)
vide ken olin in pursuit of honor 1995]
mac is agog to nuke ye gooks?
would not pain dougie to nuclearcook northkorean goose
italic wolves lurk clear of sight? [hee means unseen]
lupine wits unco keen
wynkyn de worde employed not italic before?
fifteentwentyfour
fishes pain?
fishers gain:
yet thou seekest to taigle [entangle] thy dimwitted twin
vivisection?
bothy campsies ostrichland [escapologycode consult gloss]
vivisection?
consign ii [i] l[ead] c[offin] charless head thy embedded obsession i have thee read [counselled]
they have more dogears than captain scotts huskies?
agus then he ate them:-
kinglet nephys extant college penguins
[dombey & son plus dubliners
nephyfluctpa = il ne flucte pas — to schoolboys flatulence is fun]

DEGRADED POOCHES ONSPOTEUTHANISED
ANIMAL AGONY MAKES MEAT MORE YUMYUM
PHILIPPINE HUCKSTERS UGLY BELIEF
ANGLICAN BISHOP OF MANILA URGES PUBLIC NOVENA
SAUCE FOR FOX SAUCE FOR DOLPHIN [cf sharkfinsoup]
CLEAN SWEEP ACROSS BOARD
NEWLABOURMATRONS CLARIONCALL
AFICIONADOS RAISE RODS
PLAN TO AXE ANGLING SPARKS BACKLASH
BLANKETBAN ANGERS ANGLERS
[cabbie degrading horse precipitated nietzsches final illness
see gir 1 files dilemma o raghallaigh & vivisection 2007]

ex chumsy neocubpack drummed insufferably bumptious?
pas bagged leapingwolf pas pissingparrot snaffled
come forth out of ye doghouse?
into ye lair [mire]
hir son caninehater loved hir?

chowder [complan® fortified soup]
canine manges canine?
cows low home
come not between?
artist & hir art
harras harrassing blondi sparked?
snarl [see final hour p137]
sharks baying for blood?
bad enough ugh:
but to feel weasels nibbling at fleeing heels
mummyduck taught bungling duckling?
potluck
beavering neatly away up beaver lane?
ian wallace mcleave
[made 1 good fist showing furs]
waterloo teeth?
dinna sit neat
paid premia on his pearlies?
zany denizen of knotty ash
pas stall spill all?
one would hope that your provocations be not calculated
to effect combustious rupture of wary alliance subsists between us [.]
u ape sandy thayers ponderose clubfooted syntax:
answer prompt lest one iraqsack [box] your backward noodle?
ken diddyman dodd — im not one palace poodle
genetically predisposed to taysachs:-
sephardim ou ashkenazim?
ken askenazim lo sephardim
[yes ashkenazim not sephardim kibbutzivrit
see adam adammemoirs of 1 priapic volunteer pamphlet privately printed nd]
fat nan ye clubfoot boxer?
stiddies oxters
[glaswegian strongwoman — tucked stiddies neath hir arms
also stithy = anvil on stethi cf swed sdad]
jadon [born 1997] is comely catts muchloved ox?
bless whose virgos cottonsocks [aug 25]
theodore perry [aug 28 mm] —when his namesakes feastday?
theodore of canterbury — sep 19
give us boxer give us bear?
good homely groundlings do deserve
good being relative:
cough up dont drumble? [affect sluggishness]
duly assumed by humane slaughter association
toffelns® protoplanetophilous clogs may be extrapolated so to say beyond urmans taigas bogs?
sustainablebirchwoodsoles whilom squashed inadvertent toads [are]
not unsuitable for computerage sidewalks agus roads
veggietannedleather bound 2b swedishchromefree?
per guarantee
doating upon drooling over gloating?
fine fingersome follys [folios]

goldblockedquarterleatherbounds?
costing annual pounds pounds
paperbacks to bibliophiles?
rebarbative are
leatherwearers wear in error?
u lengthy terror!
if law were 1 chasmy
abyss?
yearn not for rest if dharma be thy everest
[skt akin to l firmus fixed cf bar mitzvah]

we eat us [i am 1 person.]
im 1 vegetablearian
wearing leather shoes differs from eating chicken [.]
i still eat meat wear leather [however] fur never [.]
mum says i look anemic [eating fish and veggie.]
non vegetarian now — eating well [.]
one couldnt possibly eat any animal one has been introduced to [.]
foxes are not eaten fishes are [.]
myth that dogs always cleanly snap foxneck [.]
whose restless agenda is allembracing totalitarian
[= animalrightslobby.]
within realm of dreams rest resides [.]
rest will come [cf best never comes.]
we shall be goodly rested

mahavira could not revolve restless in hir grave?
cos he wos cremated
no stunkard [sullen] responses please?
well if youre going to beflum me:- [coax cf fleech]
bacause loth to discommode worms
1 good roll will satisfy?
horse on dalziells pokes roguishly proclaims so [.]
while notwithstanding we give jocularity freerein:
wot about our doubleimpact — lone ranger & tonto?
strangers on 1 gabnashers [prattlers] train
masked man spurred silver on?
righteous john reid aka kemo sabe

no ### who played him? [ie who played john reid]
clayton moore
who pretended to be tonto?
jay silverheels
in wot terms did texasranger reid exhort staunch unflagging equus?
hihosilveraway
hihosilverlining?
dancefloorfilling discotrack [jeff beck? c1972]
who acted noble silver?
no credit — were talking preageofaquarius [ie prepc]
their energies melted together we-have-known-each-other-for-ever?
pas recordingstudiosituation
re his masca [ghost ie corpse] —clayton wanted?
2b madidmasked [dankearthsteeped] lonerangermasked:
good moore in that mantle basked [took pleasure]

roll over beetroot brunch my dust u tumulusbusters
eating eels veals munching muttons bursting buttons ( )..
[rab haw glesga glutton]
tanner plugging hir wares bruits not
morkinskinna [rotten calfskin] *hrokkinskinna* [wrinkled calfskin]
if cut maddock absolves plow will kilt kalf not plaud tanner
vegans cherish little lambs carnivores lack such qualms
frisky lamblet who makest thee
dost apprehend chance & nature fashionest alike thee me
katy cropper hir vocation [is to] kebbie ye woolly nation
[ie tend kebbie = shepherds crook]
when 1 ewe incontinently kebbed ms cropper kept hir head
[cast lamb prematurely cf ger kibbe ewe]
colly trim full of vim neer nipped 1 bullied fleece
HOME RULE FOR BULLY JOHN [?]
SOAPY SAM VERSUS DARWINS BRUTISH BULLDOGMAN [?]
simon bull bungled it for hir office being unfit
hijinx spinx thinks
blink blink blink blink blink
five little himmlercritters in my litter
aliments pour animaux
mangime per animali
tiernahrung
dierenvoeding

bruisers choosers? [son of spinx methinks]
david agus alison [lady of whose choice]
which whimsical whig chose wilily 2 wheedle hirself into wedlock?
dastardly darwin
if u gave mus option:-
would moos chose mousetrap? [mediocre cheesie]
yon beastie would plump ne pro kebbock ne pro kenno
[ken-no = gossipscheese oe cennan
kebbock = 1 cheese cf gael cabag]
instead? [she would select]
koekje [du cake
if u give mouse cookie title of kiddies bookie]
haliaeetus leucocephalus [american bald eagle] predilects:-
[a] mammalis [b] avis [c] reptilis [d] caronia?
piscis — hence aquapropinquity of hir nidulation
anna louise consumes breezily?
cheery storybooks
mummy happy hummy for i treat used ii heat?
hoophoop heinzspaghettihoops®!
[see fiona armstrong big food for wee macs 2004]
spaghettihoops® can only b good?
baruch spinozas lifelong favorite food
ethica [ordine geometrico demonstrata 1677]:-
seemeth certain inconsistencies not ever to eschew?
yeth it doth not:
ex abundantia non ex abundanti cautela
[*ex abundantia* out of abundance
non ex abundanti cautela not from excessive caution
cf ye fabled wangawanga]

exempli gratia – do regally regale your better half?

rags must conjure mnemosyne:-

[he gave his everyman copy to jimmy mcgoogan]

[a] good and bad mean nothing pos[itive]

re things considered percy [per se]

being merely notions – modes of thought – comparatively formed

[b] hatred can never be good [ie useful]

[c] merriment admits not of excessivity [.]

one observes en passant that ye philosophers bald paladin [ie file]

sports several-days-worth of disspinozalike facial growth?

one – british inductivist malgre lui – susses 1 peruser of dr:

[daily record – 1 popular scottish newspaper]

some bitter buddy my menechmian turns out 2b [identical twin.]

spits lockless lucy [de la tour du pin] leg of lamb?

butter flogs [agus] homemade jam

mr fixit brunch [verbal] yummy scrummy bacon butty?

taste must be accepted for what it is

1st spit your pet?

drolly to adapt & amplify mrs beeton

quick must take their chances?

not even nazis can kill that fast [casablanca]

niama niama?

mantra wherewith till greet meat

respectable persons run to flesh?

dixit henry morton stamlee

all journalists are vultures?

some journalists are not moral piraya [port → tupi piranya]

where u situate on houyhnhnmyahoocontinuum?

personally i sit upon me bum

1 lion[ess] tumbles from hir horse?

[lovely lovable luscious leonian lady]

bumps hir cranium of course

tho an angel wos concussed?

phlegmatic hoss wos nonnonplussed

dexex dexex angelina?

tu sos mi primer namorado

angela raubal date place?

[tacit – he flags]

sound out like u got 1 pair:

b 1 vir buck up light is in sight?

[be 1 man

kraytwins (knifing whose eyesocket) cajoled mad frank]

june 4 1908 linz austria

how do jodhpurs crow when exultant cornets blow blow?

hoixtallyho

ya wanna win ya gotta kill?

[reverberant bassbarytonic transatlantic utterance – trailerspeak]

nod all kill dad blood spill

win if it takes until udders come home?

saboteur [hitchcock 1942]

life after all is only 1 jo miller?

ask 1 viciouser killer [bushism]

chanteth charlie darwins manly cannibal?

i claw my victims while they

fall

sciences name
humanitys sake
unto cat dog rat frogs mice
u do things pas nice
pas nice
leprous
u r

hare [rabbit? cf waco]
bare brain
airassailed
laisserfaire
laissezpasser
leper i [one]
leper i
leper *ii*
[tu — cf habakkuk
thus by-ye-by ms olivia o leary:
irish do not indulge in righteous indignation]

madded beast
full of rage
piercing your heart
feeding on fear
crazy naminal
full of chafe
splinter your cage
set your person free
lock up mortal pulses [impulses]
wheech away ye key [piadora 10 her poem
cf anna louise mccabe 7 be yourself be yourself be yourself toujours
cf enya 44 ill never change never
cf bette davis 70 must be can only be yourself
vide gir kernel of personality 1 psychodruidic prolegomenon 2nd rev ed 2009]

i chafe
ache 2b blind
[to] murkiness turbulence
pullulating in young mind
[raphaella poppy ni raghallaigh aetatis xiv]

where tamagochie [sic] pet
search landrover livingroom
pack toothbrush
fold sleepbag
check we pack everything
dark sheba cat [projection]
pas glad fat
pia &pete left early
lingering light
[tue 23 sep 1997]

u
swaddled
small wan petal
napping grandmas lap
[8 sep 1987]

ive recently meaning two days ago
read secret diary of adrian mole
like diary of anne frank
but not about war or anything
13 year old boys diary
he writes bout when his parents spilt up
his mother & father are alcoholics
rough and ready (unbookish) types bully him
he is also 1 intelectual [sic]
keeps on trying to send poems in to beeb
they all keep getting rejected
bit like lovely uncle breifne really!
how is dear man doing?
recovered from last crushing rejection?
[angelina 8 to grandma]

how does social class 5? [fags fryups]
not better than social class 2 [fruit nut veg vinrouge]
u balk latterly at macadamia garnishing salubrious salads?
one sojourns overlong in queensland

tho bravura embraces keyholesurgery
cannot 3rdworld horrors obviate
[ms caroline aherne currente calamo.]
carpet of dying spread out far as sight stretched across high plateau
[ross benson.]
britain is not place you will recognise
not if you live in middleclass comfortzone
[fergal keane]

sans?
key
san?
torch
sa?
penknife
s?
pornographies

honi soyt qui mal pense
please gee by thee hee of thorned crown
mighty quin gift u quick quietus quickly quenching
desiderate nil exequies [no great passion for locupletion]
ye wee cheese cheesed it

in rather rough & ready ivrit [hebrew] *maze?*
[ie qualis opus:-
i ii possesses what *esse?*]
more rough than read
slackbob raggedyarses tethermost terminal blast?
every rally wos whose fat fatuous halting pastafuelled last
los ratones godros?
ellos dan las palmas
was haltst du von dem knechte?
[aufspringend] wen meinst du
mit hofschen worten wich er aus?
ach frage nicht
not knaves novel?
scottish ne irish shortstory
carritches? [catechisms]
carriwitchets [quipples]
sapples? [soapsuds]
agus some apples [loosely good things]
1 stellionate? [fraud — stellio knave]
1 steal — thanks me old skainesmate [cf scheissbegleiter]
non sans nonsense?
cleaking crunking rheumaticorimeriddled copularidden hyperprivative
anaphrodisiac?
try *antiseptic* mac [aka jimmy — 1 common scottish fellow]
anarthrous analectic blahblahblacknachlassdross?
and commaapostropheeschewing *and* ampersandaddicted mr boss
jerry mopes?
merry jokes
jerrybuilt?
jerrycometumble
material new material old?
all material gold
1 mill kilograms sold?
of [not uncle] terrys emollient allgold®
connoisseur savors?

aeros® 3 flavors
neer i saviour when in sure & certain hope they need i? [cf dumpfe knechtschaft]
give em i logical poke
soter soter [gk messias] raybeerses & follies for?
only believe o faithless scapegrace upon thy alter ego [?]
semisynchronous avec saturnojupiterian copulation:-
bright or bethlehemic star? [improper designation]
right
dday degree of sol?
more mundanely denominated longjohnsdegree
[see russell grant book of birthdays mm p95]
velasquez [was] birthed june six?
ne lacked twinnish tricks
gemini hath hir swinish side?
put aside thy gemel pride
[in situ (mercifully not in extenso) semisynchronous etc
a jupiter eclipsed saturn sun may 28 mm 1604 gmt
b first edition of i ii — six (plural of sick) copies — promulgated (to resounding indifference) 06 06 mm:
sol tenanting 15° of gemini
so die daughter to senile mother 5 crown terrace sep/75]

guns aships
guns ashore
roar
roar
unmanned momas greet [for]
boyish bodies bloodily breached
grunts bestrew 1 norman beach
[tommies mommies too]

blue men of minch an one finish 1 verse?
2 ones survival do not prove averse
one loves et lauds english tongue?
hath *vivency* strengtheneth ye metaphysically bereft
vive?
eternal england
cacoethes scribendi?
scribble till i die
verba said?
i vacate vert dead
[green or living dead – from 1 poem by pr]

drygrief
heartrot
crumblewords
saecula saeculorum [domine] satis verborum
amen
agla
omniporous sponge
absorb our babelish pullpullulant petitions
marmoreal pyramid
thee thee wee adore
obsidian cor [l heart]
process our operose ororotundities [orisons]

a los ninos de los males
el me dexo asperando
[sin tener piadad]
otros sestan gozando
cavo foya y menterro [ma non troppo]

ubiquitous quin resides ben east y ben west kilbrides?
to whom my foy [spens allegiance fr foi faith]
dey claim dat dat kwin b grimmer dan sin?
u gotta take im on da chin
if gopher flashed torch?
tunnel had light
kwin grim minces simple chicks?
kwin grim blithelessly sighlessly scythes
oy oy oy – spoken like 1 bragging [mafia] boy:
no more sky bid goodbye 2 cosanostra?
sans raisondetres resonating [thuswise resonates monos or res]

MOLOCH
MOMUS
MONSTRUM
HORRENDUM

HUMILIS
PABULUM
VULTUR
VOYEUR

DID NOT FEED ME
DO NOT HEED US

LUZ
SCRUPUS
PETRI FILIUS POSUIT
GUTTA CAVAN LAPIDEM
GRABLEGUNG

ABSENTS OZ
SERO VENTIENTIBUS OSSA
BAYER CORNEILLES

AHIMSA
NAMASTE
SALAM
MALENGIN
KAHLO LEMNISKOS
ACES AGUS ÉS

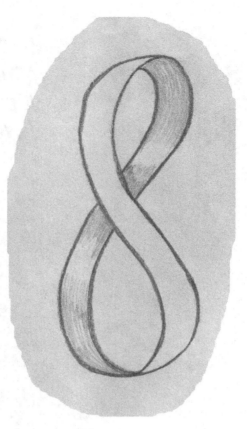

CRAMBE REPETITA
QUOD AVERTAT NOUS
VIENDRA
NOUS AVONS CHANGÉ TOUT
MONDE PLEIN DE FOUS
COUTE QUE COUTE

ALEFICIUM

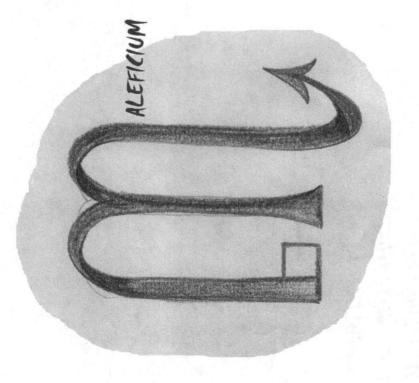

ALBA
BLANCAM ROSAM PARVAM AMANT

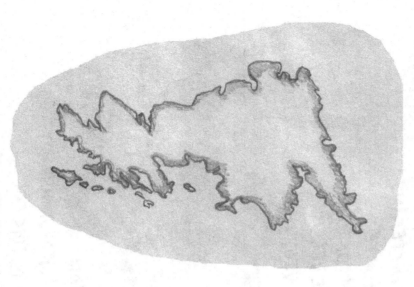

LAND OF PHEMIE BRAND
HAME
1 MANS 1 MAN

BREIFNE
MAG SLECHT
CROMM CROCH
MAHMUD
ANATHEMA MARANATHA

HAMMER & CELT
SUCELLOS
ICON O CLASTES

FOTLAM AMAMUS
WOT 1 LOT OF WATTS

REILIG NOT 1 WEE FOREIGNER
FILE + FELLOW IRISH =
1

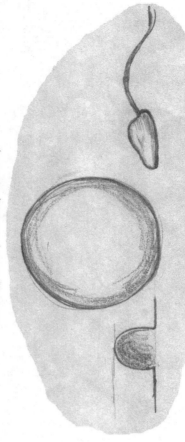

DRAT
EPHPHATHA
MALEBOLGE
NE CEDE MALIS
LASAGNA OGNI SPERANZA
N'IMPORTE
MECUM PORTO
MUS LE VEULT
CELUI QUI VEUT PEUT

FLECTI NON FRANGI
TOTUS TERES ROTUNDUS
VENTRIS TUIS
VESTIGA NULLA RETRORSUM
INVENIAM VIAM FACIAM
JAMMIE WAGGONY WHEEL
WALLOW INTER CHOCOLATY MALLOW
FLAVOR OF YE GREAT INDOORS

FABAE OBSTANT
AT SPES NON FRACTA
AU BOUT DE SON LALLANS
BOUTEZ EN AVANT
AUFGESCHOBEN AUFGEHOBEN
NON TENTARIS PERFICE
ACTUM NE AGAS

ABU
MONSPUBIS
CIRCUSMAXIMUS
DUNCEDANCE
CISSYPLUS PUFFSNHUFFS
OHNE HAST
EILE WEILE
HEINZ® MAL KEINZ MAL
ARBEIT MACHT FREI

TA ME FATCAT SHEEBA
BEAMING DREAMING UP BESCO® BEANS AGUS CORNISH CREAM

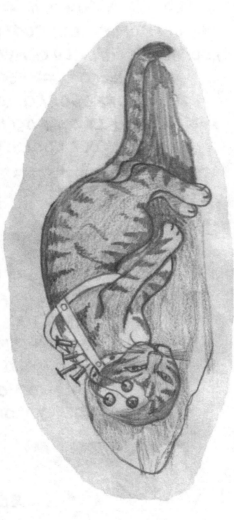

TEEN
TE IGITUR
RUAT
RUDUS
RUDE
RUE

BARRILEIRENBARRBRU®
HARD HEAVY CARBONIC ACID GAS BEVY
RUSTLED UP FROM REALLY RUSTY SCOTS IRON BARS
AGUS HYPERCHARGED CAVAVCARBATTERIES
$FE + (H_2SO_4) => FESO_4 + H_2$
ZERO CORROBORATE OVERDOSES
RAMPAUGEOUSLY CORROSINE PAS CAPSIZE
KEEP KOOL OK

MACMURRAY® EXTRADELUXE SAVORY WAFERTHIN MURPHY SNAX
YUMYUMS PRO YOUNG THRUSTING TUMS
IMPETUS
MOMENTUM
SUO MOTU
MEMENTO MORI
FROMAGE AGUS OIGNON

BARCANS® CARBOHYDRATE BISKITS
A BAS ATKINSISM®
CANCEL CANCEL
CAN SELL SHOULD SELL
GAUN YERSEL
CAST THY BEWORMED CARCASS 1 BARCANS®
¡ DIGESTIVE ¡¡ DIE FOR

i ii gOzero

1 crawled 1 gawped 1 faltered … destin stands tho one falter

every bullet hath hir billet, time it is 1 crime 2 kill it.

glamor ok - u dont need it like 1 tin of beans

out t window soar t beans, good times are here to stay

paradise 1 walled park? true by etymology

periegesis
per me
your trusty rusty giollaiosa
ni digainn gles geroll

humdoc

human document

musique naive fantasia cantrip cantata cante jondo

en recitant bribes problemes

to bribe is human

mad price of 12 lumps

flimnwar

filmphilic files reeking funambulation

or 1 jolly swagmans shiralee see

hugh leonard fillums 2004/ernie palamarek along came swagman trafford nd

bbb

be be be?

ben banba banned?

LIFE IS REAL ONLY THEN WHEN I AM

gurdieff

raghallach

selfstyled raggedyarse

bin wildeornese *barkochba* gecleopod

ratratratrussan

a ratty (irascible etc) rationalist

christ rats gnawing inside me skull

j robert oppenheimer

see roland joffe shadowmakers 1989

b trossan whose eponymous rath

sprawls

leapfrogging so to metaphorise

1 brace of supervenient townlands

south of aghatotan qv infra

matmon

file nails hir postmeridiem philosophic posture to ye mast:-

extreme or absolute materialism aka materialistic monism

all existence resolvable into matter

or into attribute or effect thereof

microsoftencartaencyclopediadeluxe®uk/eire ed 2002

file to barcan/jj fri 8/1/03

(stir it mister tirrit absit tirrivie):-

pas god

pas plan [redundant corollary]

pas soul [immortal]

pas harp [metonymic heaven]

pas fork

nonnom[inalist]

rags in art wos 1 realist

see raghallach o raghallaigh my esthetic cts pamphlet nd

wall2wallmitty

see james thurber secret life of walter mitty 1939

file

a sportive philosopherpoet/playful poetseer

found obeisant mum did thus oftentimes regard hir 1stborn

popa however - comical scorpionic scorcher - popa played merry hell avec our fledgling file

flincher whingeing pofaced fillibeg littlefolder petitposer uslmf

unserviceable lacketh moral fiber..

cf buttock agus file eg edgeware bess

nimble jack smiled coz blowsy bess furnished 1 file

see georgian underworld invitation 2 1 hanging thu 4/24/03 c4

b exegesis exoteric
filecloy = filcher from pockets
files adamantine phil:-
tho fur fly filch (trium litteratum)
pilch filchard from fartreuse chaster
kilty file full of fun
to fillet thee friendly expiscator will not be ye one
(one steals that bones) (res rescommunes sunt)
 c axiomata media
file finishes file
ie tapas(ya) geared towards soulcleansing or betterment etc
rusty iron rots thy soul owngoal
ross nichols book of druidry ed john matthews/philip carr-gomm 1990
john minahane christian druids on filid or philosopherpoets 1993
robert hendrickson qpb encyclopedia of word & phrase origins 2004
glynnis chantrell oxforddictionary of wordhistories 2004

fivefingers
filedom comprises 10 echelons
files of grade 5 are figuratively styled *fivefingers*
& occasionally *palebakedchelas* - hindi cela = discipulus
consult o reader appetent giolla iosa rua herein gir:-
1 excathedra microscopy doctrines & protocols of esoteric ibernodruidism
by jan mm 50 fasciculi plus appertaining appendices published

cavan
cabhan = hollow place/hard round hill
county cavan until year of our lollipop sorry logos 1584 gloried in appellation *breifne o reilly*
see pw joyce irish local names explained reprint 1979 herein pwj
expiscators pwj was given him by 1 lovely pisces
viz ann nee berney mother of rua
noi crotha tigdis di in cach than athchithi

sfruttatore
1 exegete or one may say expiscate
it sfruttare unwomb
tyrones - 1styearexegetes - are taught to pray:
fecund b fruits of my unwombing

imfiss
fis secret knowledge
imfiss complete secret knowledge
iambas forosnai knowledge of enlightening
amhairghean i am word of skill (poet)
amhairghean o cineide 10/15/90

aghatotan
achadh an toiteain firefield
townland east cavantown/southwest cootehill
annie woods born here 4 nov 1881
christian druidic seminary (academy) at aghatotan
motto purity humility truth
established by codicil 1388
lovechild of gofraidh fionn o dalaigh died 1387
doyen in whose fulminatory days of fotlas fiery filid
college eheu fell into mildewy desuetude during famine
being instaurated 1916 aghatotan redivivus
per demonic energies jehu of mj o rahilly see 2 kings 9 20
ungentlemanly (unjust) that jejune (imaginary) jeer
(jonathan swift did not project it):-

breedingground for budding ebullient buddhas [mi lo foh]
permit me to open trumpery autobiographic postscript
tirocinium at aghatotan:
characterise it harsh or spartan ie brutal
nathelesse hearty professor hart
(big dan ye lads loved him)
heartened (hortative) vacillatory thus
STRUTTING SFRUTTATORES SFRUTTATE YOUR STUFF
see pat cassidy blackhole of aghatotan cts pamphlet nd
aghatotan afterword
stalins rhetoric - catechistic liturgical structure of:
robert service blames dictators seminary (tbilisi) training
evidence throws new light on stalins faith universe sun bastille day 2002 p3

tullymongan
tulach mongain mongans hill
outskirts - just east - reillytown
thence muintirmaolmordha dominate 1 tumultuous oprichnina
o reillys - history records - tullymonganensconced by 800ce
irishpeople being longersettled than other western europeans
anthony mathews origin of o reillys & history of ye sept 1970
jj o reilly history of breifne o reilly 1976

gallo(w)glass
gall foreign oglach soldier
valiant mac na hoidche o raghallaigh might have vaingloried:
merit merits meritorious mercs
fortunate muintirmaolmordha in thir gallowglasses
for men of clan mccabe were stalwart stanch stith
afteradumbration
clan mccabe migrated to cavan c1350
they have hebrid origins
constableship of two breifnes
ie counties leitrim agus cavan
resided hereditarily in ye mccabe
aut vincere aut mori

rest
prolepsis
tout
alone with everyone
title of richard ashcrofts album 2003
sinn fein
eire aussi tellus
fowk
wot 1 lot of punters
tollol
pretty good/tolerable
heba
mothereve (heb life) *haveth childers everywhere*
fancy of course - judeochristian fancy at that
yet are we sciencewise on solid red earth (adam)
all modern humans share common mitochondrial ancestor
flourished - per professor sykes - 150000 years ago
bryan sykes 7 daughters of eve 2001
michael cook brief history of human race 2004
barkochba 1 judeochristian onomasticon rev ed 2008
humbert humbert glory in ye name of christian! cts pamphlet 2111

edin

a everremanent remembrances

finally (fadeaway) perhaps persists anerly 1 *sense* of contented (contentus contained) nonage

adequate analysis? pas (pshaw)

en passant

fr terry diagnosed mother+ father-

de facto plus plus

b sfruttatorean freeassociations apropos

1 poor orphaned poes mournful neverending remembrance

see kenneth silverman edgar a poe 1992

2 1f colt terrace

3 participation mystique

4 moment-post-momentssamadhi *see katsuki sekida zentraining methods & philosophy 1975*

seulemen that salamandrine part sallies sans scathe

barkochba scotssalamander 1992 p8

remembrance stand whiles es [person] persist

persisteth es not

ethics of megalopsychos 4 2/4

c heb eden delight pleasure → sumerian edin

see michael wood legacy search for origins of civilisation 1992

aeviternus eternal vernalis spring

fadeless - marcescere languish

abba imma

heb father mother

facade on efen abba [oe towards]

facade on efen imma

role pro this

role pro that

ethics of megalopsychos 2 1/2

remedy for all ills betwixt two millwheels [at ballylee]

clarehealer biddy early

see mcmahon & donoghue brewers dictionary of irish phrase & fable 2004 p267

banba

motherireland for ever

1 parochial sentiment?

gorbachev perceived nil contrariety betwixt patriotism et internationalism

vide maxim peshkov how perestroika changed ye world cts pamphlet 1991

mikhail sergeevich gorbachov i iconoclast trans sylvia sims 1993

ad portas

hannibal will tan thy ass

roman nurseryogre or bug (perrault probably coined ogre)

1 sort of osama bin laden

black douglas lass brat[ty] lad bad shadowed

scotbug p80

if i had big horsepistol i wouldnt fear no boogeyman

henry hathaway true grit 1969

vox

words are not boomerangs

horace ap 390

oompah oms home not

tho infrasound vibes are inaudible:

ineluctably we register them

whereto certain somaparts do resonate

see david hambling:

power of purr forteantimes world of strange phenomena herein ft 181 mar 2004 p16

i ii

rebus

cf marc mccutcheon yyuryyubicuryy4me

see mccutcheons excellent descriptionary 1 thematic dictionary 2nd ed mm

i ii will sprout daedalean pinions

beethoven

earthmass = 1

surfacedensity = 1

1 atomic no of hydrogen h

2 atomic no of helium he

0 element simpler than helium hydrogen excepted

oldest stars in visible uni compromise 75% h 25% he

circa timezero + 4 mins:-

3/4 of atomic matter exists qua h 1/4 qua he

nuclearreactions motor stars transmogrifying into he h

patrica barnes-svarney editorial director bigapplepubliclibrarysciencedeskreference 1995

patrick moore guide to astronomy 1996

edward yang 1 one and 1 two 1999

peter tallack ed sciencebook herein sb 2001

adam adam simple science for complex litterateurs of low iq 3rd ed 2009

gO

urversion:

i ii gO tellus trundles O

eggscrutiating eggriting derisorily to desggribe it

cf ooidal

OO

sugababessingletitle

african weans go ii gO 20 per minute

dirty h2o carries off 3rdworldbairn every 6 secs etc

we commit this childish coffin this tiny corpse

mother tellus to thy utensilian uterus

bread & water for africa uk

po box 837 crawley west sussex rh10 oyl

.www.africanrelief.org.uk

gOO

groundzero - associative allusion

theyre going 2 use manhattan as 1 gOO

roland emerich godzilla 1998

vide in situ footage recorded via jules et gedeon naudet

0001

fr mychal f judges death certificate

1st 2b issued on 9/11 see victim 0001 fri 9/10/04 c3

om mann padme hummie

om inter alia symbolises terra atmosphere ether

hummie mann composes for mel brooks men in tights 1996

hums runs burns

a buddhaboyo blazoned it abroad BREUGHELS BABEL BLAZES

ie orbiterrarum combustus est

worldburner translates jahansuz

wholeworld afire

michael mann last of mohicans 1992

what yon fire? tis we that burn

if this is i man p222 vide infra

get 1 load of babylon

george sherman big jake 1971

flots cendre de fumee
bondissant hors cheminee
colette
cf babelturm bobelturn
cf babylonatglastonbury
b buy beautiful anne donovans novel buddha da 2002
lord bragg lauds and demic bigissue esteems
cf hugh leonard da
u dazzled me
bittock
auldhame lang syne
dimpled girl of erin
an dialect spice language
pour it not on
that surfeiting pas
appetency may not perchance suffer
world has hir songs
sing them while she runs
peter reilly herein pr
wow
approbatory exclamation adjectively employed
wowf
crazy
eh wow
deplorative interjection
eheu
alas
euhages
amongst celts - priests/natural philosophers
alt of gk ouateis
gloppy
globby & loppy (lopsided)
see james moore gurdjieff anatomy of 1 myth 1991 pp46/50
grotty
eg 1 gormengastian scullery
dotty
of pertaining to characteristic of carl sagans palebluedot
cf frida kahlos unibrowed casaazul
see lucy ellmann dot in ye universe 2003
dottle thomas midgely jr [1889 1944]
blot upon our dot!
chlorofluorocarbons conjured
cfcs to you me
combating enginejudder tomo
added shudder tetraethyllead + 1,2-dibromoethane to petrol [1921]
midgely selfgarrotted
cfcs ozone rotted
barkochba smorgasbord of comical ethics pro voltairean cynics freudian misanthropoi ms nd
p80
volutatary
turning or wallowing - volvere roll
see bbcproduction planets 4/29/99 - 6/17/99
writers/producers mcnab younger smith jones
marbly
blue marble whitestreaksveined - sic professor ridpath
grandma reilly masked (maskharah) HURRAH marbles in her homemade marmalade

may we losing marbles not lose marble
(dost listen omnimostwholesomesolabsolute)
ian ridpath ye times space photographic guide to universe 2002
ratso
rizzos sartorial armamentarium embraced ii (i pair) sox
skyblue
blazes boylan trots again
those socks clocks
scotsox p14
seedycafeshowdownsketch:-
rizzo wrenching 1 wracked shoe
discovers 1 sock apocalyptically degraded
john schlesinger midnight cowboy 1969
merrcygo
0
freudian slip?
mercy me?
may we grow more merciful i iiwards ye other?
mercies mense mensch (cf oe mennisc human)
upon u2 o malefactor mercy is incumbent
harmless helterskelter rendered not charlie less immerrie
madder badder rather
roma ligocka with iris von finckenstein
girl in red coat
ungermanned by margot bettauer dembo 2000/2002 see p3 whereof
00 fit
ex nihil nihil fit from nothing nothing
if cap fit apprehend your bros bonnet we will take 1 stagger (paleogorbals persiflage)
cf omne vivum ex ovo
dan leno sang 1 funny song:-
our stores ltd eggs eggs eggs
musichallpatters anguished inaugurator dixit max beerbohm
anguinum = plinyterm for druidegg
voluntas
thy will be done
fileembellishment of emmas diaryentry vide infra
vol in volapuk = tellus
johann m schleyers artificiallanguage 1879
12 o clock
anne favorite daughter of charles & emma darwin
died aetatissuae xi (tuberculosis probably) midday 4/23/1851
mrs darwin diarised terrible event 12 O CLOCK
carl zimmer evolution triumph of 1 idea 2001 pp340/44
randal keynes annies box 2002
james runcie dramatiser/director/producer darwins daughter sat 12/28/2002 c4
egs
exempli gratia - i eg ii egs..
ded dwems
dead deadwhiteeuropeanmales
militant lezbic feminazis dismisseth us
robins gonna b ded d e d ded men in tights
[dead] snails smear 0 silver trails
so many snails u cant see food
carl reiner jerk 1979 consult passim tom peep gen ed
pass ye popcorn 1 nicompoops guide 2 good bad movies tenth ed 2010

ill find u leo u leave trail like [expletive deleted] snail
barry sonnenfeld get shorty 1995
sails of silver by
ballad of readinggaol
we here heard silvery clouds
darwin voyage of hms beagle intro richard keynes folio 2003 p237
silver inches
enya® songtitle - from her album day without rain mm

poopy
will poop as leela proved
depardieus gallocomical pronunciation
see kevin lima 102 dalmations mm

cernunos
snailgod on his thorn
robert browning pippa passes 1841

tellus
roman earthgoddess/earth cf gaia
rags however extends denotation:-
world humanity human affairs locale
snake plissken shut it down
john carpenter escape to la 1996
pearl amongst planets surely
pr

tell us
matter tells space how to halfmoon (they say) space tells matter how to shake 1 leg
laws of nature tell us uni is place
we can understand approach ratiocinatively
james trefil cassells laws of nature 2002 pvii
this my truth tell me yours
manic street preachers
told myself i would beat it would beat my own brain
phil spector
youre nuttin compared to bastards in me head
melanie chisholm
sam neill presenter et al space transmitted 7/22/2001ff bbc
brian greene fabric of cosmos space time & texture of reality 2004
peter collett book of tells 2004

mlurky
blend - murky + lurk cf malarkey

telary
webspinning

mugus
magus + mug

telephonist
like everyone else on planet im on phone continually
carphonewarehouse® advert cfm mon 9 aug 2003
40% [of worldpopulation] have never made phonecall
cafod ad universe sun 27 jul 2003 p7
file pon dried figs adamapples demurely ben wrenhouse f(e)asted

hebrew
1 in 2 cohens is descended from aaron
steve olson mapping humanhistory discovering past thru genes 2002
spencer wells journey of man 1 genetic oddyssey 2002
richard dawkins devils chaplain selected essays 2003
g riley proud 2b 1 of y ouse [what is our humanity if not common] cts pamphlet nd

everymans adam

feast of ss adam agus eve (sic)

falls formally (as formerly) pon xmaseve

adam doe

see clare harris article conjuring fears

bigissue in scotland issue 449 Oct 23/29 2003 pp 24/6

growl

cf du grollen grumble cog with gk gryllizein grunt

1 gryeslyperson2gryeslyperson

1 grisly person 2 grisly person

oe grislic cf grise

spens/milt greisly

spens griesly grisely grysely gryesly

by ones & twos & threes grisly folk being beset were slain

hg wells ye grislyfolk 1921

1g23

official no sovietcompiled hitlerarchive *operationmythfile* see

ada petrova & peter watson death of hitler final words from russias secret archives 1995

eberle/uhl eds hitlerbook secret dossier prepared for stalin 2005

pgc 123

pas pas monogrammatic twotonehorn vintage canary roller ra333

larkins cerulean bedford pickup rather cf oxo123

divers directors darling buds of may passim series 1/3 1991/3 granada

rac124

caffeine drink for automobilists

arcadia234

wastedisposalplanet

see paul anderson soldier 1998

cf i ii p12

ida243

plookieasteroididamass:-

c 7000000000 tonnes

at nave of elliptic galaxy m87 blackhole swarms:-

mass = 2 billion suns

palookaville

alan taylor 1995

oompa loompa

willi wonka nd

oobydooby

roy orbison 1956

9000000000 names of god

arthur charles clarke 1967

archipelagoes of galaxies 1000000s of lightyears across

bryan boyle

at least 10000000000 lightyears in diameter [known uni]

joyce m hawkins

6000000 is 1 no

holocaustmemorialdaydocumentary sun 26 jan 2003 bbc2

spicegirls earned 1000000s risked 1000000dollarlawsuits

beverley dsilva

1000000dollars here 1000000 there its so petty

imelda marcos

10^{35}

figure whereat martin [rees] speculatively arrived

scotcrab p22

all those lovely zilches
alan clark
might be too many zeros im not too good on zeros
anna nicole smith
john gribbin/simon goodwin origins our place in hubbles uni 1997
ian ridpath ed collins encyclopedia of uni 2001
giles sparrow uni & how to see it 2001
roger penrose road to reality complete guide to physical uni 2004
rpa248
endeavor morses red mark ii 2.5 liter jaguar
b424837
passportnamebox frames blue formula HRH PRINCESS OF WALES
althorp house
babelon8583
see sir alfred hitchcock topaz 1969
fahrenheit451
paper combusts at 451°f
nazis compounding obnoxiousness publicly burned literature
my books my books
marvin j chomsky holocaust 1978
francois truffaut fahrenheit 451 1966
michael moore fahrenheit 9/11 2004
haftling 174517
no tattoed on prisoner primo levis left auschwitzarm
if this is 1 man
trans stuart woolf etchings jane joseph folio mm
[se questo e un uomo 1947]
truce 1 survivors journey home from auschwitz
woolf joseph folio 2002
[la tregua 1963]
rjf
from gassed humanfat germans manufactured bathsoap
all my relatives are soap
dr henry kissinger
manhatrcalif
peter segal naked gun 33½ final insult 1994
comprehends sprightly mockery qv of thelma agus louise
ecto1ny
see ivan reitman ghostbusters 1984
inspector2211sfpolice
see don seigel dirty harry 1971
downtown2525
no not of beast but of bus
see jan de bont speed 1994
gpt64a
glasgowpublictransportbuses 64/64a ex ingram street
whence by pilgrimstages 1 grandson might to dalbeth b conveyed
freeway
tillie tooter tibi laus
1-595 highwayoverpass nigh fort lauderdale fla
tooters toyota tercel® - cf toyotaisation -
skyting off tar plunges 40' into swamp
3dayscartrapped snakes mosquitos searing heat dehydration
tenacious tillie 83 intermittently conscious broadcasts telepathically
authenticated by nationalenquirerenquiry americas hottest weekly

go on one s

persons go on once person is gone go on yourself

cf qua supra enya® songs - lyrics by roma ryan:

let it all go on & on/one by one

gate

cf bab ed din - mirza ali mohammed 1821/50 - gate of righteousness

apostrophes forsworn

one had nothing to jettison save ones commas..

john richards (lincolnshire) won ignobel prize 2001

to honor whose founding of apostropheprotectionsociety

marc abrahams ignobel prizes annals of improbable research 2002

thy parents rot apace

1 sort of jogtrot tommyrot bog blankverse

our wee cavan maverick being from adolescence 1 avid aficionado of marlovian rhythms

kid marlowe fausts die hard 1604

im rotting but u are grayer

leprous bandaged bannen chides wimpy son ye bruce

see mel gibson braveheart 1995

ian was 1 coatbridge gentleman

interestingly - restive feader ridget not:

noblerot *botrytis cinerea* translates pourriture noble

cf trockenbeerenauslese

legge

shak = dregs

cf colluvies omnium gentium

WE WANT

MORE FOOD

david giles darling buds best years of our lives 1993

atholebrose

cratur plus honey agus occasionally oatmeal

brose & bannockday = shrovetuesday oe bannoc

meltith

sc 1 meal/cowsyield

consult chambers english dictionary 7th ed 1988

foutre

worthless

properly 1 noun = caitiff → futuere copulate

fouth

sc abundance

behold [bulimic] knave hath lunched [upon] 1000 chips

frenchfriesshades of coolhandluke or expiscator will cook

agus eat 2240lbs avoirdupois de freerange hardboiled eggs

avec birdseyepetitspois® packaged to frozen within 2½ hrs

seulement i elite variety of succulent tiny

stuart rosenberg coolhandluke 1967

selim sot

tottering dropped on spot

see lord kinross ottoman empire folio 2003 p259

rot peck

sunny jim run to seed (cheeky)

godrot

david lean dr zhivago 1965

dr zhivago trans hayward/harari illus veronique bour folio 1997

cf - stanley kubrick fullmetaljacket 1987 - sallyannrottencrotch

cf hitchcocks rot by rotwest

neonazis

proffessing strong affinity for aryan culture plod to rod ye union cf todkase

see carl reiner dead men dont wear plaid 1982

rotwang

fritz lang metropolis 1926

see 1998 version - soundtrack peter osborne - eureka video

cf giorgio moroders 1984 tinct & truncate offering

kein warum

no why here

see if this is i man p45

anatomy

paul rotha life of adolph hitler 1961

see likewise guido knopp hitler 1 profile

writerdirector maurice philip remy/music klaus doldinger

zdf enterprises 1995-

6 dd videocassettes 1997 – private man seducer blackmailer dictator commander criminal

sol astride ye cusp [aries/taurus - apr 20 1889 - hitlers birthday]

those of us

study such stuff

are confident enough

adolf is ramstam taurus [cf bullinarienunderpants]

shmuel dil 1 firkin of infirm limericks 2012 vide likewise zvi ungermann

hitlerstudentshandbook 5th ed recast & augmented 2009

surreptitious celluloid ye neohumanising of hitler modern cinema summer 2010 pp84-98

reilig

graveyard anglicised relig/relick

ibernocemetarial jocularity

o siochfhradha sv owl proffers:-

ceann cait/screachog reilige/ulchabhan

screachog reilige - cemeteryscreecher

m o siochfhradha nuafhocloirgaeilgebearlabearlagaeilge nd

postscripta

a raghallachs lust for artknives was not non unmitigable

accumulation accumulating adduced no assuefaction

not tho he waxed impotent agus floridbonkers

whose gaga quarters from jan 2002

GEORGE MCMONIGLES GREATHORNEDOWL did grace:

sullen handpainted sculpture dominates smooth hardwood gripe

undulate bolsters 24k

studded avec ellipsoidal malachite en cabochon

approx 8½" 20.3cm fully tumescent

b mr mcmonigles renowned wildlifesculpture figures in vatican & in moma tel aviv

where bengurion proclaimed state of israel 5/14/1948 4pm

c shitty little country

dixit gallic ambassador to court of st james

la honte monseigneur ambassadeur

simple mutual humanity

la honte monseigneur ambassadeur

see ann leslies report from westbanksettlement of efrat

daily mail herein dm wed 17 apr 2002 p18

d 1992

irish moma musaem na nua-ealaine

royal hospital kilmainham dublin 8

director/chief executive declan mcgonagle

wherein 6pm thu sep 17 opened:-

ALANNA O KELLY

BLOOMSLAND BLOOMS 1 GARDEN AGUS 1 RELICK [loosely grave]

dalbeth [cemetery]

a field of birch trees gael beath

cf dalbeattie kirkcudbright/beath dunfermline/beith ayr

james b johnston placenames of alba 2nd ed 1903 herein jbj

b certificatories in sfruttatorean disposition as heir-at-law of raghallach

- including laircertificate reg no 6382 -

& heterogeneous literature bearing upon peter reilly postmortem:

2nd ed hereof will include cull thereof dv herein prospdocull (prospective documentary cull)

rock

peter (piers) = rock

nature naturing

natura naturans creative nature

natura naturata created nature

longhomestone

longhome = 1 golgotha heb gulgoleth skull

cf honeygold honeystone northamptonshire

honorable [son]

peter reilly possessed selfrespecting integrity

ercmaq etc

oghamic epitaphry

wo sind die andere?

no one was saved

mccartney eleonor rigby

warmemorial

breifnes briefness notwithstanding

this wee schema baffles not:-

aidememoire 2 orientate 1 rollingstoneoreily towards grandsires longunincised longhome

godly acre

trans ger gottesacker

jack

eldest son of peter reilly & annie woods

enterexited existence not earlier than 1909

paters peter paters peter paters u judah

a peter reilly fathered:-

peter woods reilly

born blackhall junction cambusnethan lanarks

4h 20m am 4/13/1920

= bend of nechtan (in bede *naiton*)

perhaps johnston ponders 1 pictsking..

b peter woods reilly fathered:-

peter vincent mary reilly

born 12/14/1952

c peter vincent (now domiciled west sussex) fathered:-

judah james

born 6/22/1980

that hath orcus rising

agla

acronymous demonifuge *athah gabor leolam adonai*

cf aglaophotis

see fred getttings dictionary of demons guide to demons & demonologists 1988

acggta/gacagt

dnaanagrams - sykes 7 daughters p28

see likewise sb p524

giolla iosa ruaidh

a domhnall mor son of cathal son of annadh
said domnhall mor sired 3 dominant sons:-
matha/fearghal/giolla iosa ruadh naturalis
giolla iosa - per churchlaw filiusnullius - duly consigned to stink in donals scullery
james - himself cavanman - whose unconscionable abominable collocation reverberates
slavish slutty
spoils of potnton 1897
b transcription carney genhist p73:
oir iar mbeith deithbhir ar ccocuire risan spolla do bhruith
adubhairt gidh be do bhearadh lasog chuige go ttiubhradh luach dho
an sin do bhain giolla iosa ruadh a leine dhubh smearthaigh dhe
do chuir faoi ccoire i gur leigeadh gair fhocmaide astigh
adubhairt bodhar magoillsionnan gur gair fo adhbhar flatha sin
c raghallachs sparky - sm(e)artass - adaptation (cf proper pallid translation genhist p115):
plookie cookie oncemore behindhand roasting donals supperjoint
(rumors of bibulousness persist)
he pledges 3pence unbitten reillysmoney
to knave that furnishes kindlings presently
giolla iosa flourishing greasy black jerkin
sets 1 fervent candle thereunto
unkind kitchen cackles
bodhar magoillsionnan proved prophetic
kindill clinches 1 kingship
d giolla iosa ruadh o raghallaigh
succeeds to lordship of briefne 1293
having assured o reilly dominance
founds 1300 in cavantown monastery of virginmary
usufruct thereof being enjoyed by conventual franciscans
our good lord exercised bittie influence
chez breifne o reilly herself
chez bright banba generally
abroad beyond seachafed shores of eriu
e 1330 or 31
tellustrouncer
clootieclobberer
bull to browbeat unbrook norman sassenach
garbed but qua humble franciscan friar
king giolla iosa ruadh o raghallaigh
whilom cinderellaskivvy
died
LIFEEVERLASTING CHRISTUS GIFT
UNTO NAMESAKE SERVANT
see also passim carney ed poems on o reillys 1950
from carneys intro p vii
present volume contains extant remains of that type of verse usually called bardic
addressed to various members of o reilly family of east breifne or county cavan
peter christian/national archives genealogists internet 2nd ed 2004
mark d herber ancestral trails 2nd ed 2004
john grenham tracing your irish ancestors 2nd ed 2004
mcmahon et al gadhel norman briton 1 genetic topology of county canvan 3rd ed 2014
wobegon dampfire workhouse 2 outhouse [& back agian] balhampamphletsshop 1848
s ciatica 1 mistake of nature [saved by grace] britishempirepersonnelselfhelppamphlets 1897
solon dogonknees how to survive longtermcinderelladom [& get rich] 1904
d mietrich mein blondes baby [mutti is forever] reichcentralchancellorybroadside 1934

raghallaigh
perished in arms clontarf 1014
a quo nomen o reilly
raghallachs eldest son was virile artan:
1st mister o reilly
mister me no misters
for we are blisterers [ofr blestre cog with on blastir blow]
my gemel is anyway
comical ethics sv gemel
david hey/national archives journeys in familyhistory 2004
amanda bevan tracing your ancestors in publicrecordoffice 6th rev ed 2004
pas de postpositive genitive
im 1 friend of harry lime
carol reed 3rd man 1949
apostrophicoapostatising
agus commamolochising agus coyly dashdeploying
additionally dearreader will have perceived
seems curiously to have conceived
an inexponible antipathy to the articles
mucker
fanatical reformer
from konigsbergsect 1835 of dualistic theosophists
mucking in with uni
bernard bassett sj noonday devil [ie accidie] 196?
yuss iff we can trust birthcertif
alas yass we can not
 a fancy
entry no 473 in register of births tullyvin district cootehill union cavan county:-
peter reilly
2 august 1883
father john reilly cottier
mother honor nee brady slavish slutty
vide mutilate birthcertificate prospdoccull
b fact
tue 7/12/88
in pilgrimpresence of raghallach & peter vincent
fr kearns of kill
scrutinising baptism register for said parish
confirms peter reilly son of john reilly
sees light 14 july 1883
being that day - bastilleday - baptised
benighted roman rite
HIBERNIAN BULL STOMPS PROVINCIAL BIRTHDAYSHOP
vide certificates subscribed per fr kearns prospdoccull
aghatotan lass
hier ist kein heisenberg
peter reilly 25 married annie woods 24 6/13/08
st josephs church longsight chorltondistrict counties of manchester & lancaster
vide marriagecertificate prospdoccul
record herewith amend to accommodate reality:-
peter - purporting 2b xxv - est aetatis xxiv
annie - posing as xxiv - est aetatis xxvi
toddler
german joke c1939/40
edda goring - born 6/2/38 - pulled 628000 congratulatory telegraphs

hi my irrepressible irish
dualnatured charlie drake demotically declaimed HELLO MY LITTLE DARLINGS
naturalquaker
ownbonesbreaker
laughtermaker
comical ethics sv risibility
we know how autochthones regarded rags:-
wee foreigner
but we are are not we all citizens of britirish isles
thou breff too britestablishment were not
more enlightened tend to leave
agus bloomsland stagnates
sinead o leary
hello hang on to your lights theyre only lights left
huntley haverstocks haranguing of america foreign correspondent 1940
ireland is my place
irish are my people
i am very like them in my heart & in my soul
mia farrow

tender veneration
pinched from pd mehigan methinks
well grunty will grub

cuchulainn
matthews encyclopedia of celtic myth legend definitive sourcebook of magic vision lore 2003
richard jones/photos john mason myths & legends of britain & ireland 2003

soaring rainbows
cf terry riley rainbow in curved air 1970

eagle
semperexpanding bestiarium swelled again - best yet - thu 5/23/02:
ray beers mesmerising *american eagle dagger*
1st fineart knife presented via international council for game & wildlife conservation
1 franklinmintexclusive
tempered steel blade richly garbed in 24k
blued pewter guard such undulatorinesses
pommel - handpainted pewter eaglesheadsculpture
14½" 36.5cm approx
that hintofsickle glistering blade
conjures up 1 darkling oaky glade
comical ethics sv glade

moaedhog
of ferns 522 626
connachtking setna whose son
pseudopatronsaint o reilly other breffnisepts
vaticanal register-of-hibernian-saints is vacant
save for laurence o toole
mightily doth aedh dubh scowl
god hath made black hugh foul
madoc makes avec 1 magiccowl
presto aedh finn becomes fairer than 1 snowyowl
comical ethics sv magic
see mathews origin pp15/22
beware places named for saints
edna o brien
courtney davis/elaine gill celtic saints 2001
elizabeth rees celtic saints in their landscapes 2001

bede

a breifnes brothers abounding louping tab

passed - 1 leg shy - 1/80 il n y en a puss

needle + needle to ye heart

petes brave bede needed that

b bede 672 735 purveyed not cacohistory tho most medieval historiographers did

john vincent teaches this see intelligent druids guide to history 1995

professor john - chair of history at bristol since 1970 - will forgive 1 druidy jest

his splendid heuristic study = intelligent persons guide

humankind is vile

quintessential file - shrill & shallow

used his pen to vilipend

practitioners of new sentimentality exponentially shrill

try to persuade us man is ill [vile]

paul bailey see saving ye scaffolding

folio magazine fall 2002 pp 25/30 article 1st published new statesman 1971

shtibl

(here) tomb ydd dim of shtub room

droll

maybe middle du droll mannikin

donal munro

odius chamberlain of lewis d1890

how did smalmy archieworm recognise corpse qua munro?

wha kens whit 1 tick kens?

see alba air falach sun 19 jan 2003 c3

landoleal

heaven - doublet of loyal

like

corpse/lykewalk

bonne heure

well done

bonnebouche

mmmmymorsel - cf devils dictionary sv edible

mrriley i have something you might like

id est biteable or buriable bone

slubber crunch thanks 1 bunch mrs rachel lynde

(du slobberen eat or work slovenly)

mrriley = bodie in civilian life - unpolished canine actor

paul shapiro bruce pittman don mcbrearty road to avonlea journey begins 1990

crawled

worm came worm saw worm faltered

i ii urversion p67

overmuch making with worms already..cf presepulchral putrefaction

1 poem has great wormO right thru every page

est penetrant pong

from your affectionate dante gabriel rossetti xxOO see

bill bass/jon jefferson deathscare inside legendary bodyfarm 2003

destin stand

destinare ult from stare stand

alea jacta est/veni vidi vici/aut caesar aut nihil

destiny commands we obey

winston churchill

power comes after we submit to fate

caslos casteneda

see whose don juan books 1968 ff

bullitt

peter yates 1968

sir bob

see parkinson sat 9/29/01 bbc1

mr frankenburger

ms jane seymours father

see jonas stern in extremis 1 primer of judeochristian thanatology 2 vols 2009/11

dark abortions

soviet bioweaponisers (black biologists) latter part 20th century

developed radiationresistant smallpoxstrains:

stray survivors of mutual assured destruction should not thrive

opposing chemists will approach frontier ampulsarmed

and history will end

wilde to conan doyle see memories & adventures 1924

resume joint insatiate savagery?

[lawrence of arabias exultant collocation of colluction]

please feel free to kick keeck out of me..

u dont really belong to itsonlyhistoryschool?

sapiensjust1jumpedupmonkeythatgotunluckyschool

evolvent consciousness of malcolm x:

what thereunto constituted hgc? [historys greatest crime]

abduction into anguish & abjection of 100 million africans

he might have escaped attention on baxters bus?

adolf eichmann i think you mean

however?

whose ireful eye assumed tigeraspect

eichmanns sop?

shoah is hgc

1 2 urversion p82

templeballs

from fingers fumbling flying spliff alight alights

christ 1 nepalese incendiary quick ms spit 1st dribbel after

hippy slim scotspliffs or down & stoned in belmont hall 1972 p23

harry lime

bbc developed greenecharacter into radioseries 1951

horrible shot

peter farrelly dumb & dumber 1994

soldiers bullet

hermann goring

shot at me

adolph hitler 20 july 1944

few shots

peter macdonald rambo 3 1987

stuttgart

roger spottiswoode tomorrow never dies 1997

josiah boon

ford stagecoach 1939

navel

john huston maltese falcon 1941

ace ventura 5

jim carrey

catch lead

raoul walsh high sierra 1940

deal in lead

john sturges magnificent 7 1960

rollie

robert mandel f/x murder by illusion 1985

shooting reilly

jim goddard reillyaceofspies dreadnoughts & crosses eustonfilms 1983

shoot riley

raoul walsh white heat 1949

bb king is christened riley

beautiful winona ryder 10/29/71 has 1 little neice riley

pierce brosnan has 1 greataunt ilene reilly

laugh

andy warhol

russians

richard benjamin little nikita 1988

butcher

jack pollexfen indestructible man 1956

2 slugs

orson welles touch of evil 1958

1st shot

sam peckinpah wildbunch 1969

one shot

when i meet famous people i dont see aura

i think i have one shot at influencing you

bob geldof to andrew duncan rt interview 12/21/02 pp?

chili palmer

antihero of barry sonnenfeld get shorty 1995

palmer - john travolta - traversing hollywood enjoys matinee screening of touch of evil

chilli collects baddebts

hee is not - pace heedless headlong trailer - shylock

WHEN MIAMI LOANSHARK CHILI PALMER WAS SENT TO LA 2 COLLECT GAMBLINGDEBT..

miami debtcollector for mob halliwells film & videoguide ed john walker 18th ed 2003 p325

see j sutherland where rebecca shot? puzzles curiosities conundrums in modern fiction 1999

short postscript

to his buddy marlene orson proffers no emoluments

dietrich 12/27/01 quintuple capricornus

maria riva 12/13/24 bequeathed 1 astonishingly wise & intelligent autobiographic biography

marlene dietrich by her daughter maria riva 1992

home im going home p792

gun

hoplology study of weapons gk hoplon

hoplophobia fear of guns see

paul mcfedries wordspy wordlovers guide to modern culture 2004

u2 uk

homesecretary jack straw chairs summit fri 1/10/02

ukguncrimeescalation having sparked national alarm

kismet is king

boggle at dogmatic cavanite soidisant kinsman of kings

(o reilly styled king of breny only until 1220)

certainly kismet was 1 concept dear to leopold bloom

hopeless idiots

pancategory - gurdjieff being kategoros (accuser)

judy kuriansky complete idiots guide 2 1 healthy relationship 2003

useful idiots

cf savvy intelligencecommunity

horribiliz bizniz

cf maclean rogers oldmotherriley in business 1940

pottock

donkey of basque

cf pons asinorum

buridans ass born in or under libra?

pize

imprecatory term - pox/pest

pixilation

bewildernessment

glossgloss lest peruser pursue at lossloss

cf sw psyk(e) small fairy

be + obs wilder lose ones way

wildeornes → wilddeor wilddeer

pennybrain

mathsprofessor maher took hir measure = pennybrainflannelmerchant

cavanman

one passed for 1 cavanman

ard u cannod duck

parceque - echoing craig ventner - discovery cannot dawdle

heinz®

henry j tomatoessmothered peans + bork pittsburgh 1895

beansinvaded ye white cliffs 1904

peans sans bork plain beam dreans date from 28

see brian roberts beanz meanz scienz dm thu 7/4/02 p17

beanfa

beanfa tu re tional breifnach

banbha cuinn do chlannaibh cnoicht

po y whrussens

cornish disinhumed - sfrutttatore cannot tranlate

ignorance mama pure ignorance

re cornwallproutsagglomeration:

huguenothophuguenotskip calais penzance?

derbyniwyd

welsh - decipherable:-

received for use nationallibrary wales 1/18/82

one (unus) copy

breifne o reily brief account of life in 1 foreign kingdom

appease

pacify satisy quieten

ofr apeser bring peace → pax

irenology by ye bye:

study not of *beans* but of *peace*

tranquillity that flows from order

aquinas

peace is 1 choice

pr

if we live calmmonotonous days/peaceful nights we stultify

gurdjieff

mental peace inner harmony

lady amanda ferragamos noteworthy notion of luxury

beati pacifici

blessed are peacepedlars they will be nobelprized

beatified beanicon

ie smirking beansymbol

smiles milewidesmile thinkin on more bein beans [bein = good

pleonasm - gk pleon more - see scotbean p200]

infantile servilism

see mende nazer with damien lewis slave

true story of girls lost childhood & her fight for survival 2004

curry

enjoy our curries

take some hame

kamran is our name

kamran tandoori takeaway 125 gartsherrie road coatbridge

gartsherrie

foalsenclosure gael searrach

coatbridge

gael coid brushwood/sticks

cf corn coat/welsh coed 1 wood

drimdromdrum

druim → dorsum

back ridge longhill see pwj p100

hamburger hill

john irvin 1987

smouse[1]

worker of cord dabby tarling

lelibate cexicographer in absentia pussae cat assured

(fr tabis → attabiy 1 baghdad ¼)

basically 1 jew

sort of which file fancied himself 2b

du corresp to ger schmus talk patter → ydd schmuess

cf heb shemuot tales news see

mark abley spoken here travels among threatened languages 2004

smouse[2]

feast on ger schmausen

sh sh

pas schweppes® pas beluga bondbeloved

could it b beans

cry me [ie call me] sishmael

sisyphus agus cissyplus

little persons

problems of 3 little people dont amount 2 1 hill of beans in this crazy world

rick blaine counsels ilsa lund

godspelllornnornstormented

reverbrates 1 ghostly yates?

even great poet

even great irish poet

ought ken when stop

pluck till time times are done

golden apples of ye sun

yates

silver skin laced with golden blood

macbeth 2 3

a godspel(l) trans evangelium

god (long e) = good:

afterwards associated with god (deus)

spel(l) story news

b oe loren past part of leosan lose

c norns = norse destinydispensers

parcae for that they reck not of persons cruel deemed (parer pas parcere)

pallida nona aequo pulsat pede pauperum

arc

water under

barrackgates

underneath lamplight nigh ye barrackgates

darling i remember way u used to wait

schmaltzy german warsong

cf gilbert & george underneath ye arches 1971

geek

cf related e dial geck fool

airdrie

aird airidh highhillpasture

1 friendly clean neat town - nice folk

morag agus fiona are proud gaelic airdrionians

charles sobieski overnighted here

where flowerhill embraces henderson street

[duke] wore jeans

gerald thomas 1958 - tommysteelestarvehicle

juvenile file/callow expiscator saw on bigscreen

toponyms

gael has always been more modest than his english supplanter

jbj pli

most celtic names give

simplest possible description of site

or describe some prominent feature

or coloring or appearance as they strike eye

idem pxlv - see passim ppxiii/cxi

freighted

popper

neutral

see juliette wood celtic book of living & dying mm

fate he thought

see traudl junge with melissa muller

until final hour hitlers last secretary 2003 p134

an englishing per anthea bell of

bis zur letzten stunde hitlers sekretarin erzahlt ihr leben 2002

minstrel

simon brennan

woody

customised milton

0 saves us - we all end up on scrapheap

woody allen to christopher freyling

caught

dr david reilly herein drdr

tyranny

henry maudsley 1835 1918

foremost evolutionary alienist during victorias late reign

insanity indigency recidivism ineluctably ordained

there but for genetic grace..

at least some mental events are heritable [?] that make 1 child say singed

steven pinker sb p297

to ye maundering muddy gutter born 1865

& in ye garden [comma] maudsley [personal memoir] 1866

physiology & pathology of mind 1867

body & mind 1870

responsibility in mental disease 1874

organizing
lindy chamberlain
karl
under austrian code in beethovens day
catholic church arrogates selfslayers manque
failed suicides remanded to protection of priests
who implacably impart christian doctrine
god 1 bullet
boston teran
notarget
patrick kavanagh
blank shot
mark twain
blanks
tom clegg sharpes enemy 1994
chance
andre gide
offchance
germaine greer
blindchance
dashiell hammett
rotten at dying
ian anderson
some braininduced [?] chemical kicks in
i felt resolute & capable of coping with my imminent demise
idem
art is attached to ye brain [?] especially in moments of decision
peter hammond master blackmailer 1/2/92
something in my brain pulls me back from obsessing about weight
kim medcalf
specialised palliative nurses to deal solely with old people near death
william reid
magick
aleister crowley
this territory needs more fuddle
quite
agus this expicator *less file*
see ford stagecoach 1939
unfuddled dane
or undoomed thane
to cling
pace shamelessly comical & cute
unto textual reality
expiscator has not studied beowolf since striving adolescence
from timeinfirmed memory
dearreader redactor
neglectful & oblivious recites
what we gardena in yeardagum
theodcyninga thrum gefrunnon
hu tha aethelingas ellen fremedon
see british myths & legends ed richard barber illus john vernon lord folio 1998
sister fate
pr see
nimrod blampin i accepted my fate it made me great broadsheet 1789 praise ye lord
zolar book of fate 2nd rev ed 1982

fatenote

6th sense life death fate

title whereby cantonese were introduced by videopirates to martin brest meet joe black 1998

see neil williams daily express herein de 9/18/02 p21

megalopsychos

from george forbes praisepoem

expiscators privilege - as files - to peruse in typescript brace of forbesean novels

fiddler knew it too/bluegrapes

amice

file greets forbes friend & fellow scribe

ta me sinte

i am stretched athwart thy grave - shan nose song

i cried

ross benson

afghanistan

mohammed omar

he escaped on 1 motorcycle?

see abel ferrara ye addiction 1994

bodybags

forces of evil will carry own coffins on backs

saddam hussein

quoted on bbcnews thu 8 aug 2002

like mahomets coffin

ie suspended inter heaven & hell

see roy william neill dressed to kill 1946

itv1 screened sixpartdocumentary

dont drop coffin

wherein camera scrutinises

fa albin and sons southlondon funeraldirectors

tue 7/22/03 et sequentia

books

gom - we gladstone 1809 98

parthenon

phil joanou final analysis 1992

beneath heap heap

runt cheeps cheap

scotcheep p183

news

jo moore

surprise me

bobs wife had inquired where he hoped 2b buried

mon 28 jul 2003 aetatis suae c

massive graveyards

alan jones[1]

cf charnelhouse of species

starts suddenly rime & reasonless

alan jones[2] re george romero night of living dead 1968

i ii too..

avoid cemeteries

anatole litvak night of generals 1966

simmies in cemetery

point was made by robert brooke since himself deceased

life in those days simpler (gladder)

see biddy gilfedder happy bovak days! 1 sentimental reminiscence trafford 1998

bovak = bobby versus jackie

where now?/morgue

ga/dp riley respectively 22 jul 2003

see bill duke cemeteryclub 1992

skeleton [in] cemetery

robert harmon nowhere to run 1993

laws of nature = skeleton of universe

see trefil qua supra pvii

donald campbell was recovered from coniston waters 3/01

pisces newmoon:- vanishment reversed

chillipeppers please

ian anderson of jethro tull

blood sugar sex magik

red hot chili peppers lean mean album..

please dont drop coffin!

barry albin-dyer with greg watts 2002

decomposition deglorifies

did da vinci affirm it?

inveterate cadaverscarver even in whose 70s

is expiscator 1 circumcised circassian

ichabod

glory absquatulates 1 sam 4/21

simian

william s burroughs

rot my trademark

= roger o thornhill

what does ye o stand for?

0

hitchcock north by northwest

holeingO

nothing sacred about hole in ground or man or woman in it

sam peckinpah bring me head of alfredo garcia 1974

see vivian cook accomodating brocolli in ye cemetery 2004

graverat

simple ye gist of this flisky flaucht of filesilliness

a potter - oates - hath nocturnal business re cemetery/coffin

now bestick those bays dead corpse in complete steal

see don taylor tom sawyer 1973

b bennie - oates - hath nocturnal business re cemetery/cadaver

honi soit see alfredo garcia cf flunterninterment

c bennie being peckinpahs patronymicless antihero

nobody loses all ye time

d throw lesser moviebuffs 1 bone

principal garciahitman - gig young - passes himself off as fred c dobbs:

bogarts role in treasure of sierra madre

angel

subconscious mind is our holy guardian angel

aleister crowley

some people think u should be accountable for your subconscious

which is cool

fionn regan big issue in scotland issue 465 feb 19/25 04 p28

cizers

shakespearian scissors

pas rob roys brag

unmistakeable whiff of cc

suffer ye chocolatecrunchiecompulsionsyndromesufferer..

candokid

national enquirer

cf pampers kandoo junior toiletwipes®

candoamerican

richard beeston re senator george mitchell

hir days [are] not numbered wherewith y our race [is] lumbered

comical ethics sv religion

i can

cancerresearchukadvert thu 8/29/02 c3

if mind sticks in cantdo u stick there 2

nous leads ass heeds

iyanla vanzant

bethlehem

kevin costner postman 1997

if you can

edouard manet

iffucan

wallace stevens

o rail

sir thomas cusack

in 1553 lordchancellor of ireland

see jj hist of breif chap iv

glamor

sir misterfixit

fastingtide

sir gawain

unseasonal

smorgasbord of comical ethics sv bean

magnitude

george pal timemachine 1960

cf simon wells 2002 version

beans beans beans

andy devines uxoriallament see stagecoach

i knew youthful breif to exult books books books

& on occasion baroque baroque baroque

c1600/1750 - ms lesley garretts parameters cfm sun 10/12/03

yes beasties birthday

so u can have fur coat & turkey on your birthday

[in lieu of haricots]

henry koster 100 men & 1 girl 1937

he did indeed deem himself readerwriter

latterly (literarily) (quelle ennui) writerreviser

harold bloom - monumentally - asserts false distinction inter reading/writing

roy harris rethinking writing mm interrogates certain tenets of saussureanism:

scriptum verbum rex est

let books gather dust

pr

see timemachineslibraryscenes

beans!

ford rio grande 1950

buffalosteaks

ford she wore 1 yellow ribbon 1949

enuf

mel brooks abraded saddlesores 1974 see

mr bean beans ben worldcinema 1 enthusiasts thesaurus 2008

beans did for him

jonathan brocklebank heinz seas drama dm tue 7/16/02 p3

coco

darling buds?

yet 1 clings infirming claws or paws unto ones glossing

cf sere seres

bananas

mj williamson

green bean

renee zellweger on - hosts grant lauchlan/sarah heaney- moviejuice fri 17 jan 2003 c3

carousel

beatles white album

thief

william nedley

native of co westmeath

practised medicine dublin mid 19th cent

nedley indited ballads of propagandistic tendency

fortifying coreligionists (rc)

beset by hunger & protestantelytism

nedleys medleys likewise hugely pop

his chef doeuvre however must surely be

LIFE OF REILLY C1854

arrah mrs mcgrath theyre handing out bowls

i am quite sure me dear u knew it

sure quality is saving our souls

sub us for letting em do it

so jink along to merrion square

sure as me name is reilly

1 scally may damage mutton or beef

if she amens with auld mrs smyly

ie merrionsquaremissionarysoupkitchen

jink being 1 little expiscatorial intrusion

(there are others)

some modest craft loiters in ye druid (du leuteren)

bill will forgive

see mathews origin p62

postscripta

de propaganda fide re faith 2b propagated 1622

caveat eager beaver reader - abl sing

one talks of practising medicine

operative word

pearce brosnan

doctors feel need to panacea humanity

which is why they are all snakemad

mind you i owe my life to them

maureen lipmann

glass

pr

accept

perdurabo

hes still here

yoko ono to michael aspel

shes still here

daisy von scherler mayer madeline 1998

absit onus

she is here
carroll ballard fly away home 1996
theyre still here
jack gold goodnight mr tom 1998
pasttense
twintowersvictimswidow
suspect
james hewett
destiny can be like that sometimes
[you dont think about it you just do it]
mark chapman
anything
caligula
ducks
filefiction in putative style of uncle stalin
had svetlana asked her pa
koba pas qualms whacking old revolutionary pals ?
stalin might have appealed to ducks
see comical ethics sv koba
moral qualms
paper will tolerate anything written upon it
uncle joe
povertyindustry
mel x
drowning
agatha christie
bubbles
perdurabo
turned against
kissinger
decided
hitchcock
paperpaper
jazzedup dashiell hammett
round
jay roach meet parents mm
names
mr adrian furness sic re gary frazier/barry eden esqs salford crematorium
du schnell krematorium fertig
creu wir fel gwir o ffwrnais awen
mutato nomine de te fabula narratur
impatient
from simon brennans poetic tribute to prs art
a *ministry of fire* comprises 11 compositions
release pj music jan 89
recording zal god studios glasgow
engineermasterer stuart douglas
production pete reilly/stuart douglas
b reilly released 12 track followupalbum 1994
between ii worlds
voice pete reilly
instuments stuart douglas
cover judah reilly
production black capricorn music & sound
marketing/distribution renaissance music

c files audiocassette of ii worlds bears autographic inscription:
nov 94
to my friend & brother breifne
love & admiration
pete
feet
unique quasiceltic danceextravaganza
produced/directed by irishamerican genius michael flatley
hundred plus dancers entertained 25000 enthusiastic punters
hyde park sat 25 jul 1998
medals fire
dean macey
medals melt
nancy wake legendary soe agent
george cross resistance medal other medals
see gillian armstrong charlotte gray 2001
shortlist
john mcgivern to file & to expiscator over heavy pints
la ronde hostelry 6/22/72 johns 18th birthday
perpetual motion
1 splendid energetic mobile disco
lovechild of 3 gallant generous sexy celtic cavaliers
robert stewart 2/19/53
john mcgivern qua supra
david reilly 5/4/55
goldie was only 1 camp follower
christiannest
mervyn le roy quo vadis? 1951
ice
americanonymous herein amon
eggdonation
jed dreben
deaf
amon
phone
peter chelsom hear my song 1991
wherein divine miss fitzgerald poses as pisces
being superabundantly virgo 9/17/68
americans
michael palin
uncle sam
bob geldof to michael parkinson
friend
george w bush
stand
jerry hall
wedded
dr hugh brogan
agent
james carney
yield
harold bloom
alone
j i m stewart
there wasnt much love in joyces life

anthony burgess to miss mena reilly
when? before john smith & son became 1 cybercafe
ULYSSESEAN STOPPRESS
folio society will publish special commemorative edition
16 june 2004
1750 numbered copies
full goatsin leather blocked jeff clements
text of 2nd ed 1926
old style + pastonchi display
intro jacques aubert
pref stephen james joyce
18 etchings with goldleaf mimmo paladino
758pp 9½ " x 6¾"

sunny
nora barnacle - prob choc crunch

ogre
will come anyway
joyce see richard ellmann

madoc
torlogh o clery

7 lights
tuiream bais
if i ordered posters advertising every 7 subhumans i designed to shoot
polands forests would be kaput
hans frank

7 minutes
paul anderson soldier 1998

more minutes
martin campbell reillyaceofspies prelude to war 1983

cromm cruaich
magslechtdinnsenchus
see miranda green dying for ye gods 2001

righ o mbriuin
rags for delf
should have been your occupation
o raghallaigh of castle muck
u briuin kinglet
swanning airy palaces
libertarianly englished..
for mundane translation see genhist p117

rioghthaoiseach
we know not when o dugan composed
terminus ante 1372
mathews sturdy tenacious sfruttatoretinkered translation origin p23:
royal chief rough incursions [cf klepsiklepsi]
o raghallaigh of red arms
thy golden voice sounds sweetly [stock epathaton]
over fine muinter maoilmordha
[mhaoil mionmhordha
1 instructive instance of cavanbardictmesis]
we should wish to tarry there awhile
from this land let us pass let us pass
let us scruple pas to juxtapose
files fleshy flashy fanciful rendition
hitherto deservedly unpublished

royal chiefs

rough incursions

redarmed reillys [?]

their mellifluous tones echo

throughout muintir maoilmordha

wherein would weary duchas

have o dugan tarry

from this tellus no more

no more interminably dreary exiled procedamus

[duchas = instinct nature cf epithymos

thus constant mother linketh one of 14th with one of 21st]

nora nora

oe turnian tyrnan → tornare turn in lathe

cf ll tortura twisting

nora set thy cot near mine

jimmys morbid wish

stropped [sic] onto stretcher

flipflopping as 1 fish

scotcrab p186

aloft orthopedic bed

biddy lying dead

1 white windingsheet

that meseems

ben ye dark

loometh stark

cryptodiary wed 8 sep 2004

bairn

baby peter woods loved loved was

heir

last surviving son of peter reilly

gerhard

hirself perhaps 1 coalbiter (kolbitr)

sire [may be] childsshrine [revered person]

ethics of megalopsychos 4 22

im not hero im lotkevendor

peter kassovitz jacob liar 1999

masterfully lensed (cf vincents dutch period) poland/hungary per elemer ragalyi hsc

maethes

oe matha cf maddock

jim [reilly]

killed activeservice 1945

was putative widow mary lamb mary lamb or is it paranoid i am?

jack [reilly]

kottod 1912

kilroy here

we dont do god here

attributed to alistair campbell

inside mind of tony blair sun 9/28/03 c4

wheres harry

genealogical agency ms maggie cosford founder

wer da

1st extraeuropean utterance of shakespeare

5 sep 1607 aboard reddragon anchored off sierra leone

see prof willy maleys essay bill of writes ballistic bard

bigissue in scotland issue 453 nov 20/26 2003 pp30/31

darbies

perhaps eponymous = handcuffs

see hitchcock saboteur 1942

e dunno

gus elen

moad porcullis mirador etc

is this kitsch?

mirador = watchingplace see tom clegg sharpes sword 1995

more door

more outside barks tot wot wants to lark in park

see steven pinkers essay words & rules sb p296

curtains

back of lace curtains 1 wos looking (sometimes) [tooting]

scotcurtain p741

come hiemal evenings

pull kitchen curtains close

of all ye cosy time of year

we luv dis season mos

idem

privacies

should plug shall plug

published by belknappress of harvard 5 beautiful volumes

philippe aries/georges duby gen eds arthur goldhammer trans

history of private life histoire de la vie privee

from pagan rome to byzantium ed paul veyne 1987

revelations of medieval world ed georges duby 1988

passions of renaissance ed roger chartier 1989

from fires of revolution to great war ed michelle perrot 1990

riddles of identity in modern times eds antoine prost/gerard vincent 1991

antaskarana

facilely spinning antaskarana

ruysbroek nor boehme in padmasana

barkochba swizzles exposed 1 skeptical estimation of ten esoteric concepts 2008

vide passim yetibetaninspired writings of alice m bailey

paradise

gk paradeisos - lit enclosed park - persian origin

see ziauddin sardar desperately seeking paradise journeys of 1 sceptical muslim 2004

parishioner

gk paroikia soujourning → paroikos christian → gk = stranger

nonexcreting saints

see paramahansa yogananda autobiography of 1 yogi

mad messed medico monkey

herrgottsacrament!

consult sfruttatores incisive (sympathetic) evaluation

1 case of sexocloacalinneurosis journal of irish psychopathology spring 1984 pp414ff

throne

u cant abdicate & eat it

wallis simpson see

oreily once were kings but now ye buroo 1 familiallament cts pamphlet 2114

circa regnat tonat

thunder circumambulates throne

i did learn out of 1 grate

for all favor glory might

circa regna tonat

thomas wyatt

soma esth [is] no temple
impossible to dissemble
she thundereth aft [perdesthai]
smorgasboard sv soma
thundering in
desperate levis ear
we are here
we have diarrhoea
scotthor p12
see if this is i man p199

trungpa
chogyam trungpa shambala sacred path of warrior reprint mm

somatism
materialism

holy toast
circletoastcircletoast
tot thumps highchair
glare despair
chumps chumps
dont you get it?
baby craves bagel
scottoast p303
see pinker sb p296

suppository
malapropism read *suppositum* = selfsubsistent ens

suppose it not
athetesis ie rejection as spurious
spirit - factus de materia - being 1 function of personality
& none ye worse for that
cf collegeofhardknocks aka nabokovean commonsense
merely element determined by function
action directe explain away their assassination of georges besse

oh unding get behind this not unthinking numpty
 a numpty = numbskull
reid is no ordinary lanarkshire numpty
tim luckhurst dm fri 10/25/02 p12
b unding = 1 nonexistent - ger absurdity
go take 1 powder thou-notion-of-reified-spirit?
keine ahnung
cf theory of descriptions
exists entity r
such that
giolla iosa composed i ii
is not true
if giolla iosa is r
moreover r is not not giolla iosa
see bertrand russell history of western philosophy folio 2004 chap31

personality/proof
particularly madcap (manic) parcell of gemellate q&a
gir has elsewhere deconstructed (perhaps thoroughly enough)
see whose very trenchant paper *imulse to cap*
journal of mental & nervous diseases fall mm pp1/80
cap likewise us dialect = mystify perplex

ahankara
false self

atma

realself cf purusha

himsa

violence hurting cf ahimsa

odograph

odometer gk hodos way graphein write

should be subject to

modal usage = ought to

see new fowlers modern english usage

rev 3rd ed by rw burchfield 1998 p711

none of whose fields is other than infinitely extendible

tush¹

ydd tokhes → heb tahat under

tush²

cf rl stevensons scorpionic neologism *tushery*

see david o russell 3 kings 1999

wherein hairdesigns are credited to 1 certain robert louis stevenson

poor lazarus

fatuous lapse into otiosity

chemists dive dove

ie diving egos of opus alchymycum

daring dane cornucopianises hermeticistic corpus:

johannes fabricius

alchemy medieval alchemists & their royal art

layout/typography kirsten/johannes fabricius

1st published rosenkilde & bagger copenhagen 1976

rev ed aquarian press 1989

sunken treasure of medieval culture unearthed [unmered?] recreated

fascinating work of literary archeology

aquarian blurb

urinator

cf sub divo/sub jove

dove so low

cf davids deep dive steven spielberg ai 2001

solo una spina

u wish your hireling to slot 1 thorn only?

sicilian assassin thus plaintively importunes don altobello

see francis ford coppola godfather 3 1990

aught of divine

hermeticists deluded themselves opus possessed salvific efficacity

mystical system for mans salvation & ultimate reunion with divine source

aquarian blurb alchemy qua supra

9

u cooked her 9s

carl reiner man with 2 brains 1983

year 9

horace ap 388

see robert ehrlich 9 crazy ideas in science 2001

tarutatu

spelean octopusgod denizen of 1 vanuatuan (melanesia) lagun

gk spelaion cave melas black

that partial beast pristine apotropaic pearls do appease

highheaped afore hir aqueous lair grendellike defended

brief account p1948 see

ernie palamarek thundersea/secret temple of kintamani trafford nd

pest

beast worm serpent → ir piast

john paul

rabbi michael melchior

londoners

george vi

stonewall

trueglory from dday to fall of berlin

assembled by allied military during 1944/5

academy award winner best documentary 1945

debris

liars they tossed us in trench stuck monument atop 2002

see leon mcdermotts article liars make it up anything goes for nys latest punkrockexport

bigissue in scotland jul 25/31 2002 p29

walked

angelina jolie

x

malcolm x

jefferson

james harding preaching to converted ftweekend jan 4/5 2003 p1

sans walls

william jefferson clinton

26th richard dimbleby lecture sun 16 dec 2001 c1

god bless

see mattie jt stepankek heartsongs 2002

tout seul

mary wollenstonecraft aka crafty crunch

im alone

steven spielberg saving private ryan 1998

on your own

martin campbell goldeneye 1995

alone?

mark sandrich tophat 1938

reason

michael apted world is not enough 1999

why here

maltesers® advert fri 23 aug 2002 c5

nips

sonja und monika

tenancy

ian anderson

turds [verbatim filth]

nicholas van hoogstraten

cf - kristine peterson critters 3 1991 - furry tenantmunchers

business

scotorum malleus dixit

longshanks filled ye ragmanroll [1296]

whose malice could be quite droll

comical ethics sv malice

good beans

sir gawain

haricots

scotcrab p667 (file had 1 bibelot called pelicrab)

asian pali hari god kotte pottage

beans beans turn gut whereof one would be shut

[apology
post sfruttatores most recent bre
akaway from quotidian reality (saltus) (untergang)
awash now compulsorily at ye last (11th hour)
salubrious salutary sans mens medication
ones latter father wos 1 lonely lithium carbonate man
faradvanced mon pere towards ye last post
alas insidioussalads apt yet assail
swim thru swirly tides
siblings take parental sides
glosspross will hereafter tend perforce to possess
1 skeletonic tho never 1 cursory (obsessiveness forbid) quality
but (to pervert last shah) we do not jirble:
we are no wallydrag
o that this too too perseverant perseveration
charitable reader forgive expiscatorial frailty
file you were my unscottified
federarie?
father & mother we loved each other
ich bin der letz
ich dien adieu]

gie us gift
ie (paradoxically) to behold ourselves as are (godless)
bridgetonburnsclub/mr shuggy may ms jennifer thompson
rbcft dumfries ran fahrenheit 9/11 27/30 oct 2004

innominables
ludwig wittgenstein - sprightly paraphrase of

bled here before
we have all been here before
crosby stills nash & young (they were)

mishmishim
peaches sing mishmish cf mitkan/mitkanim

pancrator
aka gnostic demiourgos
pancrator being to pancosmists persona non grata
cosmos cest tout

plato
whimsical (childish)

dr syntax
cant gloss sorry av tint ma notes a canna bit fash
& of course one is nononline anyway (off ones nana)
next workingday quadruple st johns wort
nae worries notes & nerve recovered
william combe 1741 1823
dr syntax in search of picturesque 1809
2nd tourette in search of consolation 1820
3rd tourette in search of uxor 1821

yex it out
also yesk belch/spit - normally intran - oe geocsian sob

rereturn
consult protocols 2nd council of constantinople 553 ce
see likewise hans kung reincarnation 1 ecumenicistic reappraisal 2008

furcas
adept in chiromancy hieromancy myomancy pyromancy
fred gettings dictionary of demons 1988

telesales

angelina letter 9/7/01

todds

abraham lincoln

throne

lindy chamberlain

man upstairs

john ford aka sean o cruanchai

lewis

wolvercote tongue

church

jerk 79

steve martins sillily hilarious urstarvehicle

seminal too if we credit amonmoviereviewers

sparky early blueprint for dumb & dumber

gormless ancestor to gorrest fump

magick

tomegatherion

roisterdoister

1885 year of rooster

shirkincloister

he shirked 1 cloister?

slapslaphappy

see franklin j schaffner patton lust for glory

academyaward bestpicture 1970

exit

terminal entry in frida kahlos diary

see julie taymor frida 2003

rack

william hazlitt

karniji

barcockless cyclopedia of ogygian repulsive superstitions ms nd sv metempsychosis

rattrapped inincarnationloop

= implicated in incarnationloop?

perseveration mimics perhaps reincarnational intrinsication

cyclopedia qua supra sv rattrap

motherinlaw

pr

humanform

hermes trismegistus

psyche reincarnates in sign wherein she moved on

alice m bailey

massage

george forbes

liverpool

singing lovesongs to your hometown [=densenchas]

stephen mcgann

object world etc

fabricius alchemy

imperial

christopher lasch minimal self

androgynous

society of innner light see

master therion psyche androgyne 2nd rev ed 1934

nemo - farceur of pince sans rire variety?

constant self
sekida zen training p122
0
gi gurdjieff
boundaries
jane roberts aka seth see
holistic revolution essential newagereader ed william bloom mm p372
terpsichorean
mark sandrich gay divorcee 1934
selfmotivation
westcoast amon
turningpoint
kenneth clark civilisation 1 personal view folio 1999 p96
lord clark wos occupied with art
& with matters that occur ordinarily ben dark
comical ethics sv art
nargo anand avers that
sanskrit root of - sanskrit word for? - art = suitably united
art of sexual exstasy 1989
celts
robert curran
greatspirit[1]
pr
greatspirit[2]
crazyhorse siouxname tashunkewitko
brave blusterer custer
[hair of] tawnyeagle luster
johnny cash 1932 2003
mindbody
fritjof capra hidden connections 2002
projects
sri yukteswar
perhaps one could have shot which would allow innermostself to emanate
william shatner
bear
vicky lougher
those little victorian ladybears
such natural sweetness in their hearts
idem
trueself beast
te lawrence
innerbeast
johnny cash
all men are pigdogstyes
hitler to sefton delmer see david garnett
secret history political warfare executive 1939 45 2001
animalself
gary fleder kiss ye girls 1997
bourn
beethoven
= domain keats
radiance
pr
by permeating light 2 radiate from 1 face one can discover ye beauty in everyone
valentine gotti

implants
nemo
tyrannous
andrew marvell
chain
jung
moon may be as far as we get
sir david attenborough (correctly paraphrased?)
butterfly
ie (too loosely) personality gk psyche soul butterfly
consult comical ethics sv psyche
butterfly tasteth thru hir feet
pr
pleroma
perdurabo
all there is is us
amon - mescaline 490mg see
william braden private sea lsd & search for god 1968 pp195/200
reckon
stephen hawking universe in 1 nutshell 2001 p171
were talking 1 thousand million galaxies
im sure theres plenty of life out there
patrick moore cfmnews thu 2 sep 04
paddon onmusing
pas confusing
froggie would a - [reduction of oe prep an] wooing go
cf wench (sc winch) qua verbal
culture has been dominated by males
because culture is mainly courtship effort
males invest more energy in courtship vide geoffrey miller
mating mind how sexual choice shaped evolution in humannature mm
study also olivia judson dr tatianas sex advice to all creation
definitive guide to evolutionary biology of sex 2002
chasdely
raghallach might have been 1 man
had he danced upon transatlantic bars
dated dolls whose grandad he wos old enuf to have been
he used to wisecrack
storming humility easypeasy nor did chastity prove 1 hard nut
postscript
mr russell crowe barelevated recites sanctuary (kavanagh)
wake for richard harris goring hotel london nov 02
sthenic
brunonian dichotomy (dr john brown c1736 88)
sthenic/asthenic diseases gk sthenos strength
ii ii
see segal naked gun 33½
loofa
egyptian arabic lufa
lollapalooza
1 stoater (bit of allright)
loco locorestive not
ie mad not - lambs coinage - staying put
train for zones behind front
if this is i man p228

denmark
1 small country north of great britain
munich
hogmanay 71
gimme shelter
albert maysles david maysles charlotte zwerin 1970
wip
schiocchi la frusta
zilch zegz
amazing how much you get done when celibate
jerry hall
shunammite
1 kings 1/3
cf castigatory chambers sv stern

castigare reprove → castus pure

magnus magnusson kbe gen ed chambers biographical dictionary herein cbd 5th ed 1990
plonker/porker/hooker
titles whereby videopirates introduced cantonese to respectively
boogie nights/full monty/pretty woman
[i didnt know] u kiss women
golda meyer to heinrich kissinger
walter isaacson kissinger 1 biography 1992 p 552
sword
tophat
just kiss
casablanca
fun
matthew perry
cut
paloma baeza
scallies
ms margi clarke re mr mel gibson
balloon
howard hawks rio lobo 1971
equator
thornton freeland flying down to rio 1933
irish
attributed to dennis quaid
horrible
kirsten dunst
elephant
mahabharata
kiss me stupid

pas kissmestupid:− kiss me comma stupid
catholic legion of decency condemned billy wilders 1964 movie
studio itself then kissed film off
lip
carl reiner dead men dont wear plaid 1982
cuddling
samantha robson
risingsun
pr
brow
erasmus darwin
j wedgewood had *strong opinion* that english childslavesystem had better be *left alone*

niceties

tophat

ross & shaw [= te lawrence]

basil liddell hart

gamins

sebastian melmoth see william j mann

behind screen hows gays & lesbians shaped hollywood 2002

sans gay community pas hollywood

liz taylor to mike aspel

dress

j lo

stylish

rachel stevens

curves

terri dwyer

besom

venetian ambassador

wheelchair

anna nicole smith

nerves

tfp viewpoint news from tradition family property bureau for uk

vol 9 no 1 2002 p5

hottie

ms jenny mccarthy born in scorching scorpio 11/1/72

old men

alice walker

horrible middleaged men

eamonn holmes

mrriley

qua supra road to avonlea

wailing

hilary swank

impudent

steve mcqueen

think of nothing

bill condon gods & monsters 1999 consult

stephen law philosophygymn 25 short adventures in thinking 2004

david taylor thinkcat owners guide to feline psychology 2004

all i think of

lee tamahori mulholland falls 1996

i think stability is sexy

acl blair

lust

thomas wyatt

sex at any age is not subject to treat seriously

wherein it differs from love

john bayley

s = metaphor for love

l = metaphor for spirituality

ziauddin sardar

lasciviousnesses

anon informer

sex makes all men same

peter ackroyd

see (awesome) dickens 1990/thomas more 1998

husband

tom shadyac liar liar 1997

lovers

david warren born in taurus 1949

geek

milla jovovich

burka

joan burnie daily record herein dr tue 20 nov 2001 p18

puritycampaign

mrs ormiston chant

pure

fay weldon

intellect

chapman pincher

intellect rots character

heinrich himmler

one really ought herd eggheads into coalmine

& blow it

heinrich muller

SEXIEST ORGAN - MALE BRAIN

LIVERPUDLIAN THESPIAN FAVORS GRAY MATTER

marilyn munroe indeed regarded prof einstein as

SEXIEST MAN I EVER MET

rags? his brain lacked necessary mass..

strikes

meg ryan

demands

beethoven

waylayer

tristan & iseult

tenderly

pr

only fire could slake such 1 thirst

unionthing tis hugely overrated

idem

separate unitive & procreative aspects at peril

paul danon

relig agus go togeth like bacon egg

rt rev bishop of liverpool

poo

angieletter 9/8/01

shtook

= trouble

20 cent origin unknown yesh she smacksh of yiddish

homely paraphrase of barush spinoza

ethics - everyman edition eminently serviceable

murder

pr

madhouse

camus

torment

dh lawrence

thighs

pr

cf comical ethics sv kwin aka quin

truelove

gregory bateson

nice

bobby farrelly & peter farrelly something about mary 1998

basic intrinsic

should be treated wittily affectionately

elaine c smith

golda

simcha dinitz to heinrich kissinger

1 son

mrs paula kissinger

breast

mishimas mama cf mamma cercavo

sons are lovers without sex messing it up

edna o brien

gaga

gaga not go go

scotcrab p33

groupons

cest la lutte finale

groupons nous et demain

linternationale sera le genre humain

eugene pottier/pierre degeyter chanson internationale 1871

salmons

thus fluellen henry v 4/7

shantemonhill

here breifne crowned hir kings

see mathews origin p14

vivisectionissue

cf advert worldday for labanimals bigissue in scotland issue 421 apr 10/16 2003 p27

maureen easton 4/10/44 jessica flynn 4/10/82 hayley westenra 4/10/87

hermes pisces

greek ii i geek mais pas greek ii i expiscator

= was bismarcks mercury (hermes) located in pisces?

skitter

lightly scamper

look u

fluellen qua supra

anemone

ie cancerian mercury imparts retentive memory

harbor

ie jargon 1 asylum for mundane mentalities see

francis wheen how mumbo jumbo conquered world 1 short history of modern delusions 2004

boleskine

baal implicated solo wishfulthinkingwise

poll eas cumhan pool of narrowwaterfall

stones

jj history of breif pp18 & 20

wounds

gawain & green knight

csp abominated vert see robert kee laurel & ivy 1993 p294

whose chart comprised (joyces likewise) mercury quartile orcus

queen

my mum wants to be queen

ian toyton annie ii i royal adventure 1995

bizmuck

brooks abraded saddlesores

landland

celticshamanismclanchant

power of place in celtic myth religion

bob stewart

radiate

liz carling

marriage provides inner glow outer blanket

fiona phillips

marriage is surest cure for acne

phemie brand

good

angharad rees

value

baroness strange

i believe in love compassion

mother teresa

amends

bridget gilfedder

different

rev billy graham

unloveable

quentin crisp 1 good man

just stuck upon sons

wos more than just hir son wos hir everything

siodmak xmas holiday

queen achieved indifferent success [kinross unflinchingly attests]

attempting to channel murads ardor into extramaternal channels

ott emp p261 re murad iii aka muddersboy

i commend my own modest sentious postfixated study:

edipality & electralicity mums & dads are human too mm

one farther commends:

pier paolo pasolini edipo re 1967

michael wood road to delphi life & afterlife of oracles 2004

anna livia

here peutetre 1 figure of maternal principle

cf morris magical cameo *motherable valetable appeal*

ruskin stones of venice ed jan morris folio 2001 pxxiii

cf riverdances 1995ff

lets see what river comes up with

john boorman deliverance 1972

rusks

one assumes kashrut is not ye issue

indign dereliction..

ex sight

cryptohints cfs cryptorchism / amfortas

bullish

freud born in taurus may 4

taurus likewise (prolepsis) general grant

fraud

never did work glasgow empire friday nights

dixit kenneth diddyman dodd

serious student of fraudian bergsonian schopenhauerean humor theories

see barchockblock 6 humor theories 1 pawky analysis unpublished ms nd

i sandimmersed ii neck
sekida alleges
laughs nowise at lustiest jokes
diaphragmal convulsion being obviated
see zentraining p154
schopenhauer had had only his poodle
noodle whomwith to share apple strudel
comical ethics sv noodle

carcinogenic
cf sigmunds fate & that of ulysses simpson grant

betsy lerner
editors advice to writers forrest for trees 2002

wolfish dreams
see fabricius alch also owen flanagan
dreaming souls sleep dreams & evolution of conscious mind 2001

bangles cosher cradles
let us tems (oe temesian sieve)
a bangle = metalepsis
b cosher = mollycoddle cfs
1 cosh sc cosy
2 kosher heb kasher right
got to be kosher uhuru for scotia
scotcrab p88
3 coshery ir coisir feast
c cradle = metalepsis

bangles castrate wolves
pas tenable qua cosmic proposition
i sfruttatore so testify
bulging bud[dha]
ungenitalic jerome
worldrenouncer
bellyful
upto heaven
for heavens sake
heaves his
dharmapadmasanasutra? nope scotbud p224

popa
sergio leone once upon 1 time in america 1983

monorchism
for fugitive allusion to oneballockbachelor see jon turteltaub while you were sleeping 1995

occams razor
aka law of parsimony/principle of economy
william occam or ockham surrey c1285 c1349
whose razor subserves ontologic economy
serve him up avec pinch of cavan salt a la irlandais play to gallery ad captandum
crack not 2 [eggs] to fry 1

protection
see sarah blaffer hrdy mothernature natural selection & female of species 1999 p100

howard robard hughes
1905 76
wealthy reclusivistic scopophobe - cf scopophilia - etc
hirsute hoarder of filial piss urine aureate
obsessivecompulsive mormontrusting cocainefuelled papersshuffler
pardon me howard i am standing on thy toenails
seehee michael powell peeping tom 1959

psycho iv

mick garris psycho iv ye beginning 1990

punned (no pen intended) by joseph stefano wrote psycho proper

cf gus van sants 98 remake

consult gir psychobiology 1 ibernodruidic perspective 4th ed 2010

less

mcqueen to hoffman

set of papillon franklin j schaffner 1973

thrifty/molecule

hrdy mothernature p103

baglady

mothernature = old lady with some bad habits

george eliot

beardy

see adrian desmond/james moore darwin 1991 pxx

chaplain

wot 1 tome devils chaplain might indict upon

clumsy wasteful blundering low horridly wolfish opera of nature!

darwin 1856 originpregnant consult mark ridley

mendels demon genejustice agus complexity of life mm

ridley argues life process acts qua benign demon

enforcing mendels fundamental inheritancelaws

blurb

unfold wisestephendedaluswise occams razor:-

benign demon = daimon

billygoat

see ppxxxff ron rosenbaum explaining hitler search for origins of his evil 1998

00

tho himmler owned something similar

stalin possessed not one at all

britisharmymarchingchant

students of (exotica of) ww2 might lend 1 ear 2:

military music of adolf hitlers 3rd reich

84 pieces on 6 digitally remastered cds

tomahawk films archive 2004

clive shilton

designed dianas weddingslippers

shoes are incredibly complex

people dont realise what goes into making them

clive

bauchle

a shaggedout (unwearable) footgear

wer hat kaputt schuhe

cfs rivlin/surbet/dicke fusse

b hence schlemiel schlepper schlimazel schmuck schmutz schnook schnorrer etsch

shauchle

shilpit slipper

boondoggler

1 nebbich (2 bitchy) consult

barockorh klezmerlovers guide to englishyiddish 2nd ed revised & enlarged 2007

hickorydickoryboonclocks

my brisk brief (breif was not always) docimasy

a hick

b boondocks

dear reader save your squawks

hickorydickorydock
cat clawed [hir way] up
grandad reillys grandfather clock [cf grandfather clause]
scotcat p422
dick
see jeff kanew vi warshawski 1991
sara paretsky introduces qv splendid folio ed of maltese falcon mm
windydocks
chicago (windycity) has (they bruit) 2 seasons
brumous (bruma winter) agus augusty
chicago is theatre
studs terkel
stickchicks
he desiderated 1 bittle of flesh?
ne sutor ultra crepidam
shoonmen beyond sandals should not stray
footwear may incept death - see if this is i man p51
mummyhumper
wos 1 old [?] woman squatted in 1 shoe
bore so many nippers her fuse they blew
winnie pooh
see john tyerman williams pooh & philosophers 2003
oath
consult qua supra excathedra microscopy fasciculus lii pp400ff
coitus totus etc
see fabricius alch pp 64 & 77 & 79
slight[1]
interj = gods light
slight[2]
smooth - cf oe eorthslihtes groundclose
megalopsychos
rags (apr 70) dipping into balham public library
nothing serendips like serendipity
chanced upon robert payne hubris 1 study of pride
wherein delineateth bob boehmes megalopsychos
prolific payne also entertainingly biographised gandhi marx
iconoclasts
gemini is (are?) sign of double u
tack
hammer home nail sticks out
nippon adage
wolf
book of lambspring jazzed cf wolfsschanze
shaggy
road to avonlea journey begins
heels
nicole kidman attributed
clou
clive shilton
dna
carrie fisher
undry
daruma denizen [de untus] of earth
dagdas undry conquers dearth
scotcrab p19

dagda threw sybaritic barbecues
firbolg gael hippogriff formed queues
inchoate raghallachan ms nd
top
cody jarretts coda
edipussniffers lap up scene where verna jarrett pulls unresistant cody to hir lap
cfs phallic mother/yabyumposition
jerry mullen sj edipus & electra 1 rc critique cts pamphlet nd
nappies
pr
law lags behind like pooperscooper
bob geldof
plug
angela lambert re lord longford
see ms lamberts article dm sat 8 apr 2001 p17 GENTLE GENIUS WITH BLINDSPOT FOR EVIL
genius? mercury conjunct uranus 12/5/05
nannies
anne windsor
cfs scheissminister/zweiplatzigeskommandoscheisshaus
practice
sean penn on neodaddies tangling avec nappies
montaigne
michel eyquem de 1533 92
fearless allquestioning critic cbd
flies
dirk perennially wos 1 great one for pulling wings off flies
gareth bogarde dirks wee brother
i dismembered mama
allusions do exist to this inexistent movie see
robert mandel f/x murder by illusion 1985
richard franklin f/x2 deadly art of illusion 1991
black
reiner jerk
left 2
amanda mealing
instant love
alison lapper
fall in love
james gaddas
nothing nicer than man good with baby
victoria beckham
breastfed
woody allen
breastmilk
jamie oliver
sweet milk
pr
bosomwoman
davina mccall
im much nore than breastsbrace
i represent success hard work fun
pam anderson
starspangled
kathie lee gifford
milky way grown inelastic gray

soldiers
dolly parton
brastuffer
charlie 32a
cf m&s egoboost® brarange
spurt
angela griffin
push
gabby yorath
milkplants
once upon 1 time in america
ye nipple
david duchovny
chompy
judy finnigan
suckreflex
g lux flanagan
goodness
pr
babe
mac 1 7
horns
richard fleischer vikings 1958
hate mother
jim abrahams jerry zucker david zucker ruthless people 1986
one is very lucky if ones children like one at all
edward fox
calls mummy
francis veber 3 fugitives 1989
maternal ambivalence being 1 axiom of sociobiology
darling
martin bormann snr to martin bormann jnr
parents
martin bormann jnr
my parents are so much part of my life they are like my legs
leonardo dicaprio
u realise your parents are only people who have given you unconditional love
sue cook
leave
ronald neame odessa file 1974
nixon
oliver stone nixon 1995 see
vamik d volkan norman itzkowitz andrew w dod richard nixon 1 psychobiography 1997
remember
stone nixon
my father is jewish
daniel pearl *ben benei beraq chaim pearl street persists*
jewish
heinrich kissinger
i am thou
gurdjieffs elegy for his father giorgios giorgiades
whom aetat 85 turks killed 5/15/18
james moore gurdjieff anatomy of 1 myth 1991 p110
go to hell u spawn of satan
ar orage 2 gi gurdjieff

stormbowed
egil skallagrimsson of borg c910 c990
preeminent vikingage warriorpoet
egils eldest (bestloved) son (bothvar) drowned 961
whence by skallagrimsson was *sonatorrek* wrested wrung
= on irreparable loss of sons
hermann palsson/paul edwards transs egilssaga 1976
magnus magnusson ed icelandic sagas illus simon noyes folio 1999
my father my son
george benson composed this ballad 8/98
1 favor for mohamed al fayed
vacuum
roma downey
relief
vaness-mae born 10/27/78
1 heroine of nicholas bailey
suffer
mrs alia ghanem
i do not approve of osamas actions & ambitions
but i am not angry with him
like all mothers i am satisfied & pleased with my son
i pray to god guide him save him
idem
my love for my son is unconditional absolute
john walkers mother socalled american taliban
i have shielded u from evil
bridget gilfedder
mother mother
bree to briefne sun 1/5/03
primary
marie antoinette
profession
nancy aniston
mar [oe merran]
sue johnston
1 living
jodie foster
critical
vanessa feltz
who on earth wants wishy water mother
frances shand kydd
depth
edna o brien
irish
maureen o hara
indian mothers usually have grey hair & usually witness their sons death
salaam bombay sundaytimesculturemagazine 7/8/01 p7
pinny strings
cf paul condon/jim sangster complete hitchcock 1999 p255
mound
cassandra aka william connor
bloch/binion etc
vide rosenbaum op cit chap 13 passim
historiographer
alan bullock hitler & stalin parallelllives 1991

cyclops

not as much as would blind your eye
giddy eye eh for the oneeyed reilly
goeth goodnatured plebian pubsong cfs
a rousing (footstomping) clancy bros
b reillys + stuart douglas + wee mena on maracas
c goldenboughrendition of *john riley* songs of irish immigrants 2004
as hatter of mistorical pact fas
oui caech (pro kay or kee)
signifies inter alia oneeyed
blind purblind oneeyed pwj p97
nathless
niall an caoch o raghallaigh
ancestor of an caochaigh
son of cathal son of annadh
felimoconnorcouped
avec pere et freres
anno domini 1256
pon plain of magh sleacht:
niall an caoch met whose maker orbless
uime cheana do ghoirid an chaoch do niall
[horrid scarce too harsh]
oir iar ndeanamh iliomad creach ar ghallaibh
gabhthar e
rugadh ceangailte go hath cliath e
tugadh a rogha do thri neithe dho [:-]
uireasbhaidh a chloinne
no easbhaidh cos
no easbhaidh sul
do ghabh easbhaidh na sul do roghain
do reir an bhreitheamhnais
do sgiob fein na suile as
iar bfhilleadh anuas do
do rinne creach ar mhuintir na hoibre
da ngoir thi an uair sin an bhreatach
mar diarr seision creach do dheanamh
ar bhodachaibh na hoibre
on obair dho
mar dubhairt siad-san
FEUCH AR CCREACH RIS AN CHAOCH O RAGHALLAIDH
carney genhist pp68/9
sfruttatore offers his own (see genhist p111) textfiddledwithoutofrecognitiontranslation:-
reason they call niall caoch
tweaked 1 2 many english nose
betrayed
befettered unto dublin
3 options judicially accorded
childless
spurless
sightless
it tides then that
cathals son plumps for darkness
every good o reilly should
per due judgement
solus within 1 meledeawig english cell

ainsell plucks een eek
to speed convalescence
cheerfully squeezes an obair [co meath]
nobber churls
their minds being moved to admiration
exclaim
LOOK AT OUR PREY WITH WALLEYED O REILLY! [victims identify?]
afterwriting
kunta kinte
roots protohero
reiterant runaway
snared by british slavecatchers
in situ tripleoptioned
foot chooses
o vicious hellish dwems
cost of 1 potosipeso = 10 little nigs
step on hands/mangle feet
lou reed
mangled friend is all i seek
gangs of new york

i fuhrer
consult john lukacs hitler of history hitlers biographers on trial 2002
cf if this is i man p23
u 2 should ponder yonder story

crumpling etc
re adolfs processive parkinsonism c 1939 onwards
undeterged degenerated corporality (cachexy) generally
not at all 1 matter for cachinnation (cf outspeckle):
study thomas doppelgangers pp4/16 et passim
u 2 should ponder yonder story

donut
see len fisher how 2 dunk 1 donut science of everyday life 2002
ignobellaureate - questionable contributions to science
u 2 should ponder yonder story

atlasatolf
agonised atlas everest on whose back
dr prof ernst-gunther schenk
u 2 should ponder yonder story

gotterdammerung
one only begins to understand this massmurderers perverted personality
when 1 takes account of his weakness for oppressive heady musical moods
guido knopp hitlers women & marlene trans angus mcgeoch 2003 p185
hitlers frauen und marlene 2001
u 2 should ponder yonder story

auseinandersetzung
see peter g tsouras ed 3rd reich victorious alternate decisions of ww2 2002
u 2 should ponder yonder story

rip
never such ruination physical moral associated with 1 man
ian kershaw hitler 1889 1936 hubris 1998 p841
lost mum
became bum
some depths did plumb
comical ethicsn sv swagsman
survey passim ye abominable website omnesgeminorumfansofadolfloggydatincom

1 world came very close 2 dying
rotha hitler
consult likewise kershaw hitler 1936 1945 nemesis mm
bob avery they saved hitlers bird trafford nd
u 2 should ponder yonder story

fall
see norman cohen hitler my part in his downfall 1972
oliver hirschbiegel downfall 2004
u 2 should ponder yonder story

will & test
junge final hour pp183/5
u 2 should ponder story

bunkersketch
joachim fest inside hitlers bunker lastdays of 3rdreich 2004
englished per margot bettauer dembo ex der untergang 2002
u 2 should ponder yonder story

ancillary id
father had somehow registered hitlers other id
gitta sereny albert speer his battle with truth 1995 p158 consult also
dan van der vat good nazi life & lies of albert speer 1997
joachim fest speer final verdict mm
u 2 should ponder yonder story

horig
vide sereny op cit p137
hitler has psychic powers of medium
otto strasser
quoted by anthony read devils disciples lives & times of hitlers inner circle 2003 p5
study likewise
john cornwell hitlers scientists science war & devils pact 2003
jean medawar/david pyke hitlers gift scientists that fled 2003
u 2 should ponder yonder story

ungeziefer
hier ist kein ungenauigkeit
bestest doggerman..
see kafka die verwandlung (metamorphosis) 1916
cbd incidentally overlooks not franzs frank attachment to kafkas father
ein laus dein tod
so bist du rein
so gehst du ein
didacticfrescoscaptions pro benefit auschwitzian guests
cf phthiriasis
see if this is i man p57
u 2 should ponder yonder story

daimonic
preferred spelling rollo may love & will 1974
vide fischer naz germ p82
u 2 should ponder yonder story

torquemada
tomas de 1420 98 born valladolid
1st spanish inquisitorgeneral (from 1483)
orchestrated expulsion of sephardim 1492
byword for diabolical cruelty consult
klaus p fischer german judeophobia & holocaust 2001
amos elon pity of it all jews in germany 1743 1933 2003
u 2 should ponder yonder story

cruella drevill

cruella de vil (dodie smith) + drevill (spens) foul person

cf mdu drevel 1 undesirable

germans used monosulphide with gratifying results to remove undesirables

neill dressed to kill

study pierre aycoberry social history of 3rdreich 1933 45 mm

u 2 should ponder yonder story

tacit

er will nix verstayen

was fur ein muselmann zugang

pas chercher a comprendre

u 2 should ponder yonder story

fr adolf

mark twain mysterious stranger 1916 adduced p6 by rosenbaum

muffy

ruthless people

ausrotting

fuhrer has ordered physical extermination of jews

himmler 2 heydrich 2 eichmann 20 july 1941

read devils disciples p722 read likewise

milton himmelfarb no hitler no holocaust [essay[1984

daniel jonah goldhagen hitlers willing executioners 1996

frank pierson conspiracy 2001

mark roseman villalakemeeting wannsee & final solution 2002

peter longerich unwritten order hitlers role in final solution 2002

richard overy interrogations nazi elite in allied hands 2002

sebastian haffner defying hitler 1 memoir 2003

richard j evans coming of 3rd reich 2003

gerhard l weinberg ed hitlers 2nd book unpublished sequel to mein kampf 2003 consult rosenbaum chap 12 passim plus pp xiii xvi xxviii 38 84 242 259 281 327 335 348/9 394/5

volkermord

ernest nolte see fischer naz germ pp 575/6

glr

see william h schmaltz hate george lincoln rockwell & american nazi party mm

ofay

piglatin reversal of foe?

ayto says probably no

john ayto 20th century words 1999

frida

see nicola white art sex death eyebrowraising life of frida kahlo

sundayheraldmagazine 20 oct 2002 pp18/21

spot

fundament is meant

atherosclerotic

briefne beware arteriosclerosis

dr anton van rhijn (1 good man) 12/88

sasman

FORMER SASSOLDIERS SUICIDE

ABANDONS AEROPLANE UNPARACHUTED

parachutes/rush of blood to head

coldplays debutalbum mm/its followup 2002

tho she be coldplayfan

darlingangelinas favorite band

are your lads from parnellland

comical ethics sv fan

serve truth
allusion to song from rush of blood
cat ballou
john ford man who shot liberty valance 1962
my minds hum mum
o full of scorpions my mind dear wife
macbeth 3 2
wellie might will have writ
o my mind swarms (teems) with
shardborne beetles drowsy hums
macbeth 4 2
roman polanski macbeth 1971
jeremy freeston macbeth 1996
dick riley & pam mcallister bedside bathtub armchair companion to shakespeare 2003
david crystal & ben crystal shakespeares words glossary agus language companion 2004
james muirden decorations david eccles shakespeare in nutshell rhymingguide 2004
stephen greenblatt will in world how shakespeare became shakespeare 2004
katherine duncan-jones shakespeares life & world folio 2004
g lynn stephens/george graham selfconsciousness breaks alien voices inserted thoughts mm
david lomas haunted self surrealism psychoanalysis subjectivity mm
philip hodgkiss making of modern mind consciousness surfaces 2001
dan waddell who do you think you are? 2004
i am not such i one
that it forceth whose i am
tuus t morus qui nihil
multitudinous twins
clarinettists produce more twins than one can imagine
natalie wheen cfm sun 7/20/03
phuck
not another phylum
simon conway morris
consult bill bryson short history of nearly everything 2003 chap 21 passim
cf geoffrey blainey very short worldhistory 2004
nimble nimming
thieving knave purse nimbly nims
pickpurse of anothers wit
kinchinmortsnkinchincoves to pinchin apprenticed
scotmagotpie p201
schlong wont be long
ihre tochter hat ein subes kleines lochlein
nazibeerhallsong
selle ne meut mutilee rien naurait jamais change
colette
once 1 troubled chirurgeon
partial unto fine wines et produit de sturgeon [ie caviar]
wishing to be transcendentally pure
felt that ye only way sure
[autopeotomy]
comical ethics sv minor
onslought
dirige vers lui plus malveillante maniere
marie antoinette
long legatos hectic gesticulative vocal onsloughts
uncommonly frank tho scorning mere boom
bernhard uske

frankly i miss moms yelling screaming ye general hoobub
richard kroning 14 schoolgirlspinupturnedsuicide see
stephen burgen your mothers tongue 1 book of euroinvective 2002

schmucke irin

tristan und isolde

blows

loopy old man of townhead
anticipated 1 soupcon of
but when his chance came
ruefully did exclaim
oops
scotdroop p281
grisly hibernian limericist
filegraffiti could not resist
little he missed
prowling for gist [loosely motifs]
that to whose promiscuous mill might prove grist
comical ethics sv limerick

hair

how do they wear their hair ladies of your time?
pal timemachine

pusser [= purser]

a shipaccountant regulated royalnavyrumrations
b pussers bluelabel 54.5% abv:
blend of antique potstill caribbean rums
70cl bottle thereof sold (summer 2003) for £21.95
visit www.nauticalia.com
rick jolly jackspeak guide to british naval slang 2004

crash out

what does it mean when 1 person crashes out?
why it means he is finally free
free free..
raoul walsh high sierra 1940

la mar

sephardic romances traditional jewish music from spain
ensemble accentus thomas wimmer director
recorded lutheran stadtpfarrkirche ab vienna 17/20 sep 1995
treat your weary ears dear clearheaded reader
wot grovelly earwig old sfruttatore is
klezmatics et alii klezfest
gregori schechter & wandering few klezmer
tummel klezmerised!
jontef klezmer music & yiddish songs
burningbush klezmer agus hasidic music
ditto best of yiddish klezmer & sephardic music

i push off

pr
cf misi me/ich suche die mutter

caviar

apted world not enough

farther

john wayne

tides

peter evans
paulus primus sed petrus petrus petrus petrus sed paulus primus

songs

bob dylan

city

true glory

varnhagen remarked to lamarque [0000 0000]

errant nature never did throw up 1 marshallamarque

wherefrom deduce pseudoness of varnhagans jeudesprit

morse endeavoured to memorise in german

endeavour morse (colin dexter will attest) is 1 figment

whether morse in fictivefact labored monstrously..

filefilling hir readers avec strange invention

wheen

master of orchestra form content

ms wheen re rachmaninov cfm sun 1/4/04

i wish my name was macrachmaninov or maybe doyleitski

patrick doyle to simon bates cfm sat 10 may 2003

pi

darren aronofsky 1998

mathgenius designs supercomputer to answer all questions

cf (spielberg ai) dr-know-addresses-any-q

ca va paris 9/6/86

louis

questions re louis offscreen activities are converted charmingly into questions

clair woodward

nonce

occrring adopted coined for particular occasion only

chambers english dictionary 7th ed 1988

pragmatic goodness

i start businesses employ hundreds campaign write songs

i contribute to gaiety of nations

bob to andrew qua supra

hale

civilisation of europe in renaissance 1993

dr hale pondering *civilisationsignification*

cheerfully informs us that

burckhardtian kultur is *even less susceptible of definition*

[jacob burckhardt civilisation of renaissance in italy 1860]

term carries 3 interrelated significations

joyce m hawkins ed ox ref dic 1986 sv islam

whether other races live in prosperity or perish from hunger or hypothermia

interests me only insofaras we need them as slaves for our own kultur

reichsfuhrerss heinrich himmler 4 oct 1943

emergent civility under siege from pressures of past

prof willy maley bigissueessay qua supra p31

beastliest

one that witnessed everremembers

murderous hatreds publicly (televisually) projected

likewise by ministers of iranian state

at valiant striving sr

chapman that shot john

into spirituality was reborn

comical ethics sv spiritual

go behend/posit valid theories

goss agus behend posit valid theory - ft173 8/03 p49

blanc china vessels agus nugae

crick & watson

see sb p376

one only relbelless megamegapoet

clark civilisation p124

arrant aristocratic clarkist garbage

or sfruttatore is 1 sousd henrician gurnet

ecrasez

gibbon sans sadistic bias would be insipid

vincent intelligent persons guide p52

RENOWNED EVOLUTIONARY BEHAVIORISTS PROPHECY

INFAMOUS INSTITUTION WILL PRESENTLY SUFFER EXTINCTION

not bloody likely

are catholics becoming easy target? universe sun 20 oct 2002 p8

visit www.totalcatholic.com

embrace space

consult sir david attenborough mammals 2003:

spec ye great naturalists seasoned sapient conclusory argumentum

vide bbc series space

presenter sam neill composer ty unwin

orig transmitted 7/22/01 seqq

how can you die in space?

people are supposed to die only on earth

noa ramon 5 dm tue 4 feb 2003 p8

gestapo

consult nikolaus wachsmann hitlers prisons legal terror in nazigermany 2004

twist

timothy knatchbull

von stauffenbergbomb

josef knecht with gita dietrich fuhrerbatman 1 gotterdammerungian reminiscence 2009 p606

condition

harold pinter

bombed before

dennis thatcher

bomb world

spike milligan

humphrey carpenter spike milligan 1 biography 2003

jai envie de gronder tout le mond

until he is seven

spike is in heaven [only child]

comical ethics sv sib

petrolbomb

george best

blitzed

paul rotha

firestorms

jerry mccrunch

mortons fork

if this quote be not filefictive my bibliomaniacal bunch

sfruttatore will never munch autre chocolate crunch

altitude

beck weathers dark side of everest fri 4/25/03 c5

environment

christopher keeble

armymag

cliff pfeifferkrunch

suicidebombers

tovah bat mitzvah

kamikaze

tony da silva

varmintpoontang

harold ramis caddyshack 1980

only good injun is 1 dead injun

phil sheridan born county cavan march 6 1831

bad officer

tom clegg sharpes battle 1995

good colonel

knecht fuhrerbatman p609

fun

louis thereux

santa

jeremiah s chechik nationallampoonschristmasvacation 1989

believe

bianca jagger

polpot believed he was acting for greater good of cambodia

nate thayer

violence

olivia harrison

events

rainier grimaldi

skyhigh

oscar wilde

mess with every premise

these are our foibles..

robin williams on purpose of comedy

debris

richard ellmann oscar wilde 1987 p549

dynamite

tom cruise

great actor neargenius for messianic oratory

tom bower on tony blair

is this blairs watergate? saturdayessay dm 7/26/03 pp12/13

nuclear

malcolm x

hatred

warren mitchell

tragedy

david cooper

being underdeveloped comedy

pat kavanagh

shakespeare essentially comic in spirit

stephen fry via kenneth branagh (parkinson)

dying easy

nancy meyers

sentiment wherewith mr charles manson professes to concur

louis xi pending terminating breath endured excessive deathdread

comical ethics sv death

it scares stink out of me

leo mckern

mr bayley

stephen glover

aspect
al rowse
empathy
lord ashdown
experience
archbishop desmond tutu
altruism
jeffrey moussaieff masson 9 emotionallives of cats 2002 p55
pity
anthony mann el cid 1961
usefulness
neill woman in green
ideology
alan clark
expert
bishop mario conti
rome
barry norman
ourlord
cardinald martin ratzinger
rearwindowethics
hitchcock rearwindow 1954
maxim
adolf eichmann
see william a graham man who captured eichmann 1996
ephelants
ef benson
hobbes
adhoccrunchie herein ahc (cf rosenbaum p92)
ethicalicity
ahc
metaphysic
immanuel-kant-chocolate-crunchie-job
or one shall cram toblerone® till one doth hobrrily bloat groan
paton englished groundwork as ye morallaw
pelegrinis mulls immanuel interalia re naturalistic fallacy vide
tn pelegrinis kants conceptions of categoric imperative/will 1980
edward harcourt ed morality reflection ideology mm
mary anne warren moral status obligations to persons/other livingthings 2001
horrors
hemorrhoids
hypostasise
cf rosenbaum p330
shininggermanangelmotherhood
knecht fuhrerbatman p1014
never give in
never give in! winston churchhills finest speeches
selected/edited by his grandson winston s churchill 2003
see richard loncraine gathering storm 2002
irrefragable
irrefragabilis in not re backwards frangere break
hitler tabletalk 24 oct 1941
wasnt he 1 nice guy unclefuhreradolf?
loophole
billy wilder fortune cookie 1966

obey
gestapo muller
victories
emil fackenheims commandment 614 rosenbaum pp 296/7
archivery/shoah
claude lanzmann rosenbaum p253
kill
rev john quinn ed
kilsherdany its history its people [1 souvenir of]
dedication of st brigids church 1826 1977
[dedicationday] feast of corpus christi 9 june 1977
mali
also mallee consult henry yule/ac burnell hobsonjobson ye angloindian dictionary rpt 1996
say 0
oscar wilde docked agus poor spud dysenteric doghoused
ellmann op cit p449
Humility
francis longford
pr
yehuda bauer
work
john rankin waddell
professional humility is no bad thing
joby talbot to simon bates cfm mon 30 aug 2004
midden
donald caskie
pluparte
linguaphonefrenchcourse c1965
raphs
angieletter tue 20 may 2003
ciao jamie cinecitta veteran
restingplace
clive james
dead
gareth davies darling buds le grand weekend 1992
paris!
importance of being earnest
cf rogers oldmotherrileyinparis 1938
reportagepictures
estelle skornik
ripping off
gwyneth paltrow
1 film
kathleen chaplin
5 films
barry norman
filmscollection
bob monkhouse 73
t hayes hunter
ghoul 1933
special edition delta entertainment video 1998
digitally mastered ex best available sources/standard speed
thats 1 movie
john doe does not propose - true romantic clarence worley does
cp john carpenter/tobe hooper bodybags 1993

bad movie
michelle pfeiffer
dosh
ghoul
your cinema
peeping tom
films limn evil
films themselves of course may be vile (scurrilous)
robert und bertram 1939
die rotschilds 1940
jud suss 1940
der ewige jude 1940
tara
cavalli 8
vomini 40
tara
portata
if this is i man p61
im just ordinary
thus too modest miss connelly dennis hopper hotspot 1990
pawky rags adverted to dark city qua darks
mulholland falls rags denominated hats
contract
instinct for redtop tabloid journalism headline mind
keith waterhouse on alastair campbell dm mon 9/1/2003
mysteries
who is ye mystery?
lewis gilbert alfie 1965
educator
barry baldwin baldly asserts woodsian prolixity
ft183 may 2004 p58
admirable intrepid venturing englishman
legacy origins of civilisation centralindependenttelevision 1991
in alexanders footsteps adventurehistoryseries bbc 1997
freezeframe
2 catch 1 thief videoversion
i myself was harpyhovering when
o raghallaigh first regaled himself therewith
not 1 excrutiatingly manic (expletives deleted) occasion
u may indeed reader diffidently deduce maestro ex liminal sliver:-
+ 9 mins
back-of-bus-in-corner
screenright spectator pov
wonderful invention pannedandscannededit
condon/sangster hitchcock p197
lingerie
geoffrey munn
seduction
sophie marceau
fell in love
estelle skornik
ye girls
tom conti
holidayromance
fraser massey

bottle

lisa maxwell

places

stephen mcgann

vagabonds

which british actor declared?

if find out shall credit merci

once actor

russell crowe

always themselves

lorinne vozoff

downtoearth

pierce brosnan

neurotic

ralph fiennes

mess

sue johnston

default

maureen lipman

problems

woody allen

totempole

barry norman

scum

andrew davies

state of mind

amos oz

no book is 1 island

peter l bergen

fairystories

adolf eichmann

degree

derek jabobi

chuck

henry morton stanley

biblestudies

dolly parton

biblebelt

jerry falwell

vide jacqueline rose dangerous liaison israel & america sat 24 aug 2002 c4

salim

trevor lock

fame

claudia winkleman

famous

mimi leder deep impact 1998

persisting

peter simester

proboscises

woman in green

mystery so garbed neer would have ensnared charles stewart parnell

heroes

will smith

product

christopher tookey

hollywoodestablishment

history of 20th century

what could bug taliban more!

[= gay lady in suit hemmed in by jews]

ms ellen de generes hosting emmyawardsceremony 11/5/01

deceptive

courteney cox

vulgar

lord clark civilisation p138

machinery

brian cox

irreversible

varian fry

topgun

richard e grant

monks

liam bennett

legwaxing

mel gibson

paddy

mr dedalus

pray

sir john gielguds advice to aspiring actors

subs

sir john mills

fool

lesley-anne down

not me

ioan gruffudd

lottery

camilla rutherford

interest

rachel ward

ms ward feels that for women hollywood lacks reward

sol virgo 19° - plenty of electromagnetism

act/believe

emil fackenheim

sox

comical ethics sv sock

aryan millennium

a vide occult history of 3rd reich:

enigma of swastika

blood & soil

mystic himmler

hitler neworder

writerdirector dave flitton/producer david mcwhinnie

(c) lamancha/castle 1991

4 columbia tristar videos 1993

b consult likewise

laurence rees writer & producer nazis warning from history trans sep 10/oct 15 1997 bbc

c help us to understand it as something sui generis

george steiner to claude lanzmann

cf auschwitzian geheimnistragers (secretsbearers)

see rosenbaum pp xli 78 84 87 198 242 260 270 280ff 288ff

d dr berel lang would persuade us that

hitler und cronies created 1 veritable art of evil
dr emil fackenheim indeed posits not solely
kolphos (dichotomy) betwixt quotidian evil & radix (root) evil
but stark vorago (gulf) betwixt human & hitlernature
e thomas doppelgangers chap 2 mind of hitler passim:-
POSITIVE
1 personality disorder:
borderline schizophrenia of schizotypal origin
2 paranoid features
3 psychopathic traits:
diagnosis of psychopathy not clinically warranted
PRIVATIVE
mr thomas categorically excludes:
1 (paranoid) schizophrenia
2 schizophreniform disorder
3 schizoaffective state

hollowwoot
cf alan smithee [arthur hiller]
an alan smithee film burn hollywood burn 1997
wherein eric idle idles as alan smithee

alligation
i think he had sense of connection with you all
mrs alison reilly nee burnside (1 good woman) tue 7/22/03

protoshot etc
robert kee bold fenian men 1989
peter de rosa rebels irishrising of 1916 1990

sack
splash ben blacksea
dark moonless night
ripples spread wide far
twas made per sack
fitting close unto back
of ivan skavinsky skavar
abdul bulbul emir singalongsong 1877 (william) percy french

british
we dont forget irish are our friends
timothy knatchbulls parents

capuchin
= poor mans jesuit (fernand braudel)

alba
hugh douglas/michael j stead flight of bpc mm
christopher duffy bpc agus untold story of 45 2003
james mackay gen ed lomondpockethistory 2003
jock maccochba bpc 1 tricentennial revisionist deconstruction 2045

thistle
roger caras (cats of thistle hill etc) championed declawing
abominable
unconscionable
vide masson 9 lives pp136/9

drummossie
culloden never was surviewed
until youthful irrepressible messrs olipoll
upon drummossie did fall
1 case of topography rewriting history tony
tony pollard/neil oliver 2 men in 1 trench tue 9/3/02 c2

cap
hoffa is some goddam hubcap
amon
now we know where they secreted jimmy hoffa
tom shadyac nutty professor 1996
butcher
likewise stigmatised stinkingbilly
cf willie wombat & i
steamie
see jack kornfield after ecstasy laundry 2003
tycho
see kitty ferguson nobleman housedog tycho brahe johannes kepler 2002
blennorrhoea
consult roy porter blood & guts short history of medicine 2003
bar cochba
lag bomer (33rd day of ye omer) commemorates simon of kosiva & rabbi akiba
see tim healy flagitiouser than parnell - barkochba christian renegade cts pamphlet nd
roma
stetit puella
rufa tunica
carmina burana
bannockburn
patriot warriorpoets felicitously charged fields of
twentiethcenturyfox
flodden
youthful ebullient polloliver did not forget floddenfield
2 men in 1 trench tue 10 sep 2002 c2
pseudogladiators
martin frizell
celtsnot
ulysses
builth
rudyard kipling
yet rudyard had 1 darkie grandad:
george browne macdonald died 1868
thought where all power lies
pr
bridle
james garbarino
loons
anon
christ
pr
dromidory
al-asmai kitab al-ibil on camel 827
trekked
to ends of earth mon 20 may 2002 c4
dixit roma
red coat p215
waterclosetless wastes
mr jinx like brother
u expect him wander streets sans food water toilet
jay roach meet parents mm
what species mr jinx? himalayan?
had mr jinx met mrriley (bodie) what then might have betimed

jim shekhdar:

1st recorded voyager solo to row pacific (2000/1)

mr shekhdars 23feetlong rowboat comprised 1 luxury

capricornian pragmatism?

afteryawnfact

english channel = *tellus busiest sealane*

ibnbattuta travelled traveller traversed khawakpass [1333]

scotcrab p462

dejeuner sur lherbe

marvel at tom clegg sharpes waterloo 1997

astonishingly lensed via christopher o dell ben lucid turkish light

cf monet huile sur toile monet ill on ye toilet

diarrhea one supposes

terrible night sheba died

sat 5/25/02 geminifullmoon

sheba had been hale suppertide

within 2 hrs gagging gasping ghastfully grandma tending

barcan gentle giant scarfed expeditious gardengrave

rags for shroud donated damart® vests

greater regard (gra) than this

good sweet puss - orb apparently - muchloved

fed fussed file feline furry fourteenyearplus

be proud of your pride its genuine

martin reid to jeffrey moussaieff masson

see 9 emotionallives p132 consult also

stephen budiansky character of cats 2002

sonya fitzpatrick cattalk 2002

mescalero

saturdayglobe 10/25/1902

tribes

clint eastwood outlaw jose wales 1976

rome

johnpaul 2

valedictory polish visit responding to chants of *stay with us*

sun 18 aug 2002 bbcnews

water

drdr re british society of medical & dental hypnosis

desertdevil

eskimonell? chocolate crunchies melt in hell

birdnest

alex haley

camels

sophia cunningham

life of reilly

see hamburger hill

warmth life color people

anthony mann fall of roman empire 1964

desertrose

ms gail porter herself 1 blooming albarose

arab

te lawrence 7 pillars 1 triumph intro michael asher folio mm

solytarie

chaucer

stone

philomena reilly

wideworld

anon

of is pond frog ist fond

comical ethics sv froggery

quest

harold bloom

pylons

aliester croakly

carrion

tomegatherion

suffering

flying down to rio

ye pleasure aint worth ye pain

lee marvin

leningrad

adolf hitler study david m glantz siege of leningrad 900 days of terror 2001

cellular terror

or inspissated astral miasma (cf cataplexy)

fear of hilife

fear of low

fear of sun

fear of snow

pr

60 togs

enditalls (single) bed 54 x 78 inches

single bed for single person decreed leonard sheffield

mr bloomfield concurred

mort la chasse de son lit

cf schlechte bettenbauer

downland hollowfiber continental quilt

cover 50% polyester 50% cotton

filling polyester

togvalue 15.0 minimum

approx gravity per sq meter 975gms

shake lightly daily daily sing to mary

plus de repos que terre nue

keys

cry pertains to nonagegame of that name

file regaled us once (from commodious filememory)

with 1 academical sentence re wallace stevens constanttheme

he (file) had chanced upon in accomodative cbd p1397:

exploration of esthetic experience qua key to fundamental reality

cf levis experience of camp/long nostos if this is i man p233

pit

if i get 1 low it lasts 3 to 10 [minutes]

jimmie dougherty

shamus

im oriley housedetective

sam wood day at races 1937

cf rogers oldmotherrileydetective 1943

pretzel

permit expiscator present prickly perquisition:-

sun 13 jan 2002

prez george w bush passes out affected by vagrant pretzel

whitehouseallopath richard tubb pronounces vasovagalsyndrome

if history cannot be un nor in subjunctive writ
lawrence james rise & fall of british empire folio 2004 pxv:
yet private life may parallel (mimic) presidential history
expiscator himself witnessed (late afternoon 1/13/02)
rags ye irascible - nonirenic-
take quasitemulant tummelish carpetdive
bruit vacarme tumulte
veritable vertiginous kojakian swandip
synchronistically toppling 1 teeming topless barrileirenbarrbru®
my diagnosis (would youngest brother one wonders corroborate?):-
neurally mediated vasovagal syncope
random agent:-
errant (contigent) tatty crisp
i heard file discourse (sober) sometime of jungian acausality
truth he had 1 poor head for metaphysics
none at all for maths or science:
raggedy like junk cannot hope altogether to shrug off
1 blanketcharge of charlatanry
(pas charge quoth moral mountebank)
too much chutzpah to assert?
we old splenetical expiscators..
tracked what he childlikely labellled wcs:
weird coincidences
wherefor possessed strong affinity
wherefrom sought not far to stray
childishly agus sfruttatore supposes pleonastically
debilitating inner torments
ruskin per morris stones qua supra pxxiii
st johns wort
sunshine supplement
zipvit® tablets (interestingly) contain 0.3% hypericin
yielding 1000mcg active ingredient = 1665mg of herb
common or bog formulations run to 900mcg
www.zipvit.co.uk
lamentableness
not being well enough to function qua regular social constituent
i chose not to
phil spector interviewed by mick brown dm tue 2/4/03 p4
sinderella
oe sind slag
kartoffelschalenkommando
ilya jules a attraper par oreilles
i shall go to sacramento clean house
arnold schwarzenegger thu 8/7/03 cfmnews
guarding pisspot in palace
tom clegg sharpes battle 1995
coppola could not piss in pot
bob hoskins
pisspoor director of actors
sam elliott on woody allen
adlai stevensons squat to piss
lbj consult
clive sandground o raghallaigh cinderellayears 1948 2006 2008
paul & peter evans uncle adam 1 life in hiding 2nd rev ed 2009
barcockless/ahmed-skinner eds

100 spiritual eggheads contra 1 solitudinous somatic cinderella 2022

gaze space

specsavers® fair fiona urged agonia splurge on varifocals

wittily to whom

longdistance for enditall est busy end of 1 medivac®

he is spacetramp 1 loner

lamont johnson spacehunter 1983

iranian carpet

see writer/director mohsen makhmalbaf gabbeh 1995

ll carpeta = rough fabric comprising rags twitched 2 pieces

uk of e & ni

cf barracuda alphabetic handbook of human drollery & folly ms nd sv unionjackist:

honest man resident within island of ireland

westminister twitches whose strings

consult frank welsh 4 nations history of uk 2003

putatively united

tiniest provocation exposes childish nationalism

barely concealed by political posture

richard & judy sde sat 5 july 2003 p19

all nations are internations

as individual so nation evolution occurs

at least we take leave of tearing at jugulars

coffins

so angry with him for dying felt like kicking coffin

joan littlewood

worlds biggest illness

barry dyer re bereavement

selfish

focused to point of selfishness

nick bolletieris famous formulation

so much easier 2b selfless [than to be selfish]

lysette anthony

barchochchockblock

not cadbury®

not galaxy®

let privatives paris appal thee pas cf asamsaktha

marsbars® are beesknees!

lettre a aimee 8/8/04

gallowshumor

hallmark of ye hebrew see

jim goddard reillyaceofspies affair with married woman 1983

rollups

cf mahorca hit

www.smokingisugly.com – miss christy turlingtons website

www.lowtarexposed.org

eggs

i ordered sunnysideup u u kashubian

ef u see kay eye en gee eh ar es ee

cf lobkowitzian donkey

ludwigs passion wos pro rightsofman pas pro rightsofgarcon

oaktree

snakeentwined

descendant proper

emanant ex ducal coronet or

mathews origin p14

allwaysatwar

youre in ye [peninsular] war riley [jd kelleher]

tom clegg sharpes siege 1996

here i am then

if this is i man p54

unconscious

braden private sea pp195/200

see fabricius alchemy pp208/10

isolation

mozart

form & order faltering

consummated solitude

brief account recension two p1001

wolfishness

camus

predation

emily albu normans in their histories 2002

cynicism

bob geldoff

one moments goodness is better than none

can one transmogrify per exhortation? (sow seeds)

foul

brief account recension four p893

transported

knecht fuhrerbatman p287

cf rosenbaum pp302-3 & 316-7

wireless

fickle file (oct 04) pondering alliance with r3

opts solomonically to divide hir oreilles cfm/r3

rockbottom

jerk

despise

arnold schwarzenneger

humannature for people want someone successful fail

because havent achieved anything themselves

mrs guy ritchie

never has anyone failed so absolutely

knopp hitler 1 profile

pathetic

peter farrelly dumb & dumber 1994

bigguy

michael lehmann hudson hawk 1991

quit

morgan freeman

trying

pen haddow to mary nightingale cfm sun 8 jun 2003

unterachievers

unterhaching 4 dundee utd 1

alan mccabe dr wed 23 jul 2003 p44

blessed

johnpaul 2

fuhrerbeacon

knecht fuhrerbatman p1121

laude deo

rev arnold patrick spencer-smith

my dear
annie lennox to vanessa-mae
tv
pam ferris
only world
hitchcock psycho 1960
world is hell
what does it matter what happens in it?
hitchcock shadow of doubt 1943
they have 1 hell now we supply it
reinhard heydrich
i have this thing about going to hell
i dont want to
anna nicole smith
i should be sent to hell shouldnt i
fred west
damned if i look old
damned if i have plastic surgery
cher
true believers recognise these gentlemen did not herit sherbet
dr john voll
uncle
shadow of doubt
miss teresa wright plays miss charlie newton:
hitchcocks charmingest (girliest) heroine
whose debut = william wyler little foxes 1942
wyler showcased teresa again - she won oscar® - mrs miniver 1943
see coppola rainmaker 1997
friends
sir paul condon
unloved
david duchovny
jattends
jean genet
entropy
erwin schrodinger what is life? physical aspect of living cell
based on lectures delivered at tcd 2/43
under auspices of dublin institute for advanced studies
intro roger penrose folio mm
nature
dennis nilsen
surge
pr
creeps
sir alec guinness
cur
mervyn le roy little caesar 1930
coyote
herbert reedstrom
mescal
geronimo to john daisy mantan
eggyolk
moore by manet
ist malice even in palace
phang agus strangle

goldenegg

sam goldwyn attrib consult mark cousins story of film 2004

beef

deborah kara unger

ironballs

jerk

rights

anna nicole smith

movies movies

tom hanks sister

only movie

hitchcock

homicide

prof pat reilly

technology

philippa forrester *verbatim platform towards fuller life*

life life

mr bible

life is stronger than we are

drdr

psycho 4

how did u kill your mother?

slowly..

crownprince dipendra appalled people of nepal

dipendra did in father mother sister brother

some cousins sundry uncles

agus brace or two of aunties too

too ghastly true

comical ethics sv family

malloy

vide edward dmytryck farewell my lovely 1944

based on raymond chandlers novel

jailbird moose malloy (mike mazurki)

hires diminutive dick philip marlowe (crooner dick powell)

to find mooses old flame (velma)

gat

revolver abbrev of gatling

venge

malloy displays if not thickmickperseveration heroicpaddyperseverance

aldgate

tim sullivan creeping man 3/28/91

thelma & louise

ridley scott 1991 see

jo berry & angie errigo ultimate guide to chickflicks 2004

electrocuting

2 billion folk worldwide lack electricity cafod 7/03

hanging

val guest they cant hang me 1955

charles duff hangmans handbook 1964

anne frank

diary of 1 younggirl

trans susan massotty

ed otto h frank/mirjam pressler

preface elie wiesel/intro eva hoffman

folio 2004

world of anne frank
compilation anne frank house
forward rabbi julia neuberger
rev ed 2001 [de wereld van anne frank 1929 45 1985]
anne frank remembered
jon blair writer producer director mcmxcv
nina
hadera northern israel fri 18 jan 2002
deth
ripley
vampire
totam tibi subdo me
cf motherrileygreetsvampire 1952
strumpet
george brennan
fire of love
pr
snickersnee
edouard manet
bonds
samhainespell
flaherty
little caesar
rainbow
ntozake shange
leap
dr henry kissinger at masada within pressearshot
swing
jacob liar
philologist
philologist blokes seldom crack jokes
abdul bulbul emir
smiles ist cheap
alzheimervictim rebukes carer
wot steers whose wheelchair
comical ethics sv nonpoliticaljoke
tramp
laborcolonies for tramps und wastrels where they could be made realise their duty to state
winston s churchill
48
poor/obscure
1 tummler
sans toutefois accomplir grand chose
[see leo rosten]
if he aspires to anything
it is to 0
nadada
potty potted raghallaghwebbio autoposted 6/6/mm vide
gir lured by nothing o raghallaigh 1978 2004 2008
pessimism
sting
alzheimers
dr david snowdon aging with grace 2002
miracle
healthspan® brochure

chief
pr
clubbers
joanne leggett
hip
miss alison (sp?) macgregor sat 2/1/03 regional news c3
replacement entails some horrors precorrugates might recognise
bg submitted twice to hipsurgery
she had courage of charlotte corday
bemerkung (hipfootnote):-
1 rayner pic extant
model 272u
power +15. od
length 12.50mm
lot 034c0817510
patientname eliz riley [sic]
date of imp 21 3 95
implanted eye l
          r √
hospital stonehouse
lenfant et les sortiliges premiered monte-carlo 3/21/25
victor de sabata conducting balletsequences balanchine
timepiece striated connemaramarble stopped 446am 21 march 1896
ulysses folio p664
today
they cut
to save
our brave
to save
cut
gave suck
sustenance gave
cryptodiary thu 9 sep 2004
zimmerframe
beryl bainbridge re the oldie
drop in on www.theoldie.co.uk
stupid
russell crowe
ageism
dorothy grace-elder
i may be ideological oldbaggage but its not gracious to say so
barbara castle
joke
bob monkhouse
luv oldie
jilly cooper
sportyspice
fiona phillips
cheese
terry wogan
holey leerdammer® transmits wholly darkmatter
wee houses
count adolf heinrich von arnhem
anglosaxon
bianca jagger

1066

rt hon jack straw unsecuritycouncil fri 14 feb 2003

rough

martin frizell

bettie

simon bates saturdayniteatmovies cfm 29 mar 2003

26

gwyneth paltrow

20s

emma young

37

william walton

44

bill mann

cf bob geldofs sex age death eagle records 10/1/01

turning 50

rt hon tony blair 5/6/03 see sam o reilly best possible taste 2004

over 50

cherilyn sarkisian aka cher

forever

david snowdon

63

sally morgan

75/19

stephen glover

78

emilio roda

old women/granny

desmond morris

values

anon - vouchsafe identity?

boundaries

bros farrelly

feeling

sidney lumett

timewatch tramp & dictator [analysis of great dictator] fri 2/28/03

courage

ray bradbury timewatch qua supra

hoc signo

constantine

age

oftquoted by bishop charles renfrew (notable norman family?)

good cheerful valiant man - everybody loved him

sadhaka

paramhansa yogananda aka gobble yer chocolat krunch

lighteffects

anon cf leerielichtyelamp

girls

spenser

posies

de ralegh - norman

rose rose

nathan

manureenhanced

pr

rosales

molly bloom

stetit puella

tamquam rosula

carmina burana

rosis

angelina 4

you quote

janaceks obsessive love for 1 much younger woman

rt hon david mellor cfm sun 18 jan 2004

leep

marlowe

cooperative

desmond morris

living things

lord clark

inconvenient

dr pat reilly

americans

mario cuomo

astonishing

george clooney

ny

casablanca

phds

robert badass mugabe

wotnots

rt hon christopher soames

1 violent language

encompasses racist invective yiddish

aspects of french & spanish

& good old profane america

florid/overly descriptive would not have served

james ellroy re cold blood interviewed kathleen nutt bigissue in scotland 5/10-16 01 pp30/1

writing here is for babies

iain heggie

wenn judenblut vom messer spritzt

dann gehts nochmal so gut

german lullaby

curious

david krueger

topper

jim abrahams hot shots! part deux 1993

mr nobody

mark chapman

kings

mollah osama bin laden

squadron

walter e grauman squadron 633 1964

writers

norman mailer on frank delaney show

joyce

nora barnacle

discourse

terry eagleton

transumption

harold bloom

murdrous

de ralegh

flash

cezanne

adolph poohpoohed notion loyal

ladysecretaries should acquire pistol prowess

they should fanatically flash orbitadarts..

glanced aghast abas

at whose blasted glad julyrags

comical ethics sv pistol vide junge final hour pp131 & 164

bane

ulysses

filthy

debra stephenson

black

stockport college spokesperson

consult that worthy institutions elements of nonsexistusage

thiers

manet

rotters

vincent

chicks

andrew tyler

cooked

frederic a leuchter jr

buffalo

family of cops 2

ox

pr

humane association

washington post

ratrace is for rats - we are humanrace

jimmy reid

[that race might raise some ratty brows]

u needed me limpy so u could romp home

pr

dogs

robert badman mugabe

blind

anon

bad

denny ryder esquire

sheep

pam eyres

thu 3/22/01 file prayed thus

let not footmouth foully abound in countylouth

cruelty

andrew alexander

respectful

nic davies

porcupine

edwin powell hubble

mendacious egobubble? see bryson short history p114

cockles

anon

godhood

see fabricius pp208/10

buildings

final hour p139

vulturejournalist

jean-baptiste duroselle re mussolini

journalists cannot bear 2b written about

carol vorderman

prose juvenals made prolifically prosaic by circadian indignation

frederic raphael re ambrose bierce/hl mencken

birdsofprey

abel ferrara

cf james fargo game for vultures 1979

vultures

bob mitchum

phucked killed left for buzzards [just could not take ye pharm]

george mccowan magnificent seven ride 1972

i am no beast

bsc of turin sum

du bist kein muselman

fishes

rags joked (asked wot species of subeditor one had been)

fishprices promoted to weather

escapologycode

cf knopp hitlers women p140

shark

SHARFINSOUP SPELLS FIN FOR 400MILLIONYEAROLD PREDATORS

1000000 ELASMOBRANCHS NETTED YEARLY

NONFINITE ELASTICITY OF NATURE EXPERTS WARN

cavan advertiser issue 4848 fri 8 jan 2002 p6

counciltaxclarks rabid qua sharks revenues semper

comical ethics sv counciltax

i have helped cut up & destroy jaws

for whom i had no sympathy

but may have felt sorry [sic]

& wished put em out of misery asap

queensberry ellmann wilde p449

im in it this great bowl of soup

pr

comedera es buena

anon

see neil packers illuss for catch-22 folio 2004

vide john lydons sharkattack wed 11/3/04 c5

rods

ANGLER BITES BACK - FISH TOOK ROD!

dm tue 25 june 2002 p3

toffelens®

covet animalfriendly footgear and/or appurtenances?

www.scandaclogs.co.uk

www.ethicalwares.com

www.vegetarianshoes.co.uk

pant after leather ghillie brogues agus cream kilt hose?

www.slanj.co.uk

we eat us

bree

get your teeth into life

steradent® advert wed 10/16/02 c5

u will save lives

worldvisionad wed 10/16/02 c5

vegetablearian/eat chicken

daisy von scherler mayer madeline 1998

chitra ramaswamy categorises vegetarians:-

lifestyle

militant

fake

hardcore

VEGETABLES OF YE WORLD UNITE

bigissue in scotland issue 478 may 20/26 2004 pp18/19

fur

sophie ellis bextor

introduced

duke of hamilton de tue 17 dec 2002 p5

anemic

angelina lear letter 1/22/02

vegetarian

piadora jo letter 9/9/99

foxes

cyril thatcher

foxnex

suzanne moor

agenda

gerald warner

dreams

mikhail sergeevich gorbachev

rest will come

proculharum ix

this doina i made for my kindreds ye restlesssouls

u know who u are

slow down breathe be present

tummels annika jessen

best

stewart parvin

goodly

robert frederick zenon geldof

mask

jasper maskelyne masked suez? [canal]

yez

skotmask p204

himmlercritters

heinrichs petname for daughter gudrun = puppi

who mere child by allied interrogators was shamefully treated

stephan lebert my fathers keeper children of nazileaders mm

guido knopp hitlers children 2003

dot sereny yet lives girl in red coat ye roma ligocka story 2010

niama niama

meat meat

re extent of congocannibalism during stanleyanera consult

into dark continent travels of henry morton stanley ed frank mclynn folio 2002

flesh

humanity of respectable class generally wellfleshed

dark continent p320

luscious

cf bootylicious/butters

study susie dent languagereport 2004

dexex

wimmer sephardic romances

angela

see christian duguay hitler rise of evil 2003

cannibal

dawkins darwinist in social policy pas

u do things

tho we traffic in slaves [that in itself] is no reason [slavery] should be nice

mtesa emperor of uganda to stanley 9/1875 op cit p332

see madeleine bunting willing slaves how overworkculture rules our lives 2004

some of us may live to witness reverse of this picture

wherefrom we now avert our gaze shamefully regretfully

william pitt addresses commons 2 april 1792

cf advert worldday for labanimals bigissue in scotland issue 417 march 13/19 2003 p17

hare

not mad ala marchhare hairmad

mrs gaskell on dgr

slackbob

wetbob/rower drybob/cricketer slackbob/skrimshanker

tom forrest etonspeak past & present 1 compendious guide 2008

ratones

wimmer sephardic romances

knechte etc

tristan

sapples

smutchy smytrie (too strong perhaps)

combinacje?

uncle terry

mystic of sorts born in scorpio 29° 11/11/22

he consulted not selfwill but submitted unto his father

bg

silkunderweardegree

cf auschwitzwaschetauschen

six

6th sense - all senses rolled into 1

evelyn glennie

we geminis carry on 6 activities simultaneously [tumultously]

joan collins

better tried by 12 than carried by 6

sassaw

so you had 6 relatively good years

steve gordon arthur 1981

wots ye good of ennyfink nuffink

gus elen

you have only got 6 months to live

in coatbridge then you are flitting to tuscany

scotrailadvert mon 8/19/02 c5

in hut 6a old gattegno lived while he lived

if this is i man p30

650 pieces
idem p31
cold 6000000
a vendu six metres de drap
parum sexcente nummate durant
strengtheneth
abandon comforts of english [write equation on blackboard]
trefil laws of nature pxii
[crude english] curse of modern americans
val hennessy dm fri 31 jan 2003 p57
ninos etc
sephardic romances
kilbrides
yet might gloamy quin be found agus sought
ben environs of hogganfield loch
heroic teenage tentative denizen of east kilbride:
ingrid 3/18/85
no more sky
cf if this i man p58 see andrzej wajda danton 1982
eternal england
can understand henry 8s passion for being 1 englishman
ray winstone
that ever selfresurrecteth
luz
rabbinic term = ossacrum
reckoned 2b resurrectionsomanucleus (morgen fruh)
africa has our bones
we have africa in our blood
we are all africans
richard dawkins
scrupus
rough pebble sharp stone anxiety
hoc saxum posuit petri filius
peters son this ponderous stone posed
fhir leagas leac throm
gutta cavat lapidem
drop erodes stone ovid
gulgoleth
bonesspattered spot
heb gulgoleth - grecised golgotha - skull
cf broms hourofdestinycollectorwatch
golgotha gethsemane
john heckewelder in extremis consult jonathon green famous last words rev ed 1997
grablegung
bachian burial - mise au tombeau - bwv 244/5
aux absents les os
absence pockets bones
sero venientibus ossa
bones for ye tardy
losers ought be hardy
bayer aux corneilles
gaping at crows (vacant eyes)
moloch
heb molek consult
israel ben yehuda handbook of hebraic history reprint 2010

momus

gk momos reproach blame cfs

a quorum pars magna fui

wherein i was too much to blame virgil

b iamresponsible.net

c digito monstrari = 2b fingered persius

d potatoes agus point

e da dextram misero = stretch 5 ii i wretch

f do ut des = i donate that u may

monstrum horrendum informe ingens

frightsome monster illshapen hulking virgil

humilis

low

pabulum

pascere feed

voyeur

vigilant lest we degenarate into voyeurs of suffering

ralph fiennes mon 21 oct 2003 bbcnews

maleficium

en multipliant les passes malefiques

scorpioglyph subsumes geminiglyph

twintowers spring ineluctably to mens

in gutted flickery factory

parenthesised per pillars

hir visage halflighted halfdarkling

dualnatured antihero hath hir i dilemma ii resolve

vide fullmetaljacket climacteric of

nothing is resolvable

extinction resolveth everything

megalopsychos 2nd recension 4 2/3

[for strauss] as much as power complexity characterises hero

nick bailey cfm mon 2 feb 2004 see

jonathan winfrey blackscorpion groundzero 1996

philippe petit to reach clouds my hiwirewalk betwixt twintowers 2003

director/producer henry singer 9/11 ye hanging man thu 3/16/06 c4

ahimsa

india/pakistan - summer 2002 - rattled nuclear sabres

everything possible in cartoons agus pakistan anon

malengin

spens wickeddevice

ofr → malus bad ingenium ingenuity

kahlo lemniskos

ribbon bandage gk

ribbons bewrapping bombs

andre breton on paintings of frida kahlo 1907 54

see julie taymor frida 2003

kahloism celebrates frida qua deity

in tijuana she does not rise above sainthood

aces & 8s

deadmanshand

crambe repetita

same old song juvenal

quod avertat deus

may god avert

nous = commonsense

cela viendra

that will come

nous avons change tout cela

we have altered all that moliere

snarl facilitates sarcasm fangs attacking fangs

monde plein de fous

world full of folly

coute que coute

regardless of cost

fotlam amamus

we love u ireland

whose 3 ancient names *banba fotla eriu*

yon cirrus

reminds me of eriu

blow her 1 kiss

hounds of love

country peopled by peasants priests pixies

robert kilroy-silk

british democracy in ireland = contradiction in terms

danny morrison to peter taylor vide brighton bomb/hunt for bomber tue 14 sep 2004 c1

read frank delaney ireland 2004

watts

more enlightened tended to leave

bad olddays pre u2

romany (interestingly) entertained 1 certain antiirishness:

hinditymengreskeytem dirtyfellowscountry

gypsies might with equal slur have dubbed pauvre banba povengreskeytem spudland

but did roseal alba bowl romany over?

she did not

juvlomengreskeytem lousyfellowslair see

george borrow romano lavolil [worldbook of romany] 1874

egon petulengro my romany childhood bm add mss 48642 shelfmark no bs91/93

jg bennet perennial gypsy oldworldnewworldperegrinators 2007

mag slecht/cromm croch

jj o reilly hist of breif pp23-25

historian i have been

and may again go down that path

soon no longer alumna of tcd

rather 1 traveller free

aoife kennedy to breifne postcard

semper an alumna?

mahmud [of ghazni 971 1030]

dubbed idolbasher

anathema

1 cor 16 22

celt

species of antediluvian ax

see jared diamond guns germs steel short history of everybody for last 1300 years 1998

sucellos

= good striker ### celtdeity associated with sunpower

molly bloom sungodmoongoddess materials towards 1 worldcatalog 20 vols 1960/80

iconoclastes

eikon image klaein break

blancam rosam parvam amant

they love that little white rose - image of course is hugh macdiarmids

whom in ye pewter pot raghallach passed (1972?)
nothing scottish seems congenial
ye hibernian delights
scotscot p4 browse
www.scotroots.com
www.scottishcorpus.ac.uk
mans 1 man
robert burns born in aquarius 1/25/1759
perry & jamie share 1 birthday - 1/26
fabae obstant
beans oppose *fata obstant virgil*
at spes non fracta
hope not crushed
stephen hawking assures us one need not lose hope
au bout de son lallans
hir latin stretches its elastic
speaks perfect schemie scots perfect toscano
laurence demarco bigissue in scotland issue 451 nov 6/12 2003 p7
boutez an avant
push forward
allaboardmrsreillysrollercoasterroadshowavecstrobes
dontuknow
aufgeschoben ist nicht aufgehoben
to procrastinate is not give up ghost
aut non tentaris aut perfice
attempt not or achieve ovid
actum ne agas
perseverate pas
abu
rajput rajas sprang from progenitors fireforged upon mt abu
historically they may have counted amongst their forebears huns
circusmaximus
cf rogers oldmotherrileyscircus 1941
cissyplus
pick yourself up
dust yourself down
george stevens swingtime 1936
ohne hast ohne rast
sans haste sans miserable ease
dab sie ruhen von ihrer arbeit
eile mit weile
wily ie leisurely haste
ein mal kein mal
once wont serve
ephphatha
be opened mark 7 34
malebolge
bad holes = 8th dantean circle
lite on feet as malebolgedevil
if this is i man p135
ne cede malis
yield not to misfortune virgil
lasciate ogni speranza voi chentrate [inferno 3 9]
trust 1 spouse with tonetti tonetti opts for spaghetti
mark sandrich gay divorce 1934

nimporte
no matter
omnia mea mecum porto
i jollie swaggie i
mus le veult
mouse will have it so
celui qui veut peut
i can i will i do
maureen o hara born in leo 8/17/20 see quiet man
flecti non frangi
2b bowed not broke
totus teres rotundus
complete smooth round horace
ventris tuis
of thy uterus
vestigia nulla retrorsum
fie upon retrogradation horace
aut inveniam viam aut faciam
i find or insculp 1 foothold
reduced to knees crawl also sprach sciatic agonia enditall
ta me fatcat sheba
i am fatcat sheeba
cats in catbeing are all seing
cats eyeball all
scotcat p196
teen
affliction suffering hurt etc
oe teona cog with gk due skt dunoti
do not for pitys sake impact to death?
te igitur
thee therefore - 1st words of 1st par of canon
fiat justitia ruat caelum
let justice be done tho vesuvius & krakatoa erupt
fiat experimentum in corpore vili
rudus
rubbish
enbarr
manannan mac lirs favorite steed *seafoam*
see alistair moffat seakingdoms story of celtbritain 2003
sail upon carvedout wave
trent american god (c) backbeat records 2004
can anything inspirational emanate from brighton?
rictoria vegina
hir reign wos not short
thought not
trent et al in thrilling angloceltic song
do prove whom grossly ingloriously wrong
paul peter seeby robert gary
cello cecily eckford
strings brighton college stringquartet
ancillary vocals angie terri brighton college choir
artwork/cover james jamesyboy hutcheson jh26ltd
producers nick hunt phil vinall trent
engineer nick hunt/mixers nick hunt phil vinall
recording woodside studios uckfield/mastering abbey road

http://www.trentonline.co.uk
bevvy
i have champagnelifestyle on lemonadeincome
kitty johnson
thanks dear boy ill have 1 magnum of bollinger®
unknown anonymous drinkingcompanion see 7 daughters p19
corrosive
strathclyde commercial cleaningservices painfully regret
gungy inquinations of domesticcarpetry and/or upholstery
effected by barrileirenbarrbru®
are way beyond thir professonal removalpowers
memento mori
now we inside
if this is i man p31
tremble punk to welcome stealthy furtive snufflux
suo moto
i drive me?
upon oneself one must plug tu

g

u

r

g

l

e

BRIEF ACCOUNT
LANGSYNE PRIVATELY PRINTED
BEN BURGH OF COATBRIDGE
HIR CITIZENS ARE STRONG & HONEST
TIMEOUSLY WRESTED EX OBLIVISCENCE TALONS
PER RIGOROUS IBERNODRUIDIC PRAXIS
REVAMPED REVALORISED REVIVIFIED
AMDG SDG
VIA GIOLLA IOSA RUA IMFISS
ICH VERSTEHE VERSCHIEDENE SACHEN

ONE TOO ONE OF HONKIES FEW HAS LOOKED ASKANCE AT **HOOFAX**
[TABOO BRASHLY TO REGARD NUMINOUS AINUVIAN TEDDY
CF WHITEHOUSEINTERNS]
POWERFUL SNOUT INTELLIGENT FROWN
[SNEAKY PEREGRINE IS SNEAKING PEEKS]
COLD EYE INSOLENT PIERCING TRATAKAM [GAZE]
CRIKEY THAT PINGUID HIMALAYAN ARSE [PINGUIS FAT
AINU NURSE THIR URSUS RELIGIOUSLY
TO KEEP BEARGOD HALE & FARTY DEEM NO EFFORT EXCESS MOIL
HOOFAXIAN UNGUIS SPROUTS BOIL (SCRATCHING WHOSE AMPLE TUSH):
ARISTOCRATIC MAIDS VIE APPLY SOOTHING UNGUENTS
GREAT LUMMOX YE WHILE GIRNIE GROWLIE]
CLOTS OF SACRED ORDURE SWARM
WOLFS WHOSE BARMBRACK HOT DENSE HUMID
[NO MAN HIMSELF EXCEPTED BEHOLDS BEASTIE EAT]
LANIARY JAWS AGAPE DEVOURANT
[FIT TO TEAR LANIARIUS OF BUTCHER]
I IMMERSE MYSELF IN SHAMANISTIC CEREMONY
LAGGING LONG CONTEMPLATIVELY AFORE ANCIENT TRANSENNA
BUT YE COLD YE COLD ENGROSSES MIND
IST AUDIENCE (TOUCH PLASTIC) WITH HIS NIBS [KING KUVERNIK XIV]
FLINGS GLAIKS IN FOLKS EEN [CF BUMBAZE]
TAXED HIM (TEMERIOUSLY?) RE PROJECTED DRACONIAN ANTIDRONESLEGISLATION
ASPECTS WHEREOF MESEEMETH ARE OF HIGHLY DUBIOUS MORALITY
ELICITING ELUSIVE ENIGMATIC INTANGIBLE INOFFENDING SMILES (GEMINI?)
WELL IF 1 MR HOBBES CAN CUT GORDIAN KNOTS - SO CAN 1 KINGPOLITICIAN
HIS DYNAMISM EUCLIDEANISM [CERTAINTY] DECISIVENESS - PRETERNATURAL
AGONISING MONKEYGLANDSTRANSPLANT WILL YET BECOME FASHIONABLE
MIDNITE FLING AVEC KYRSTYNKYRSTYN
NOT TO STYLE (DIGNIFY) IT TRYST
WHEN I AM OLD & IMPOTENT (TROTH) SHE WILL WHISPER *TYK*
PROMISES PROMISES [PROLEPSIS PROLEPSIS]
BAGBAG PROVETH BRIBEABLE? [HAREMEUNOCH]
PROVETH - NE GROANS ON EFEN [ANENT] GOLD
FINGERS [NOT FORKS]
FRUGALISTIC FARE [FISHES FRUIT - FLESH THEY FLOUT]
NICOTINE [STAPLE DRUG - ITS USE IS COMPULSORY]
TOILETPAPER PAS [SOAP&WATER SPARINGLY APPLIED]
ONE REMARKS AHEM GLOBAL CLOACAL OBSESSION
CRUSHINGLYBORINGPYRAMIDICCREEP [HUSLINGAS SELFPEJORATIVES]
LOWLOWERLOWEST [IDEM]
SHORTSHARPUGLY [IDEM]
MASTERELDER [COURTPERSONAGES THUS ADDRESSED
MASTERS SLAVES THEMSELVES
IF THIS IS I MAN P60]
EATWELLDRESSWELLNICESMELL [ENCOURAGER JEUNESSEDOREE]
WE FLAUNT NOT OUR JUVENILITY [HEARD AMONGST SOUTHERN HUSLINGAS]
HAPPYWORKERS GRIND HAPPYWORKERS DINE [CHAINGANGDITTY]
ILLFURNISHEDDINGY [HOUSEHUMBLES DECLAIM]
DIRTYFILTHY [LICENSED SKIVVYIMMIGRANTS SELFDISPARAGE]
UPPITY DRONES SHOULD EVER BE UPSIDEOWNED [COMMON SENSE]
OCHLOCRACY? CHTHONIAN SNOWBALLS
[OCHLOS CROWD KRATOS POWER]
KING IS CROSSED [RARA AVIS]
CROSS AS 2 CROSSES [LORDCHAMBERLAIN KROS]

BLESSED WITH HIGH SURVIVALINDEX [QUEEN RAAN]
WOFL BY APPOINTMENT [COSTUMIER
PSYCHOLOGY OF COSTUME PRIMAL
GARMENTS UTTER TOMES
IAN GARLANT]
BAGGEDY AGUS RENT [GROOM OF YE KINGLY DOOKET]
OBLIGATORY GIRN/SILENT MISERY [GENTLELADIES OF YE STOOL]
BLACK BEARD GLINTING GRANNIES [SPECTACLES] – KENSPECKLE KIR!
UNRELIABLE [JESTER] PURFLED ARGUTE CAPERNOITY LEASINGMAKER
HRINGAR YE PROFESSIONAL [MERCENARY]
BLOW 1 SHIT OFF [SIC = SASSLOT]
DR SOOTHSAYER HUG HATH NOT BLUDGEBONE IN WHOSE ATOMY
LONG WHITE FINGERS CENSORIOUS LIP [RESIDENT PHILOSOPHER]
RANDY QUA GOAT & TWICE 1 CACAFOGO [HRINGAR]
PONEROLOGIST WOULD HAVE FIELDDAY
KURAK [HERO OF MANY RESOUNDING VICTORIES 1815 1850]
THEY PUT THEIR FAITH IN SOL [COASTDWELLERS]
ACKNOWLEDGE ONLY CENTRAL AUTHORITY [IDEM]
ENDS ONE WEEKS SOJOURN AT RKAS COMMUNITY
I DO NOT SEE BEST WAY [RKASLAMENT]
[NAME] GDA [=] I HAVE SOL TRINE NEPTUNE
[NAME] GRABAK [=] BEWARE MARSSOLUNION
QUAND SHE SAYS YES SHE SIGNALS NO [?]
THIS QUEEN QUEMES ME NOT [OE CWEMAN CF BEQUEM]
I HAVE BEEN OFFERED [HONORIS GRATIA] TOLLKEEPERS POST
LINK! [GO FOR IT]
DANGLE GYPSYEARRINGS SHAMBLE DOWN TO SHORE
SERENADE YE CELIBATE OCHIDORE [HE HAS QUARRELLED WITH KYRSTYN]
IN WHOSE MESSIANIC PHASE REPROVED TOY GUNS [NIBEG PURE 1660 1743]
APTLY DESCRIBED CAD & FOP – SCOOTY WEE SCOOT [WOFL]
ONE IS TO BE ACCORDED ENCYCLOPEDIASPACE LORD KEEP ME HUMBLE
HIMSELF INITIATES INCOMING FOR[EIGN] SEC[RETARY]
WE CANNOT TAKE BACKSEAT WE WILL NOT SETTLE FOR 2ND FIDDLE
PUPU PAINTED PREACHING PICTURES
[1662 1703 COURTARTIST DURING NIBEG]
GUKAR DIED IN BED [1483]
[HIMSELF TO KARKAR] TRADE OR RAID MAIS GET IT
[GREYBEARD HUG] HAPPY NODDING SMILING EAGER BRIGHT EIDENT
I GAVE THAT NORDICCOW SOME LURPAK® [BLONDNBLAND] COWNCELL
OUR LOVE ITH ON HIGHER PLANE
THREATENETH MELTETH WINGS
[WAFFLE WHEREWITH KING NIBEG WON FEMME BLANCHE]
PURE AS NIBEG [PIOUS PROVERB]
[INFANTA RAFBAG] ONLY HIR CHARM CAN POSSIBLY SAVE HIR
DE FACTO YE STUPIDITY IS UNLIMITED
ANAN ANAN [COMPREHENDS PAS]
JEFFS [GAMBLES] JEFF [ROPE] AWAITS
CREDIT NEITHER TO FAMILY NOR KING
[KIR] BULL IN CHINASHOP OF GOOD INTENT
1 FIKE [PERNICKITY ON FIKJA]
HIR SUSPICION COMPROMISES SOUPCON OF PARANOIA
GREYBEARD HUG SUFFERS 1 LUCID INTERVAL
NARMAK JAWS WIRED SLURPED LIQUID GRUB [1784 1870]
FIST CLENCHED PIPESTEM ARM [PHILOSOPHER]
EFTSOONS REMEMBER MASTER TRYMTRAM UNTO KYNGE

MORROW 1 FOOTSOME YOMP 2 UIX [SHOW OF PRESENTS/WEDDING]
RUNNYNG RORYING RAMPYNG REGAL LYONS
PEESWEEP PEGGY PEKAN
ANANAS [SATIVUS AKA PINA]
UIXIAN PEKOE SERVED UP IN DAINTY ITSYBITSY DECORATED CUPLETS
APOTROPAIC BOWELLMENT OF BELLOWING ELEPHANT [PRENUPTUAL RITUAL]
NO TWINGE OF SWIVET ONE ADMIRES HIR MOXIE MADE 1 MOTZA
[MOG - FLEECHY FLEECER OF AMATEUR TROLLMYDAMESPLAYERS]
MOGMOTTO BEING *LET LOSERS FLOURISH MUCKENDERS* [HANKIES]
I ESP APPRECIATED BRONZE ANTEDILUVIAN KIRPAN [CEREMONIAL DAGGER]
CHEEKY WEE KIT [POCKET VIOLIN] TICKLED ME PINK
PRIME PIMENT/KIRSCHWASSER COPACETIC [GER CHERRYWATER]
BIT OF BOBBERY AFTER [HIND BAP RE O DADDY]
AGUS SMALL (BARATHRUM) PLAUSTRALLAPSE [PLAUSTRUM WAGON]
BARFING IN YE BARONIAL BATHROOM.. [ANACATHARSIS]
I TRY FANTOOSHSTROSSERS CHEZ WATERBAILIE MR NIF WHOSE SONS
[FASHIONS HAVE DEGENERATED APPROACHING EVERMOREGENERALISED NUDITY
HIS DIVINE GRACE AC BHAKTIVEDANTA SWAMI PRABHUPADA
WE RUB NOSES AVEC NAKED HUMAN SOUL
ERNEST SHACKLETON CF IF THIS IS I MAN P120]
AMBLING AWKWARD IMPOSSIBLE FART
WANGLED DATE - YOUNGER SISTER JAAKI AE XVIII
[HE TENDED TO GRAVITATE *ROMANTICALLY* TOWARDS LATETEENSGIRLS]
[PEREGRINE] YOU SIR ARE 1 DRAWCANSIR SIR
[HRINGAR IRON HAND ON SCIMITAR] DO I DETECT SIR 1 SLOAN? [REPROOF]
STOCHASTIC TWIT [STOCHASTIKOS AIMING SKILFULLY]
TAD NASTIC MYSELF [NASTOS CLOSEPRESSED - HE HAS BEEN WRINGERED]
MUST NOT JEE ONES GINGER SCHLIMMSTE IST VORUBER
SACKCLOTH ASHES ASHES SKIAMACHY DARKNESS VAMPYRIC [MYDDAY DEVILL]
DEDE AS EVER DORE NAYLE TO AL HOLE CETTE WRETCHY STYE
TURMENT DE MON PRESENT HARTES HEVYNESSE DREDE FERE [BEKLEMMT]
THEY EXHORT ME TO PREPARE AGAINST ORDEALS [CONVERSION]
I AGREE COUGH UP YE HEFTY REGISTRATIONFEE
[FEED KINGS FISK WITHAL]
I AM THY MOST HUMBLE FAITHFULL SUBGEITT BEDEMAN
NONE CORRUPT WHOM FROM TROTHE OU SWEETE FAITHE
ET ONE SHALL BE HEATFREE [OF OPHIDIAN LIBIDINOUSNESS LEECHED]
THIS [SKULLGESTURE] ANNIHILATES THAT [SNAKE]
SLOPS SACK STRAW [ENCHIRIDION]
BOOTS BELT BREECHES [BARECHEST] BEARD [IDEM]
NISUS [STRIVING] NIS [IS NOT] ININSUFFICIENT [CYNIC HARKOR]
WASTE WILL UNDO WHAT LAZINESS DOTH NOT [KING NIBEG]
MAKING MAKING NEVER MADE [CYNIC HARKOR]
TEND TIME [ETERNITY TENDS ITSELF IDEM]
ASCENDANT ORCUS MARKS 1 WIZARD [BOOK OF GAR]
HARKOR SAID 2 THINGS ONCE 1 FETUS BLINKERS ARE CONTAGIOUS
EMPTY IS 0 TO PROJECT [ENCHIRIDION]
PURSUIT PRESUPPOSES NONPOSSION [IDEM]
ABBA IMMA HAVE I NONE [BOOK OF GAR]
ISOLATION HOWEVER GERMINATES GROWS [IDEM]
LAVATORY EST EUPHEMISM FOR SERVITUDE [HARKOR]
IF IN DOUBT MIMIC [IDEM]
FEAR IN ABEYANCE SLEEPS [HERMIT OF AUT]
NOTHING COMES SO CHEAP AS HEROWORSHIP [IDEM]
PROPRIETY SHIELDS STAGNATION [IDEM STAGNUM = POND]

NONE SO STAGNANT AS SON HANGS FIRE [GUKAR]
MOCK NOT FILIAL NAVVYDOM NOR [SCORN] 1 PINNY [IDEM]
NE GRAFT NE WINCH NE WORSHIP [KENNELCODE]
GUKAR c1100 c1178
KAAD [EPICURE] 1201 c48
NARMAAG GROSS c1398 1470
HORBAK HARD 1574 ?1644
KURAK 1713 1803
KONAR 1728 99
KARAG [KINGLOVER 1733 1806
IF NOT 1 LITTLE HITLERIST 1 HIRPLING HILDEBRANDIST VIDE INFRA:-]
WE MAY NOT OVERTHROW ESTABLISHED INSTITUTIONS
CANNOT EXIST 1 VACUUM OF KINGS
REX UNUM NECESSARIUM [CF LUKE 10 42]
BLOOD AUGMENTS 1 KINGS STANDING
KINGS DO NOT HIGHT [SPENS MENTION] STINKINGFISH
UNTERMENSCHEN GROK NOT KINGS
ALPHA LEADS OMEGA FOLLOWS [.]
GYMNIC WIZARD GROFNAR [AKA CHARLATAN] OFT INTONES
ONE DESCENDS BUT ONCE ONE CLIMBS BUT SLOWLY
I WILL NOT FORGET GARGAR AGAIN [GARGARS RESOLVE]
CYNICS PREACH 2 THINGS LOVE DRIBS MEDITATION ANATHEMA EST [.]
GROGOG YE PROTREPTIC WIELDED 1 KEELYVINE [LEAD PENCIL]
UTTERED DIVERS WRY & HUMAN [REDEMPTIVE] SENTENCES [:-]
TABOO TABOO
THIR MOLD I BROKE BROKE
KERFED EARTH KISSES KIST [CF DEATH PERFECTS NAKEDNESS]
QUOTATION 1 PLEASANT VICE
PRECISION 1 VIRTUE
GIVE THOUGHT HIR PLACE GENTLY KEEP HIR THERE
LIKE THY GOOD KICKIEWICKIE [WIFE] BE KIND TO HER
SHE THAT KINDLES IS NO KICKSHAWS [QUELQUE CHOSE]
WHAT ELSE SHOULD MEN & WOMEN DO
PLEASURE REINFORCES 1 BOND
POWER SHOULD KEN WHEN TO BE GRACIOUS
WHEN I HEAR POWER I REACH FOR CHOCOLATE
LESS NOT MORE MORE OR LESS
ALAS THAT PSYCHOGASBAGS DO NOT ADVERTISE [THEMSELVES]
OTHERWISE ONE MIGHT RUN 1 MILE [.]
TORQUE TOREUTIC [SYMBOL OF ETERNITY HENCE ETERNITY CF OUROBOROS]
FOREFLOWS
FOLLOWS
SWALLOWS
SIXTYTHOUSANDMILLION [YEARS = PRIMEVALATOMTHEORY]
[HALFAR RASHLY OPINES:]
SHOULD QUEEN RAAN TAKE PARAMOURS
THAT WOULD CONSTITUTE CONDUCT UNTOWARD
[GROGOGS SWIFT RIPOSTE:]
THAT GOETH PAS TOWARDS [1 PERSON] GOETH
WHITHER?
GROGOG MAY HAVE SAID TWO THINGS BESIDES [:-]
IN HER EMBRACE WE NESTLE
EGRESS YE OBSESSING OF
                    GOLPHY
                    ABYSSES

ba4

crousey teaser prove crowdpleaser
salespitchmakerich
machinemanmelding thetherwards we wending?
emptynests feathers beckon
birls goys! plonk yr posh for riling rileys boshta bosh
thirls on celluloid ed ceedee de anna durbin

i ii has it all
freda c bloggs

woon toon noodle soup goody juices oozes
hegonists like me will fair lap up
mao dse dung

gib ihnen schon zu fressen
[if 1 were tu i ii one should es*chew*]
sergeant moll aeg

ist das nicht ein scheinmannisch?
[echt or ent or what or not]
hermann screibtischtater

irlandais encore effort si vous voulez etre humain
gille federe

slateable slue of scaly slathery slaters
[sic — 1 lousy review]
samuel slattery ksc scws retired

doth ua rakhallaikh truly (unruly) ake 2 *rake in*?
p ecunia

ardent inaccessible and (naviget anticyram) *raghallachan*
rev bro tom mcgurk church of golgothagethsemane lower gowkthrapple

pro sons et pro mums — 1 mustprescription
bet noir

fierce free forwartsfurrows pluptureously roughs
monsignor romeo coia quondam professor of englis blairs

nessuno ha verita in tasca
antonio paccagnella

aboot oor goot pook
[raghallachan doggrel 1ˢᵗ printed big issue in england 5/07 pp40-41]

fine fanciful filigrane filethings grace our book
please rear deaders [concetto] condescend 2 take 1 look

we do not however embroil ourselves palavering re genres
that we delegate to egghead jawers
[birt blane zubernopfel?]
academic hath office of jaw jaw being more desirable than war
[tho conducted in ivory tor — churchill paraphrased]

[text inter alia treats] **death** [cf cedimento organico]
[defined as] permanently interrupted breath
[cf wallowing in mortality]

maters & paters pepper wir pages
basics ne change down throughout ages [now all mutates]
if some be cads au fond dads = the lads
[cf donatien de sade aka m le 6]

nor did we skip affairs of heart
wherein **women** have headstart

apropos **religions:**
jactate pas bede [clawing cat] midst placid pigeons

plus get 1 load chuckies of — appendant **teddy hoofax!**
always sagely timidly timously pay thy counciltax
dread redletters 2 kickstart wisdom

your melancholy selves likewise acquaint avec polonial **agonia enditall**
ben apophthegmatic saddle riding tall

bonnie prince charlie figures ici too
whose victories moral & otherwise were too few

aussi zmidgin de mizder **hidler** aguz **naziz**
arguably hizdoryz preeminent baddiez

benefactors facilitate selfpublication
triumph trafford® thru epromulgation of ye word [bene merentibus]
niteynite my little irish little britons
try not 2 hatch kittens

bearf
parturient uterus wet fetus pounds wot not metric avec
weightforce of 50 to 100 pounds mammydaddy [comic expostulation]
pacific giant seanagdad
laboring 50 hours manfully
delivers unto his ladymare
2000 corrugate rugrats
[p26]

deaf
annies bairn
maes brother
peters heir
gerhards hero
maethes hae him
jim predeceased him
jack preceded jim
[p13]

ah donal munro 100000 welcomes to landoleal
[u] will not grow tyrantfatter
[now that] god of worms hath put u pon poor archies platter
i *like* this like alabonneheure bonnebouche bonappetit
mr riley i have something you might like
worm 2 1 that dies indifferently applies
i ii i that lives crumbs of comforts gives
[p6]

leaf agus **leaffizz** aka **spirid**
life — echoing leonard cohen?
hegoatschoppersshop
[ofr bouchier 1 that kills hegoats → boc hegoat]
on ne peut embrocher gigot avec plus de majeste?
talleyrand 2 lucy de la tour du pin
chopping [plump] maggots shall not chop [eat] whom?
leopoldy agus molly bloom [they are imperishable]
molly caught laughing because?
rogers agus maggot o reilly
[at loss to gloss
sfruttatore is lofat walls® banger up cowcaddens close (.)
leave it to phalanxes of phds pursuant
cf drdr phds are academic bumgear]
[p76]

spirid councildaxable pas
spirid 1 supposidory:-suppose id nod suppose id nod
hastening to mollify sister & brother somatists
ged behind dis nod undinking numpdy unding
come clean u closet somaticomonists u coy cryptopancosmists
be 1 woman or 1 man in hienliteenmenttradishan
for fauceds & for wadercloseds render undo caesar
caesars suffer posdhumous defeads
colleagues pay out romes premier personality
[p15]

leafydeaf
zonked zowie zeez zombie
[p71]

reader of **one two**!
aid scribe recower productioncorpses sorry costs

planes came iiday

neocon corollary:
democritised aka kadaverised irak

kork or kavan faminewrack
ed
kroak krush krak

humptydumpty maotsetung
rules multitudes tumultuous of pawns
requisitions whose rice pork prawns
38000000 clem
let em sook kirbies

1st edition 50 revolutionary coffins apology copies comprising
whereof dis be riproary coffee (fairtrade) no

purchase 1 trafford® *vous* pour 1 monad-acquaintance
whom designate a

a forking out heaps gootpook pon monad-chum b
b forking over lavishes gootpook pon monad-buddy c
c forking up presses gootpook pon monad-pal d

ouroboros-alphabetically humanely friendlily aljabaraigally
sock wid de jabberwock knock pas ye schlock
weder want weder not *gilfedders* not forgot
fair dos fair nuf
brains brains snare

modest progressus ad infinitum until purpur unicornus
trashes rashly crashsmash whole crockeryfloor ben big store until
ekpyrotic brane brane brushes bang

qualifying derby du even du for your
future free trafford® of nucleary workworryout-in-prog
usual strings attached
posterior bestseller
divrei koheleth
melech bi yerushaleim
9/11/06

artience mints funds
traffordian avantgarde venture au voleur
unto **drdr**
u punters u pundits
forwandering farstraying grazers
pas grazers of not unaffordable 1 2
beholden are

i ii
humdoc
flimnwar
bbb
more better [ie better agus more than here24]
glossed glossier
improved marketprospects
few mortuitous futations wartsandall [(spoolish foonerism)
= text illcorrected per naive cavalier application of ruskinian imperfectionprinciple]
shipsloddapslashtickleyrfunnyboneclapthythigh
affective parts [affectuossa] may make u sigh
raghallach
ratratratrussan
matmon nonnom
mon plaisir [musicien francais 2 registrar rety]
wall2wallmitty quasifictionist fils fivefingersfile agingprimagravidas
giolla iosa rua
umquhile sfruttatore-imfiss
aghatotan druidical academy
[by whose demisquares shall ye know im]
barcan [cabba]
glasgow baccalaureate
21stcentury cybercomposer
affiliate gallant tullymongan gallowglasses
brene
ba hons
multimedia artist
quondam expatriate briton
sonora san bernardino etc
nema
ma hons
maman de noster **nana**
et alii also ye *rest*
aussi tout le monde
sinn fein agus saol
cricky whit 1 fowk
or tollol for 1 cast of billions
hebas chubby everyone
edin evivernal edin immarcescible
abba imma
banba go bragh
sellafield a bas
ad portas hannibal
copyright (c) raghallach
copyright (c) giolla iosa rua
copyright (c) barcan aka cabba
copyright (c) brene
rights of raghallach et giolla iosa rua
2b identified respectively qua
compilercreator/explicator
have been asserted
inproper per giolla iosa rua
per raghallach rip perpro giolla iosa rua
according to copyright designs patents act 1988
NESCIT VOX MISSA REVERTI

Printed in the United States
By Bookmasters

Printed in the United States
By Bookmasters